Southern Illinois University Press
Series in
Aviation Management

David A. NewMyer, Editor

Aviation Industry Regulation

Harry P. Wolfe
and
David A. NewMyer

Southern Illinois University Press
Carbondale and Edwardsville

Library of Congress Cataloging in Publication Data

Wolfe, Harry P.
  Aviation industry regulation.

  (Southern Illinois University Press series in
aviation management)
  Bibliography: p.
  Includes index.
  1. Aeronautics, Commercial—Law and legislation—
United States. I. NewMyer, David A. II. Title.
III. Series.
KF2439.W65   1985   343.73′097   84-13896
ISBN 0-8093-1177-1   347.30397

Contents

Illustrations

Preface

THE OBJECTIVE OF THIS BOOK IS TO EXPLAIN how the government regulates the aviation industry. The term *regulate* is used broadly to describe government control over, involvement in, and promotion of aeronautics.

To achieve this objective it is necessary to answer the following questions: 1) How did today's regulatory system evolve? 2) Which agencies regulate the industry and what authority does each possess? 3) How do the agencies exercise their regulatory authority? 4) What are the key regulations that affect the industry? 5) How are the different segments of the aviation industry actually regulated? This book addresses and is organized around these five questions.

The first chapter defines key terms and provides an overview of the various segments of the aviation industry. Chapter 2 describes the evolution of aviation industry regulation. It provides insight into how today's regulatory system came about, and sets the stage for the detailed analysis of the regulatory system which is presented in subsequent chapters of the book. Chapter 3 explains how federal regulators exercise their authority over the aviation industry. Emphasis is placed upon the three most important regulators—the Federal Aviation Administration, the National Transportation Safety Board, and the Civil Aeronautics Board.

The major objectives of the third chapter are to explain: how the Federal Aviation Administration regulates aviation safety and promotes air commerce; the aviation responsibilities of the National Transportation Safety

Board, including the procedures followed in investigating aircraft accidents or incidents; how the Civil Aeronautics Board controlled the airline industry prior to the passage of the Deregulation Act; the events precipitating the demand for airline deregulation; and the impact of deregulation on the functioning of the airline industry. Chapter 4 discusses the involvement of state and local governments in regulating and promoting the aviation industry. Chapter 5 explains how a rule or regulation is formulated, and describes the various instruments of regulation that the federal government uses to assert its authority over the aviation industry. Its major objectives are to explain the rulemaking process so that the reader knows how to participate in the development of regulations or how to be made exempt from those regulations, and to explain the process by which the federal government controls the industry in order to enhance the reader's understanding of the regulatory system and to enable him or her to cope with regulatory agencies.

Chapter 6 provides an overview of four categories of aviation regulations—economic and related, safety, environmental, and miscellaneous others. Its objectives are to set up a classification scheme into which regulations can be logically placed, to enable the reader to understand the status of economic regulations in light of the Airline Deregulation Act of 1978, to give the reader a glimpse into the content of key FARs so that he or she may discern which are applicable or of interest, and to provide insight into the environmental process, including the laws and regulations which have an impact on the aviation industry. Chapter 7 discusses how the major segments of the aviation industry are actually regulated. These segments include manufacturers, major airlines, commuter airlines, airports, fixed base operators, corporate flight departments, and airmen. In addition to providing an overview of the regulations and regulators affecting each segment, actual case studies are presented to demonstrate how the regulations are applied. The concluding chapter forecasts the direction that the regulation of the aviation industry will take in the years ahead.

WE WOULD LIKE TO THANK John Smith of the Civil Aeronautics Board, Donald Morrison of Ozark Airlines, and James Bildilli of the Division of Aeronautics-Illinois Department of Transportation for their willingness to review drafts of the text. Also, we thank Royal Mink of the Federal Aviation Administration for his helpful suggestions. Discussions with Professor William Reed of the Deparment of Aeronautical Technology at Arizona State University and Gene Abney of American Airlines were quite helpful in defining the scope of the text. We thank them for their comments. Finally, we would like to thank Toni Smith, Ann Hogan, Penny Cochran, Martha Bondurant, and Joy Trocola for their part in typing portions of the draft manuscript.

Aviation Industry Regulation

1

The Aviation Industry and Its Regulation

THE SIGNIFICANCE OF AVIATION INDUSTRY REGULATION

The aviation industry makes a significant contribution to our nation's economy and transportation network. It employs nearly 2.0 million people; it is responsible for the largest share of public passenger transportation; it provides key public transport to rural America; it provides unscheduled, private transport to over 16,000 airports nationwide; and it produces approximately 3,400 civil aircraft annually. The evolution of the aviation industry has been guided by an extensive set of regulations which have encouraged growth and promoted safety. While the deregulation movement of the late 1970s reduced the federal government's role in economic regulation, the government still maintains significant regulatory authority. Before examining that regulatory authority in greater depth, the remainder of this chapter will delineate the components of the industry, and discuss the regulation concept.

THE AVIATION INDUSTRY

The aviation industry as defined in this book is comprised of seven components: aviation manufacturing, major/national airlines, commuter/regional airlines, airports, fixed base operators, corporate flight departments, and airmen. A brief discussion of each of these components is provided below. (See Table 1.)

Aviation Manufacturing

The aviation manufacturing industry has three components: defense, space, and commercial. Table 2 reveals that defense and commercial sales are the two largest components with space (and other) a distant third. Some manufacturers are involved in more than one area, as noted in Table 3. For example, Lockheed is a participant in all three phases of aviation manufacturing, while McDonnell Douglas and Boeing are significant participants in commercial and defense manufacturing.

Because this book is directed at the regulation of the civilian/commercial

TABLE 1
AVIATION INDUSTRY IN THE UNITED STATES

Total employment	1,891,000
Aviation manufacturing, including:	
Aircraft/airframe manufacturers	1,171,000
Major/national; commuter/regional airlines	350,000
Commuter/regional airlines, included in above	30,000
General aviation (including FBOs, corporate aviation, etc.)	250,000
Government	90,000
Total active civil aircraft	219,930
Airline	2,830
General aviation	217,100
Total active pilots	776,400
Total aircraft sales	3,368
Commercial transport	262
Helicopter	415
General aviation	2,691
Value of aircraft sales	$9.8 billion
Total airports	16,029

Sources: Aerospace Industries Association of America, *1983 Aerospace Year-End Review and Forecast—An Analysis* (Washington, D.C., Dec. 16, 1983), Tables I, VII, and IX; Department of Transportation, Federal Aviation Administration, *Statistical Handbook of Aviation, Fiscal Year 1983* (Washington, D.C., 1984); Air Transport Association of America, *Air Transport 1983* (Washington, D.C., June 1983).

TABLE 2

SCOPE OF THE AVIATION MANUFACTURING INDUSTRY

Employment	1,171,000
U.S. civil aircraft Fleet	219,930

Sales
    Industry components (by customer groupings)

Defense	$37.9 billion
Commercial	$19.3 billion
Space (and other)	$ 6.1 billion
Total	$63.3 billion

Aircraft produced   (number)

Transport category	262	$ 8.0 billion
Helicopters	415	$ .3 billion
General aviation	2,691	$ 1.5 billion
Total	3,368	$ 9.8 billion

Source: Aerospace Industries Association of America, *1983 Aerospace Year-End Review and Forecast—An Analysis* (Washington, D.C., Dec. 16, 1983), Tables I and VIII.

TABLE 3

MAJOR AVIATION MANUFACTURING COMPANIES

Defense	General Dynamics, McDonnell Douglas, United Technologies, General Electric, Boeing, Lockheed
Commercial/civil	
Transport	Boeing, McDonnell Douglas, Lockheed (until 1984)
Helicopter	Sikorsky/United Technologies, Bell/Textron, Hughes Helicopters
General aviation	Cessna, Piper/Bangor Punta, Beech/Raytheon
Space (and others)	Rockwell International, Martin Marietta, McDonnell Douglas, General Electric, Computer Sciences, Bendix

Sources: Aerospace Industries Association of America, *1983 Aerospace Year-End Review and Forecast—An Analysis* (Washington, D.C., Dec. 16, 1983); Standard & Poor's, *Industry Surveys: Aerospace Current Analysis* (New York, Apr. 15, 1982), Vol. 150, No. 15, Sec. 1; and *Aerospace Basic Analysis* (New York, Oct. 7, 1982), A-24 to A-29.

side of the aviation industry, defense and space manufacturing will not be analyzed in subsequent chapters.

Commercial aircraft manufacturing makes a significant contribution to total aircraft sales. The 262 commercial aircraft (out of a total of 3,368 aircraft industry-wide) delivered in 1983, accounted for 81 percent of the total value of aircraft sales, as noted in Table 2.[1] Boeing, the largest commercial aircraft manufacturer, supports roughly 8 percent of the work force employed in aviation manufacturing.[2] McDonnell Douglas and Lockheed are two other major manufacturing companies, although Lockheed has canceled its L-1011 "TriStar" program, and left the commercial market after completing remaining deliveries in 1984. The major helicopter manufacturers are Sikorsky, Bell, and Hughes. These three companies delivered 1,073 aircraft in 1981, which amounted to 5 percent of the total value of units shipped in 1981.[3] The general aviation aircraft manufacturers delivered the largest volume of aircraft, over 2,691 in 1983, but accounted for only 15 percent of the value of total aircraft sales.[4] Cessna, Piper–Bangor Punta, and Beech/Raytheon are three leading general aviation manufacturers, while Gates Learjet, Rockwell International, and Gulfstream American contribute significantly to the growing corporate market.

Major/National Airlines

Airline classifications were changed in 1980 from functional names such as "trunk" and "local service" to financially oriented names/definitions. The former and new industry designations are compared in Table 4. "Major" airlines are defined as those with more than $1 billion in annual revenues while "national" carriers have $75 million to $1 billion in annual revenues. The airlines belonging to each category are listed in Table 5.

TABLE 4
THE CHANGING UNITED STATES AIRLINE INDUSTRY STRUCTURE:
INDUSTRY PARTICIPANTS

Category	1978	1979	1980	Category	1981
Domestic trunks and Pan Am	11	11	10	Majors	12*
Local service	8	7	6	Nationals	14
Intrastate	4	4	4		—
Others	20	20	21	Others	16

Source: McDonnell Douglas Corporation, "The Changing Aviation Industry: A Manufacturer's Perspective" (Paper presented at the FAA Aviation Forecasting and Planning Review Conference, Oct. 13, 1981, Washington, D.C.).
*Including Braniff International.

TABLE 5
MAJOR AND NATIONAL AIRLINES

Majors (More than $1.0 billion in annual revenues)

American Airlines	Pan American World Airways
Continental Air Lines	Republic Airlines
Delta Air Lines	Trans World
Eastern Air Lines	United Airlines
Northwest Airlines	U.S. Air
	Western Air Lines

Nationals

Air California (Aircal)	Midway
Air Florida System (bankrupt 1984)	New York Air
Alaska Airlines	Ozark Air Lines
Aloha Airlines	Pacific Southwest
Braniff International*	People Express
Capitol International Airlines (bankrupt 1984)	Piedmont Aviation
	Southwest Airlines
Frontier Airlines	Wien (bankrupt 1984)
Hawaiian Airlines	World Airways

Source: Air Transport Association of America, *Air Transport 1983* (Washington, D.C., June 1983), 4–5.

*A former major which declared bankruptcy inMay 1982 and then restarted operations at a much reduced scale in March 1984.

The major airlines as a group experienced serious financial difficulties from 1981 through 1983, including the declaration of bankruptcy of Braniff International in May 1982, the bankruptcy of Contintental in September 1983, plus several bankruptcies in 1984. These failures illustrate the vulnerability of the airlines in a deregulated environment. Nevertheless, the ability of the national carriers to register a profit in 1981–83 in contrast to the majors suggests that these carriers were flexible enough to adapt to deregulation even during adverse economic conditions (see Table 6).

Since deregulation has opened up market entry, both the majors and nationals are faced with competition by a number of "new entrant" airlines utilizing large transport aircraft (see Table 7). These carriers generally provide point to point service, focusing their resources on large hubs such as Chicago, New York, Dallas-Fort Worth, Phoenix, and Los Angeles. Because they utilize nonunion labor, and avoid costly interlining operations (for the most part), these new entrants have been able to offer extremely low fares forcing their competitors to do the same.

TABLE 6
SCOPE OF THE MAJOR/NATIONAL AIRLINE INDUSTRY

Employment	320,000
Total annual revenues	$39 billion
Fleet size	2,830
1983 net profit/loss—majors	
American	$227,867,000
Continental	(218,448,000)
Delta	(13,930,000)
Eastern	(183,700,000)
Northwest	50,700,000
Pan Am	(51,000,000)
Republic	(111,031,000)
TWA	(12,372,000)
United	120,700,000
U.S. Air	80,644,000
Western	54,500,000
Total	$ (56,697,000)
1983 net profit/loss—selected nationals	
Air California	$ (2,927,000)
Air Florida	(39,229,000)
Frontier	(13,772,000)
Ozark	1,953,000
PSA	(9,359,000)
Piedmont	25,539,000
Southwest	40,867,000
Total	$ 3,072,000

Sources: "1983 Financial Results," Aviation Daily, Feb. 28, 1984, 313–14; Air Transport Association of America, Air Transport 1983 (Washington, D.C., June 1983), 7 and 8.

Commuter/Regional Airlines

A commuter airline is defined as a carrier which offers a minimum of two round trips a day between two points five days a week, and which utilizes "smaller" aircraft (generally aircraft with less than 60 seats).[5] Because many older commuter airlines have taken on regional importance, their industry had been renamed the Regional Airline Association. The CAB has classified these carriers into "medium" and "large" regionals.[6] Medium regionals have less than $10 million in annual revenues and large regionals have from $10 million to $75 million annual revenues.

TABLE 7
NEW ENTRANT AIRLINES STARTED
SINCE DEREGULATION (Passenger Only)

Midway Airlines	1979
New York Air	1980
People Express	1981
Muse Air	1981
Jet America	1981
Pacific Express	1982 (bankrupt 1984)
Northeastern International	1982
Hawaii Express	1982 (bankrupt 1984)
Best Airlines	1982
Sunworld International	1983
AirOne	1983 (bankrupt 1984)
America West	1983
Regent Air	1983
Frontier Horizon	1984
Air Atlanta	1984
Florida Express	1984

Sources: Airline Pilots Association, Airline Pilot, Dec. 1982, pp. 14–15; "Carriers Newly Certified or with Pending Applications," Aviation Daily, Jan. 29, 1982, backs of pp. 146–47; Aviation Daily, Mar. 15, 1984, pp. 81–82 (tables).

The commuter airline industry emerged in the early 1960s. Since then it has grown to an industry with over 200 individual companies that carried 19.5 million revenue passengers in 1983 (see Table 8). While the industry's level of activity is small by comparison to the larger carriers, the commuter

TABLE 8
STATUS OF THE COMMUTER/REGIONAL AIRLINES

Top five companies (ranked by 1983 enplaned passengers)
Mid-Pacific, Britt Airways, PBA (Provincetown and
Boston, Mass., and Naples, Fla.), Air Wisconsin, Empire
Total companies: 200-plus (December 1983)
Revenue passenger miles: 2.06 billion
Revenue passenger enplanements: 19,500,000
Freight and cargo: 566,300,000 pounds
Total employees: 30,000 (estimate)

Sources: "Airline Yearbook 1983," Airline Executive, June 1983; Aviation Daily, Apr. 13, 1984, back of p. 250; Department of Transportation, Federal Aviation Administration, FAA Aviation Forecasts, Fiscal years 1984–1995 (Washington, D.C., Feb. 1984).

airlines provide a crucial service formerly offered by larger and more heavily capitalized companies. This service is provided by smaller aircraft which allow a higher frequency of service than was previously available. Commuter airlines, nevertheless, are plagued by a number of problems, including but not limited to: fuel availability, appropriately sized aircraft, corporate image, safety, and access to the main terminals at large hub airports.

Airports

An airport is a specific location for the arrival and departure of aircraft. It also usually provides aircraft parking and/or storage and passenger/pilot facilities. As of January 1984 there were 16,029 airports in the United States of America. As shown in Table 9, these 16,029 airports are operated for both private use (the majority) and public use. There are also publicly owned

TABLE 9
SCOPE OF THE NATIONAL AIRPORT SYSTEM

Total airports	16,029
Airports by use type	
Private use	10,042
Public use	5,987
Airport by ownership	
Publicly owned	4,812
Privately owned	11,217
Airports by type of aircraft served	
Airports (fixed wing)	12,653
Heliports	2,918
Stolports	66
Seaplane bases	392
Ultralight flight parks	12
Gliderports	32
Balloonports	7
Airports in the National Plan of Integrated Airport Systems (by airport role)	
Commercial service	605
Reliever	204
General aviation	2,815
Total	3,660

Source: Department of Transportation, "Civil Aircraft Landing Facilities Increased in 1983," News (Washington, D.C.: Department of Transportation, Mar. 22, 1984).

airports (most are owned by *local* government bodies such as cities, counties, port authorities, or airport districts) and privately owned airports (most are owned by individuals). The vast majority of airports—12,653—are used by fixed wing, land based aircraft. An additional 2,918 are used as heliports by aircraft with vertical take off and landing capability, while the remaining 509 consists of Short Take-Off and Landing (STOL) airports (stolport seaplane bases, ultralight flight banks, gliderports, and balloonports.

As noted in Table 9, there are 3,660 airports included in the National Airport System Plan (renamed the National Plan of Integrated Airport Systems [NPIAS] in 1982). These airports are designated by the Federal Aviation Administration (FAA) as eligible for the receipt of federal revenues. The majority of the NPIAS airports are general aviation facilities, those serving nonscheduled, smaller aircraft. Air carrier airports—those serving the large scheduled airlines—constitute 16.6 percent of the NPIAS system, while relievers (airports which divert general aviation from large air carrier airports in metropolitan areas) account for 6.6 percent.

Fixed Base Operators

Fixed base operators (FBOs), the "front line" or "grass roots" of aviation, are located at 3,000 to 4,000 airports across the country. FBOs provide flight training instruction, aircraft maintenance service, aircraft fuel service, aircraft storage, and other support services to the general aviation community. Where an FBO is the only entity on an airport, it may also provide certain services to the airlines and manage the airport facility. As noted in Table 10, the 4,500 to 5,000 businesses[7] had over $2.5 billion in total sales in 1980, with the majority of the activity in aircraft services business. FBOs also carried over 5.0 million passengers in unscheduled charter aircraft and flew over 3.1 million hours of flight instruction, charter work, and sales support work. Because the dominant aircraft flown by the FBO is the single engine airplane, FBOs have access to the majority of the 12,653 airports and 66 stolports listed in Table 9.

Corporate Flight Departments

A corporate flight department is a division of a large company responsible for transporting its executives and cargo using company-owned aircraft. While corporate operators fly a variety of aircraft, the majority of the aircraft operated by National Business Aircraft Association (NBAA) members are turboprop and turbojet aircraft. Table 11 illustrates that there are 9,200 turboprop and turbojet general aviation aircraft operating in America. Other than those aircraft used for sales inventory, government service, and FBO

charter work, the vast majority of the general aviation turboprop and turbojet aircraft are associated with corporate flight departments. The General
Aviation Manufacturers Association (GAMA) estimated that 45,000 people
worked in corporate flight departments in 1979.[8] Since 1979 corporate aviation has grown because of a reduction in airline service to small communities,
rising air fares, and the emphasis on point to point service. These factors have
made commercial air travel less convenient for businessmen, thereby encouraging the growth and use of corporate flight departments.

Airmen

There are 733,300 pilots and 115,000 aircraft mechanics in the United
States (see Table 12). Pilots can be categorized according to the certificate
they hold including: student, private, commercial, airline transport, helicopter, glider, and so forth. The largest single certificate group is the private pilot
group with 322,100 pilots. This large number reflects the general aviation
community's focus upon flight training and the popularity of flying for
personal reasons. Other pilot groups are student pilots, commercial pilots
(qualified to transport the public for hire), and airline transport pilots. It is

TABLE 10

SCOPE OF FIXED BASE OPERATIONS

Major FBO "conglomerates": Butler Aviation,
  Van Dusen Aviation, Combs-Gates, Hangar One

Number of FBOs: Approximately 4,500–5,000
  (approximately 950 are members of NATA)

Total sales: $2.5 Billion/year
  (NATA members only—1980)

Service Sales Total: $1.8 Billion/year
  (NATA members only—1980)

Aircraft Sales Total: $.7 Billion/year
  (NATA members only—1980)

Passengers Carried: 5.0 Million/year
  (NATA members only—1980)

Hours Flown: 3.1 Million/year
  (NATA members only—1980)

Sources: Gellman Research Associates for the National Air Transportation Association, *Analysis
of Competition, and Profile of, the FBO Industry* (Washington, D.C., Dec. 1979); National Air
Transportation Association, *FBO's Today: What's Ahead Tomorrow* (Washington, D.C.,
1981).

TABLE 11
SCOPE OF CORPORATE FLIGHT DEPARTMENTS

Total employees	45,000
Total turboprop general aviation aircraft	5,200
Total turbojet/fan general aviation aircraft	4,000
Number of companies with corporate flight departments (NBAA members only)	2,756
Aircraft flown by NBAA members	5,309

Turbojet	2,143
Turboprop	1,311
Multiengine piston	728
Single engine piston	400
Helicopters	727
Total	5,309

Sources: Department of Transportation, Federal Aviation Administration, *Statistical Handbook of Aviation, Fiscal Year 1983* (Washington, D.C., 1984); General Aviation Manufacturers Association, *The General Aviation Story* (Washington, D.C., 1979); National Business Aircraft Association, *NBAA Aircraft Fleet as of 3/30/84* (Washington, D.C., 1984).

interesting to note that, in addition to their certificate classification, 255,100 private, commercial, and airline transport pilots hold an instrument rating. This rating requires special training and, when completed, allows the holder to fly in "poor" visibility conditions. The strong percentage of pilots holding instrument ratings suggests that pilots are continuing to upgrade their flying capabilities.

Data on aircraft mechanics are not as complete as the data on pilots. While there are fewer mechanics than pilots, they play an important role in the conduct of safe flight. The supply of aircraft mechanics is somewhat constrained by the relatively low salaries paid to general aviation mechanics (which account for the majority of mechanic jobs) and the capacity limitations of mechanic schools.

THE "REGULATION" CONCEPT

A regulation is "a rule, ordinance or law by which conduct is regulated." To regulate is "to control, direct or govern according to a rule, principle or system."[9] Obviously, control is the principal objective of regulation. But control over what? And how is this control accomplished?

TABLE 12
AIRMEN: PILOTS AND AIRCRAFT MECHANICS

PILOTS (thousands)

as of January 1	Total	Students	Private	Com-mercial	Airline Transport	Heli-copter	Glider	Other	Instru-ment-Rated
1975	733.3	180.8	305.8	192.4	41.0	5.6	4.8	3.2	199.3
1976	728.2	177.0	305.9	189.3	42.6	4.9	5.3	3.1	204.0
1977	744.2	188.8	309.0	287.8	45.1	4.8	5.8	3.0	211.4
1978	783.9	203.5	327.4	188.8	50.1	4.8	6.2	3.1	226.3
1979	798.8	204.9	337.6	185.8	55.9	4.9	6.5	3.2	236.3
1980	814.7	210.2	343.3	182.1	63.7	5.2	6.8	3.4	247.1
1981	827.0	199.8	357.5	183.4	69.6	6.0	7.0	3.7	260.5
1982	764.2	179.9	328.6	168.6	70.3	6.5	7.4	3.0	252.5
1983	733.3	156.4	322.1	165.1	73.5	7.0	7.8	1.4	255.1

MECHANICS: Total 115,000
Mechanics working for major and national airlines 45,000

Sources: Department of Transportation, Federal Aviation Administration, *Statistical Handbook of Aviation, Fiscal Year 1983* (Washington, D.C., 1984); General Aviation Manufacturers Association, *The General Aviation Story* (Washington, D.C., 1979); Air Transport Association of America, *Air Transport 1983* (Washington, D.C., June 1983).

Note: Many commercial pilots are also instrument-rated, etc.

Types of Aviation Industry Regulation

Aviation regulation embraces five areas: safety, economics, environment, consumer protection, and industry promotion.

The safety of the public—both those flying and those on the ground—has been one of the key objectives of aviation industry regulation. Some of the earliest aviation legislation, such as the Air Commerce Act of 1926, regulated airmen and aircraft and established lighted airways for flight safety purposes. Safety regulation also encompasses airspace utilization, aircraft operations, and airport development.

Economic regulation pertains to government control of air carrier business practices such as fares and market entry. Designed to ensure "public convenience and necessity," this type of regulation has been deemphasized since the deregulation movement of the 1970s. Today the airline industry operates for the most part in an environment governed by free market principles.

Environmental regulation seeks to protect the quality of the human and natural environment. It is geared toward reducing aircraft noise levels and has become prominent since the rising use of commercial jet aircraft.

Aside from the inherent consumer benefit of safety regulations, there are a number of regulations which benefit the flying public from a narrower consumer protection viewpoint. These regulations compensate passengers from overbooking of flights, lost baggage, and in general protect the consumer from potential abuse. The deregulation of the airline industry may to some extent erode some of these consumer protection provisions.

Aviation industry promotion is also regulated. The federal government promotes the aviation industry, chiefly through a number of funding programs. For example, the Federal Aviation Administration finances airport development, planning, and aeronautical research, while the Civil Aeronautics Board (CAB) subsidizes essential air service (this program was transferred to the Department of Transportation when the CAB was dismantled). To be eligible for funding, potential recipients must comply with all applicable federal regulations.

Sources of Aviation Industry Regulation

The major sources of aviation industry regulation are the government, the industry itself, and the marketplace.

As noted in Table 13, the aviation industry is regulated at all levels of government. At the federal level the focus of the regulatory effort is on the fulfillment of the legislative mandate from Congress pursuant to aviation safety, economics, industry promotion, environmental protection, and con-

TABLE 13
AVIATION INDUSTRY REGULATION BY VARIOUS
LEVELS OF GOVERNMENT

Level of Government	Examples of Regulatory Functions
Federal	Overall flight safety regulations
	Economic regulation
	Accident investigation rules
State	Airport inspections
	Pilot and aircraft registrations
Local	Individual airport noise rules
	Airport tenant rules and contracts

sumer protection. The federal government's specific role in aviation industry regulation is carried out by the Federal Aviation Administration, the Civil Aeronautics Board (terminated January 1, 1985), and the aviation branch of the National Transportation Safety Board (NTSB). State and local governments supplement the federal regulators.

There are also numerous examples of "self-regulation" by the individual segments of the aviation industry. Various industry associations develop programs, standards, or guidelines for their members. For example, the American Association of Airport Executives has a professional accreditation program for airport managers. This program has obviated government involvement in the certification of airport professionals. In a similar fashion, the Air Transport Association of America (ATA), the representative of the airlines, has established a number of common airline industry formats for technical information, supplies, and other items.

Finally the marketplace—or more accurately the aviation industry's performance in the marketplace—plays a regulatory role. If a product or service doesn't "sell," whether it is an aircraft, an FBO service, or an airline route, the marketplace governs through the response that this lack of sales receives from the affected segment of the industry. The marketplace was a major factor in the demise of both the L-1011 TriStar program at Lockheed, and Braniff International Airlines. In more subtle ways, the marketplace results in daily adjustments from the various components of the aviation industry. While not a formal system of regulation, the marketplace is an informal alternative now espoused by many regulatory critics who feel that government regulation has become obsolete.

CONCLUSIONS

The aviation industry is quite diverse and regulated in many ways. The remaining chapters of this book will explain how the aviation industry is regulated by discussing the evolution of today's regulatory framework, the regulatory process, the regulators, the regulations, and the various regulated segments of the industry. The final chapter contains the authors' observations concerning future directions in the regulation of the industry.

2

The Evolution of Aviation Industry Regulation

THIS CHAPTER EXAMINES THE ORIGINS and evolution of aviation regulations and regulatory agencies. It commences with a review of the aviation industry prior to regulation, and the circumstances that ultimately prompted government intervention. The second part of the chapter reviews the legislation which established the federal government's regulatory role. It examines the Air Mail Act of 1925, Air Commerce Act of 1926, Air Mail Acts of 1930 and 1934, Civil Aeronautics Act of 1938, Federal Airport Act of 1946, Federal Aviation Act of 1958, Department of Transportation Act of 1966, Airport and Airway Development Act of 1970, deregulation acts pertaining to air cargo, domestic service, and international air transportation, the Aviation Safety and Noise Abatement Act of 1979, and the Airport and Airway Improvement Act of 1982. The major provisions and impact of each of these laws are discussed.

It is interesting to note that from 1925 through the mid-seventies, the government's regulatory functions steadily increased. In the late seventies, however, the trend was reversed with a series of deregulation acts, reducing the government's authority in airline economic matters. Whether this trend will continue is subject to speculation and will be treated in greater detail in Chapter 8.

THE AVIATION INDUSTRY BEFORE REGULATION: 1903–1925

Development and Evolution of the Airplane

When Orville Wright made the first successful flight in a power controlled aircraft on December 17, 1903, there was little government involvement in aviation. There was no Federal Aviation Administration to certify the aircraft, license the airmen, or control the airspace. There was no Civil Aeronautics Board to dictate the destinations to which an air carrier could fly. There was no National Transportation Safety Board to determine the probable cause of an accident in the event that the Wright Flyer crashed.

There were also no federal funds to finance the research of the Wright brothers, who, nevertheless, remarkably solved the mystery of flight. Two obscure bicycle shop owners from Dayton, Ohio, managed to achieve what the most reputable scientists of the day, subsidized by the federal government, failed to accomplish. They did it without any formal education, in their spare time, and with their meager savings.[1] The Wright brothers spent $2,000 and four years to develop their Flyer.[2] The federal government, by comparison, had appropriated almost $100,000 to underwrite the research of aeronautical scientist Dr. Samuel Langley, which failed to produce successful results.[3]

The Wright brothers' lack of financial resources may have actually accelerated and facilitated their success. Because they could neither afford the time nor the costs associated with repeated test flights of their aircraft, they relied more heavily on the wind tunnel to test different aerodynamic designs.[4] This not only saved them money, but it also probably saved their lives. Other airmen of the day were quick to flight test inoperable aircraft and lost their lives in the process. On several occasions the Wright brothers actually refused financial assistance from private contributors for fear that it might take them away from their business and make them lax in their work.[5]

Because the Wright brothers' Flyer had little practical use, federal intervention in the aeronautics industry was minimal. However, in the years following the first flight, the airplane was improved upon. Wheels were added, the engine was moved to the front, a stabilizing tail, including an elevator, was placed in the rear, and the flight controls were attached to a stick.[6] The French put ailerons on the wings and fashioned a central framework known as a fuselage. Given the various improvements to the airplane, noted airmen of the day increased its use and extended its range. Notable achievements included the first seaplane flight, night flight, flight above 3,000 feet, international flight across the English Channel, transcontinental flight, and acrobatic flights.[7]

Practical Use of the Airplane

The onset of World War I prompted further improvements to aircraft and engines and gave the airplane its first practical use. As a military instrument, the airplane was first used as an aerial scout to monitor troop movements and deliver messages. In the early days it was considered poor etiquette to harm a fellow flier, even an enemy. Then some farsighted pilot shot at the opposition, and the airplane became an instrument of combat. Because of maneuverability problems and the dangers inherent in flying low, the airplane was not used until later to drop bombs.[8]

After the First World War, thousands of surplus aircraft became available and a new use for the airplane and air transport developed: the carriage of airmail. Although the first airmail flight occurred in 1911, it wasn't until 1918 that the Post Office initiated airmail service on a regular basis.[9] Service was first provided between Washington, D.C., and New York via Philadelphia. It was later extended across the country to Chicago, St. Louis, Omaha, and then finally to San Francisco. Surplus Curtiss Jennys and DeHavilland DH-4s with Liberty engines were the aircraft commonly used to carry the mail. When the Post Office expanded the fleet, it added Handley-Pages with Liberty engines, Glenn Martin aircraft, and biplanes developed especially for airmail by the Standard Aircraft Corporation of New Jersey.[10]

Short haul mail routes between New York and Washington and between Chicago and St. Louis were soon discontinued because airmail service offered neither time nor cost advantages over surface transport.[11] On the 2,600-mile transcontinental routes, however, airplanes could save considerable time if operated efficiently. This required a combination of day and night flying rather than the existing practice of flying the mail by day and placing it on a train at night.[12]

In order to allow airmail planes to fly at night, the development of a lighted airway was undertaken by the Post Office. This was one of the major contributions that the Post Office made to civil aviation. As the lighted airway was developed, the time for sending a letter was reduced substantially. Record time for westbound service was 30 hours; eastbound, 26 hours (compared to four days by surface transportation). Intermediate stops were made in Cleveland, Chicago, Omaha, North Platte (Nebraska), Cheyenne, Salt Lake City, and Reno where replacement pilots and aircraft were available as needed.[13] In 1925 New York-Chicago overnight service was initiated. The total cost of the Post Office airmail operation from 1918 to 1927 was $15,000,000.[14]

A use of the airplane that began at about the same time as airmail service was the transporting of passengers. The first so-called air carrier, The St. Petersburg-Tampa Airboat Line started service in 1914. Benoist flying boats powered by a 75 horsepower engine achieved speeds of 70 miles per hour and could carry one to two passengers in an open cockpit. On the inaugural flight, pilot Anthony Janus had only one passenger, the mayor of St. Petersburg.[15] During a four month period, the company carried 1,205 passengers at $5 per trip between St. Petersburg and Tampa, a distance of 21 miles. There were no injuries and an excellent on-time record was established.[16]

The next venture in air transportation took place in 1919. Aeromarine Airways flew passengers, airmail, and freight between Key West and Havana, Cuba. Three seaplanes were used and the fare was $40.[17] During the summer months the operation moved northward. Service was begun between New York and Atlantic City, New Jersey, and later that summer between Detroit and Cleveland. The following winter season, service was expanded from Miami to Nassau via Bimini. The fare was $85 per passenger.[18] Aeromarine carried 6,800 passengers in the winter of 1920 and 1921 and 17,000 passengers in 1922.[19] It strictly adhered to the schedules and, despite the lack of government regulation, imposed its own very stringent safety regulations. The company's president emphasized efficiency, pilot and mechanic proficiency, and the safety first concept.[20]

At about the same time that Aeromarine began service in Florida, interest in air passenger service arose in California. The Wilmington-Catalina Airways initiated service in 1919 between Los Angeles and Catalina Island. A half dozen small airlines arose which transported passengers between Los Angeles and San Francisco.[21] Pacific Marine Airways operated between San Pedro and Catalina; and Ryan Airlines started a regular schedule between Los Angeles and San Diego in 1925.[22]

Problems Prompting Regulation

The expansion of the airplane's practical use for military, airmail and passenger carrying purposes resulted in problems for the fledgling aviation industry. These problems included:

1. Safety. According to newspaper accounts, from 1922 to 1924 there were 470 crashes resulting in 221 deaths. Editors claimed that 91 percent of the accidents were caused by inexperienced pilots or unsafe equipment.[23] In New York City problems developed with low level acrobatic flying and the police made their first arrest of an individual on reckless flying charges.[24]

2. Lack of funds for development of an adequate airway system. A system of lighted airways was sorely needed to enhance the practicality of commercial aviation. It is not surprising due to the lack of potential return that there were no willing sponsors in the private sector to make such an investment. Although the Post Office had started an airway system of

navaids, a more extensive network was needed to extend the coverage of commercial aviation.

3. Poor financial viability of carriers. It was difficult to make money carrying passengers given the economics of available aircraft and the lack of government assistance. Thus early operators went out of business.[25]

4. Backward state of commercial aviation in the United States compared to European countries. The United States could not begin to compare with England, France, and Germany in the development of aircraft and the carriage of passengers. German airlines were carrying 80,000 passengers a year in 1921 compared to the fewer than 10,000 airline passengers in the United States. Furthermore, the safety record of Lufthansa and other European airlines was far superior to their counterparts in the United States. The major difference in Europe was the fact that the government was providing the airlines with direct subsidy, a practice that was shunned in the United States.[26]

These problems caught the attention of Congress, prompting federal intervention and ultimately the passage of laws and regulations for the control of aeronautics.

One of the first examples of government intervention was the creation of the National Advisory Committee for Aeronautics (NACA). The committee was created by President Wilson, and although it was presumably independent of the government, it was financed by federal funds. NACA was created to aid in the scientific study of the problems of flight. In fact, however, it assumed a much larger and more promotional role. In the First World War NACA supported programs to train pilots and improve aircraft. It encouraged aeronautical research in such important areas as the relationship between meteorology and flight. It supported the Post Office in its efforts to obtain federal funds to fly the mail; and it lobbied for federal legislation to regulate and promote aeronautics in the United States.[27]

The efforts of the National Advisory Committee for Aeronautics were bolstered by the actions of General Billy Mitchell. Mitchell, the only general officer in military service who was also a pilot, argued for the more rapid development of United States aviation. He publicly criticized officers of the General Staff, and as a result was court-martialed and convicted. Mitchell, nevertheless, used the testimony at his trial to highlight the inadequacies of the United States aviation program. As a result President Calvin Coolidge formed a committee led by Dwight Morrow to investigate United States aviation. After study, the Morrow Committee recommended the transfer of the airmail service from government to private hands to stimulate development.[28] This recommendation prompted passage of new and extensive legislation, and the beginning of a long history of government intervention in the workings of the aviation industry.

THE AVIATION INDUSTRY AFTER REGULATION: 1925 TO THE PRESENT

Government regulation of the aviation industry was initiated by the Air Mail Act of 1925, also known as the Kelly Act, and the Air Commerce Act of 1926. With the Kelly Act came federal involvement in economic regulation; with the Air Commerce Act, safety regulation. These acts were followed by other pieces of legislation which have contributed to the regulatory structure that we know today.

The Air Mail Act of 1925 (Kelly Act)

The Kelly Act marked the beginning of economic regulation and served as a catalyst to the development of commercial air transportation in the United States. The act had two major provisions. It authorized the awarding of contracts to private carriers for the transportation of airmail and it established airmail rates.[29]

The first airmail contracts were awarded through a bidding process on 12 short feeder routes to give the carriers the experience that would be necessary to provide transcontinental service. The companies that were awarded the contracts were the predecessors of today's major airlines. Once the feeder routes were established, the Post Office turned its attention to the transcontinental routes in order to reduce its operating costs. It awarded the San Francisco-Chicago route to Boeing Air Transport and the Chicago-New York segment to National Air Transport. These two companies later merged, along with two other airlines, to form United Airlines.

In addition to authorizing contracts, the Kelly Act set airmail rates. At first compensation was limited to 80 percent of the postage on the airmail transported. This, however, was quite burdensome since each letter had to be tallied. The act was therefore amended to set a fixed rate per pound for airmail carried by airlines and to reduce the airmail postage to $.05 an ounce. This, however, created a new problem. Because the airlines were paid substantially more to carry the mail than the cost of postage, they were enticed to send large quantities of bogus mail and freight over their own system to reap a tremendous profit.[30] The following example illustrates the problem. The Post Office was paying approximately $3.00 per pound for trasnsporting mail distances of 1,000 miles of less; and the cost of postage was only $.05 an ounce. Thus if an airline were to send a one pound item from New York to Chicago, it would cost $.80 in postage; but the Post Office would pay the carrier $3.00. This problem was not resolved until a later amendment.

The Air Commerce Act of 1926

The passage of the Air Commerce Act of 1926 resulted in further federal instrusion into and control over the aviation industry. The act established safety regulations and charged the federal government with the maintenance and operation of the airways. It also provided for accident investigation and promoted aeronautical research.[31]

Safety regulations encompassed the registration of aircraft, airmen, air navigation facilities, and the establishment of air traffic rules. Aircraft were to be marked for identification and inspected to insure airworthiness. Airmen were to be examined and rated to insure physical health and technical proficiency, and air navigation facilities were to be tested to insure their proper operation. Air traffic rules were designed to establish safe altitudes of flight and prevent aircraft collisions. Penalties were established for noncompliance with the Civil Air Regulations (CARs), predecessor of today's Federal Aviation Regulations (FARs).[32]

The operation and maintenance of the airways entailed designating federal airways, installing navigation aids such as lighted beacons, setting up emergency landing strips, maintaining the proper operation of the navigation aids, and mapping and publishing for distribution, charts of the airway system.[33]

The Air Commerce Act of 1926 was administered by the Aeronautics Branch of the Department of Commerce. In order to minimize bureaucratic entanglements, Secretary of Commerce Hoover delegated as many as possible of the responsibilities for carrying out the act to existing divisions within his department. The Bureau of Lighthouses set up an airways division, the Bureau of Standards established an aeronautical research division, and the Coast and Geodetic Survey designated an air mapping section. These three existing divisions together with the two new divisions responsible for air regulations and air information constituted what was known as the Aeronautics Branch.[34]

The implementation of the Air Commerce Act of 1926 proceeded slowly and cautiously because of the concerns that were expressed in congressional debates on the original bill. These concerns included states' rights, authority over airspace, the cost and effectiveness of dispatching federal safety inspectors to certify airmen and aircraft, and the limits of federal intrusion into the lives of private citizens.[35]

Another reason for proceeding with caution was that the Department of Commerce did not want to alienate the aviators and sectors of the aviation industry that it would be regulating. Without the cooperation of the industry, it would be difficult for the department to enforce the safety regulations. In fact in the first years following passage of the act, many individuals failed to register their aircraft and gain airmen certificates. Many of the fatal aircraft accidents in 1927 occurred with pilots and aircraft that were unlicensed.[36]

The major impact of the Air Commerce Act was to establish the federal government's role in aviation regulation and to set up an organizational structure to carry out the regulatory functions. This law together with the Kelly Act provided the initial regulatory framework for the fledgling aeronautical industry.

The Air Mail Act of 1930

The Air Mail Act of 1930 was promoted by Postmaster General Walter F. Brown. Brown believed that the United States airline industry was totally inadequate. Established airline routes were too short and uneconomical to generate a profit. Airline companies, in the hope of securing airmail contracts, engaged in bidding wars and gave little thought to safety, adequate aircraft, and the promotion of air passenger service.[37]

In order to develop his vision of the manner in which commercial air transportation and the United States airline network should develop, Brown supported passage of the Air Mail Act of 1930. This act 1) eliminated competitive bidding and permitted contracts to be let by negotiation or by the extension of existing routes and 2) computed mail payments on the basis of the capacity flown regardless of whether needed for mail.[38]

Brown used the first provision to encourage the consolidation of small companies and to grant contracts to a few large entities. These large companies, he believed, would have the financing necessary to purchase larger aircraft, be more interested in growth and safety, and ultimately advance the state of air commerce. Brown's actions also led to the establishment of major carriers such as United Airlines, American Airlines, and Trans World Airlines.[39] Because the second provision in the act paid aircraft operators on the basis of space available, they were encouraged to buy larger aircraft, and use the excess space for carrying passengers. As an additional incentive, the act provided payments for two-way radios, passenger accommodations, and other safety measures.[40]

A major impact of this legislation was the stimulation of United States aircraft manufacturers to produce passenger carrying aircraft. At the time the airlines were relying on the outdated Ford Trimotors and Fokker Universals, carrying 10 to 13 passengers at speeds of 110 to 120 miles per hour.[41] In response to the demand for aircraft, Boeing Airplane Company produced the first modern civil airliner, the Model 247. Douglas Aircraft countered with its DC series, including the famous DC-3, the first truly economically viable commercial airliner. Later Lockheed entered the commercial airliner competition.[42]

The system that Walter Brown used to foster his concept of an ideal transportation network created many enemies. When Franklin Roosevelt took office in 1933 and Walter Brown was replaced as Postmaster General, an investigation into the manner in which airmail contracts had been awarded was undertaken. Brown was criticized for awarding contracts in an arbitrary manner and showing favoritism to the larger carriers. At the urging of several of his advisors, Roosevelt canceled all airmail contracts and turned the operation of the airmail flights over to the army. Because the army lacked the equipment and experienced pilots, the venture failed. Aircraft operating costs skyrocketed from $.54 to $2.21 per mile. After six months there were 66 crashes, 12 deaths, and a loss of $3.8 million in government operating subsidies.[43] Realizing that a mistake had been made, airmail contracts were turned back to the airlines on a temporary three month basis, and remedial legislation was drafted to prevent the abuses which occurred during the Brown tenure. This legislation was the Air Mail Act of 1934.

The Air Mail Act of 1934

The Air Mail Act of 1934 restored competitive bidding as a means of securing airmail contracts. However, those airlines which had participated in the "Spoils Conference" with Postmaster General Walter Brown were declared ineligible to bid on contracts. To circumvent the law, Eastern Air Transport and American Airways, two carriers accused of collusion, reorganized and changed their names to Eastern Airlines and American Airlines.[44] An example of the vigorous bidding that took place after the passage of the act occurred in the case of the Houston-Corpus Christi-Brownsville route. Braniff bid one ten-thousandth of a cent per mile, which would yield revenue of one dollar a year. Eastern countered with a bid of zero cents per mile and won the route.[45]

The other major provisions of the Air Mail Act of 1934 included:

1. Separation of airlines from aircraft manufacturers. At least partially as a result of Walter Brown's efforts, the aviation industry had become dominated by three conglomerates: United Aircraft and Transport Company, Aviation Corporation, and North American Aviation. These companies not only provided passenger service but were also involved in all phases of aircraft manufacturing. The rationale for severing the ties between airlines and manufacturers was concern over safety. An airline that was controlled by a manufacturer might be forced to buy its aircraft.[46]

As a result of this particular provision in the law, United Airlines was separated from United Aircraft and Transport Company, and American Airlines emerged from the Aviation Corporation of America. Later Eastern

Airlines broke away from North American Aviation, which had been controlled by General Motors.[47]

2. Division of aviation regulatory authority among three federal bodies. The Post Office awarded contracts, the Interstate Commerce Commission set air mail rates, and the Bureau of Air Commerce (previously the Aeronautics Branch) operated the airways and regulated safety.[48]

3. Creation of a Federal Aviation Commission to study aviation policy. This commission recommended a new comprehensive act encompassing all of aviation.[49]

The Civil Aeronautics Act of 1938

The Civil Aeronautics Act of 1938 consolidated previous legislation, established economic regulation of air carriers on a much more rigorous basis, and assigned safety responsibilities and authority for accident investigation. Initially a Civil Aeronautics Authority, Administrator of Aeronautics, and an Air Safety Board were established to administer the law.[50] However, a 1940 reorganization resulted in the consolidation of the Civil Aeronautics Authority and the Air Safety Board into the Civil Aeronautics Board. The Administrator of Aeronautics became the Administrator of the Civil Aeronautics Administration.[51]

The Civil Aeronautics Board (CAB) was responsible for economic regulation, entry of foreign carriers, promulgation of safety standards for all aircraft flight and for aircraft and air carriers, suspension and revocation of safety certificates, and the investigation of aircraft accidents.

The Civil Aeronautics Administration (CAA) a division within the Department of Commerce, was responsible for the operation of the civil airways and control towers, policing the industry to insure compliance with safety regulations, investigation of aircraft accidents when delegated by the Air Safety Board, administration of funds for airport development, and, once constructed, the operation of Washington National Airport.[52]

A major feature of the act was the federal government's strengthened role in economic regulation. Carriers that had provided continuous airmail service for three months prior to the passage of the act received a permanent Certificate of Public Convenience and Necessity for those routes. Anyone else who wanted to serve a route had to apply to the CAB to obtain a certificate.[53]

The Civil Aeronautics Act also provided that airlines would receive mail payments on the basis of need rather than merely by contract. In this way it established the airline subsidy program.[54] Other powers granted the Civil Aeronautics Board included control over fares, mergers, international aviation agreements, and miscellaneous carrier business practices. A discussion of how the air carrier industry operated under economic regulation is contained in Chapter 3.[55]

With respect to safety regulation, the CAB promulgated the Civil Air Regulations (CARs), while the CAA enforced them. Based on the experience gained by inspectors, and the deficiencies that they encountered, the CARs were constantly revised. In 1941, for example, they were amended to require that crews be furnished with oxygen while flying above 10,000 feet for 30 minutes or longer, and that airplanes heavier than 10,000 pounds be equipped with radios and altimeters.[56]

The Federal Airport Act of 1946

Prior to the passage of the Federal Airport Act, the federal government's involvement in airport development was sporadic. During the Roosevelt administration, the Civil Works Administration and Works Progress Administration constructed new airports. In 1940 Congress requested that the Civil Aeronautics Administration undertake a six-year program for the improvement of the nation's airports.[57]

The Federal Airport Act of 1946 firmly established the government's rule in airport development. It required the preparation of a National Airport Plan to guide civil airport development in the United States and established a Federal Aid Airport Program (FAAP) that authorized $75 million annually over a seven-year period for airport improvements.[58] Later amendments extended the authorizations.

While the provision of funds for airport development added to the government's aviation promotional activities, the creation of airport standards that recipients of federal funds were expected to follow augmented the government's regulatory authority. Section 9(a) of the act stipulated "proposed development shall be in accordance with standards established by the Administrator, including standards for site location, airport layout, grading, drainage, seeding, paving, lighting, and safety of approaches."[59] In response to this provision, airport regulations were added to the *Code of Federal Regulations* (Part 151).[60]

The Federal Aviation Act of 1958

The Civil Aeronautics Act remained basically unchanged for twenty years. Several midair collisions in the mid-1950s, however, demonstrated the need for better airspace management and improved safety regulations and led to the passage of the Federal Aviation Act of 1958.[61]

The Federal Aviation Act established the Federal Aviation Agency

(FAA) out of the Civil Aeronautics Administration and expanded the FAA's role in air safety. The FAA was removed from the Department of Commerce and made a separate government agency. Economic regulation was left untouched, and a large portion of the Civil Aeronautics Act of 1938 was incorporated into the newly passed legislation.[62]

Under the Federal Aviation Act: 1) the CAB's safety rule-making authority was transferred to the FAA, 2) the administrator of the FAA was authorized to revoke or suspend a certificate, 3) the administrator was given clearer authority to allocate airspace between civilian and military users, and 4) air safety research and development was consolidated and placed in the hands of the agency.[63]

The safety regulations issued by the Federal Aviation Agency became known as the Federal Aviation Regulations or FARs. General E. R. Quesada, first FAA Administrator, went to great lengths to strengthen safety regulations as a result of the previously cited airline crashes. Copilot training programs were upgraded, flight physicals had to be carried out by designated physicians, commercial and private pilots were required to undergo instrument flight instruction, and most air carrier aircraft were required to be equipped with radar.[64]

The Department of Transportation Act of 1966

This act consolidated the various transportation agencies in the federal government and placed them under the control of a new Department of Transportation (DOT). The DOT was responsible for coordinating the activities of its various modal divisions, or administrations. The Federal Aviation Agency was converted to the Federal Aviation Administration.[65]

While the Department of Transportation Act transfers the powers of the Federal Aviation Agency to the Secretary of the United States Department of Transportation, it stipulates that the Administrator of the Federal Aviation Administration exercise all the functions, powers, and duties of the Secretary pertaining to aviation safety. Thus, although the Administrator is organizationally subordinate to the Secretary of the United States Department of Transportation, in matters of aviation safety his authority is preeminent. Rulings of the Administrator may nevertheless be appealed through the National Transportation Safety Board.[66]

While this new law had little impact on the responsibilities of the FAA, it transferred the authority to conduct accident investigations from the CAB to a National Transportation Safety Board (NTSB). Initially a part of the Department of Transportation, the NTSB was separated and made an independent federal agency in 1975.[67] A more detailed discussion of these federal agencies (FAA, NTSB, CAB) is included in Chapter 3.

The Airport and Airway Development Act of 1970

The Airport and Airway Development Act of 1970 replaced the Federal Airport Act. It marked an abrupt departure from earlier funding practices, since the federal share of airport development costs was financed by aviation user taxes rather than general fund revenues. The companion Airport and Airway Revenue Act of 1970 levied a series of taxes on users of the aviation system and created a trust fund into which those funds were deposited. The Airport and Airway Development Act authorized the appropriation and defined the distribution of trust fund revenues.[68]

Because of the new and ample source of revenues, annual authorizations almost quadrupled from $75 million annually to $280 million. A 1973 amendment increased the authorization still further to $310 million, raised the federal share of project costs from 50 to 75 percent at most airports, and prohibited state and local governments from levying "head taxes."[69] Another feature of the new act was that it allocated funds to air carrier airports in proportion to the share of United States passengers that they each boarded.

In 1976, the Airport and Airway Development Act was revised and extended for five years. Now known as the Airport and Airway Development Amendments of 1976, it increased funding authorizations from $310 million annually to approximately $500 to $600 million annually. The federal government's share of eligible project costs at airports other than the largest hubs was increased again from 75 to 90 percent. A new formula was devised for computing enplanement entitlement funds at air carrier airports, with each airport guaranteed a minimum of $150,000, but prohibited from receiving more than $10 million annually.[70]

Airline Deregulation Legislation

In the late 1970s three laws were passed which would practically eliminate the federal government's airline economic regulation authority.

In 1977, PL 163 (Federal Aviation act of 1958—Insurance Risks) amended the Federal Aviation Act to deregulate all-cargo air services. Initially, existing all-cargo carriers would be allowed to serve whatever markets they wished. One year after passage of the act, all air cargo certificates would be granted by the CAB to any applicant that demonstrated that it was fit, willing, and able to provide that service. The amendment also permitted air cargo carriers to establish their own rates, provided that they were not predatory or discriminatory.

On October 24, 1978, after many years of debate, Congress passed the Airline Deregulation Act of 1978 (PL 95-504). This act provided for a gradual transition from an essentially regulated environment to one in which the airline's fortunes were to be governed by free market principles. Major provisions of the act included:

1. Revision of the CAB's declaration of policy to stress competition, and prohibit discriminatory practices.[71] In 1985 the CAB would be eliminated.

2. Liberalizing the rules under which existing domestic air carriers could enter new markets. At the end of 1981 CAB control over market entry was to be eliminated.

3. Granting carriers the flexibility to vary their fares within a specified zone of reasonableness without CAB approval. Board control over fares would be eliminated on January 1, 1983.

4. Transferring authority over air carrier mergers and agreements to the Department of Justice on January 1, 1985, and generally weakening the authority to grant immunity from antitrust laws. (Advantages to the public had to outweigh anticompetitive effects of the specified action.)

5. Raising the standard for carriers exempt from CAB regulation from aircraft below 12,500 pound maximum gross weight and carrying fewer than 30 passengers to aircraft of less than 56 pasenger capacity or 18,000 pounds cargo capacity.

6. Establishing a new essential air service program to guarantee ten years of service to communities threatened with the loss of air service because of deregulation.

7. Eliminating the CAB in 1985, and transferring its remaining functions to the United States Department of Transportation, Department of Justice, Post Office, and the Department of State.[72]

The CAB implemented the Airline Deregulation Act in an expedited fashion. Carriers were granted entry to more markets than the automatic one per year stipulated during the first three years of the act, and the zone of reasonableness in which carriers were allowed to vary their fares without CAB approval was widened. The CAB also encouraged maximum competition, innovative pricing, and the establishment of new carriers. Dissatisfaction over some of the provisions in the Airline Deregulation Act, and ambiguity as to how deregulation would ultimately be carried out, has resulted in calls for clarification. This issue is discussed in greater detail in Chapter 8.

The principles of airline deregulation were extended on a worldwide basis by the International Air Transportation Competition Act of 1979. This act 1) modifies the CAB's declaration of policy to stress competition in foreign air transportation and strengthens the competitive position of United States carriers to at least insure equality with foreign air carriers, 2) grants foreign carriers greater flexibility in setting fares to be able to respond to escalating or declining operating costs, and 3) grants the CAB authority (subject to Presidential approval) to revoke permits or suspend the tariffs of foreign carriers whose governments place restrictions on and discriminate against United States carriers.[73]

It must be understood that the ability to carry out international deregulation rests upon the willingness of foreign governments to ascribe to free-market principles and to apply those principles in the negotiations of bilateral agreements. Despite the regulatory powers granted the CAB in the International Air Transportation Competition Act of 1979, some countries continue to employ a policy of restricting competition.

The Aviation Safety and Noise Abatement Act of 1979

The Aviation Safety and Noise Abatement (ASNA) Act of 1979 (PL 96-193) was passed to "provide and carry out noise compatibility programs, and to provide assistance to insure continued safety in aviation."[74] Title 1 of the act requires that the Secretary of the United States Department of Transportation, in consultation with other public agencies, establish a single airport noise measuring system and identify land uses that are compatible with airport development. It also enables airport operators to submit noise exposure maps to the Secretary in order to define noncompatible land use and authorizes them to develop noise compatibility programs for approval by the Secretary. The ASNA Act also provides funding for noise compatibility programs. The authority and responsibilities of the Secretary under the ASNA Act were delegated to the Administrator of the Federal Aviation Administration in 1980. In 1981, the FAA promulgated interim regulations (FAR Part 150) to carry out the intent of the ASNA Act. FAR Part 150 is discussed in greater detail in Chapter 6.[75]

The major impact of this new law has been to strengthen the federal government's role in promoting land use compatibility while leaving to the local airport sponsor the responsibility for determining how compatibility can best be achieved. By standardizing procedures for measuring noise and developing compatibility programs, and by providing funds for carrying out those programs, the law encourages systematic analysis.

The Airport and Airway Improvement Act of 1982

In the fall of 1980 the Airport and Airway Development Amendments of 1976 (amended version of Airport and Airway Development Act of 1970) expired. After two years of debate on the nature of a replacement bill, Congress enacted the Airport and Airway Improvement Act in September, 1982 (Title V of PL 97-248). The new funding legislation reflects a change in FAA philosophy in two areas.

1. More emphasis is placed on making best use of the existing airport system rather than expanding it. This is reflected in efforts to promote the joint use of miltary airports, upgrade the air traffic control system, and fund selected privately owned public use airports.[76]

2. Emphasis is placed on the airport and airway system covering a greater share of its own costs and each user of the system bearing a fair share of that cost. This is demonstrated by the fact that the Airport and Airway Trust Fund will cover 75 percent (rather than the previous 50 percent) of all aviation expenditures and that there has been an increase in general aviation fuel taxes.[77]

Major provisions of the new law deal with the level and sources of funds for airport and airway improvements and the allocation of those funds to various categories of airports and projects. During the federal fiscal year 1983–87 period, the new law authorizes $13.2 billion to cover FAA operations and maintenance expenses, $6.3 billion to upgrade the air traffic control and airway system, $1.1 billion for research and development, and $4.3 billion for airport improvements. While the first three programs are essentially internal to the FAA, the last channels money to airport sponsors throughout the country.

The $4.3 billion for airport improvements is disaggregated into annual authorizations as follows:

FY 1983	$600 million
FY 1984	$793.5 million
FY 1985	$912 million
FY 1986	$1,017 million
FY 1987	$1,017.2 million

The term authorizations needs some clarification. When the law states that $600 million is authorized for airport improvements in FY 1983, it means that Congress has the authority to set aside or appropriate *up to* $600 million for airport improvements. Congress may, however, at its discretion appropriate less than the fully authorized funding level to reduce federal spending.

The airport and other funding programs are financed in large part by a series of aviation user taxes deposited in the Airport and and Airway Trust Fund as follows: 8 percent airline ticket tax, 5 percent tax on air freight, a tax on aircraft by weight and engine type, $3.00 international passenger head tax, an excise tax on aircraft tubes and tires, a $.12 per gallon tax on aviation gasoline (raised from $.07), and a $.14 per gallon tax on noncommercial jet fuel (raised from $.07). General revenues supplement the trust fund to cover federal aviation expenditures.

Annual appropriations for airport development are allocated as follows:

50%	Primary airports (commercial service airports that board more than 31,000 passengers annually). These airports receive funds in proportion to their annual passenger boardings.
5.5%	Nonprimary commercial service airports (airports that board less than 31,000 passengers annually, but more than 2,500).
10%	Reliever airports (airports which relieve congestion at a commercial service airport and provide more general aviation access).
12%	All other airports (includes old general aviation category). These funds are allocated to each state in proportion to its percentage of United States population and land area.
8%	Noise compatibility projects. These projects can only be undertaken at airports that have an FAA approved noise abatement program.
1%	Integrated airport system planning. This includes the preparation of state and metropolitan area airport system plans. A system plan examines a set of airports within a specific geographic area and develops broad policies and recommendations to maximize the benefits of that "system."
13.5%	Discretionary funds. These funds can be allocated to any class of airport or planning project at the discretion of the Secretary of the United States Department of Transportation. Presumably these allocations are made on the basis of "need" rather than through the application of a formula.

These federal funds are used to cover 75 percent of the eligible project costs at commercial service airports that annually enplane more than .25 percent of the national total of passengers (medium and large hubs) and 90 percent at all other airports.

To be eligible for funding, an airport must be identified in the National Plan of Integrated Airport Systems (Previously known as the National Airport System Plan or NASP). Eligible projects run the gamut from airfield and terminal improvements to the acquisition of land and airport equipment.

3

The Federal Regulators

OVERVIEW OF REGULATORS

This chapter will examine the various federal bodies which regulate the aviation industry. As background, however, it is instructive to provide an overview of the regulators at all levels of government and the private sector.

At the federal level there are three key aviation-related regulatory bodies. These are: 1) the Federal Aviation Administration, United States Department of Transportation, which is involved in the regulation of aviation safety and the promotion of air commerce; 2) the National Transportation Safety Board, which is responsible for investigating aviation accidents and recommending safety-related regulatory improvements to the Federal Aviation Administration; and 3) the Civil Aeronautics Board, which has jurisdiction over the economic regulation of air transportation until the agency's "sunset" is implemented. In addition to these key aviation-related federal agencies, there are a number of nonaviation related bodies at the federal level which have a role in regulating the aviation industry. These will be reviewed at the end of the chapter.

Complementing the federal regulators are those that exist at the state level. The authority exercised by state regulators varies but can be classified into several broad categories: 1) regulation of intrastate air transportation, 2) enhancement of aviation safety through a variety of programs which complement rather than preempt federal authority, 3) regulation of environmental impacts in selected states, 4) regulation of airport development and to some extent operations, and 5) promotion of the aviation industry.

Finally, there are regulations effecting aviation at the local government level. That is, the local airport governing body generally establishes rules for the use of its facility. These rules are formulated to regulate areas of aviation not already regulated by another level of government. For example, local "regulators" exercise control over the prices charged for the use of airport facilities and services.

Outside of the arena of government regulation, is the concept of "self regulaton" by the aviation industry. The vehicles for such self-regulation are the voluntary associations of the components of the aviation industry. They include, but are not limited to: 1) the American Association of Airport Executives, 2) the Air Transport Association of America (for major airlines), 3) the Regional Airline Association, 4) the National Air Transport Association (for aircraft owning businesses), 5) the General Aviation Manufacturers Association (for general aviation-related manufacturers), 6) the Aircraft Owners and Pilots Assocation, and 7) the National Assocation of State Aviation Officials. The remaining portions of this chapter will be devoted to a discussion of federal regulators, while state and local regulators will be discussed in Chapter 4.

THE FEDERAL AVIATION ADMINISTRATION

The Federal Aviation Administration (FAA), a branch of the United States Department of Transportation, superseded the independent Federal Aviation Agency with the passage of the United States Department of Transportation Act of 1966.[1]

The FAA is one of the most powerful government agencies. With tens of thousands of employees, a multibillion dollar budget, offices all over the world, its own fleet of aircraft, and an extensive data file on airmen, aircraft, and airports, its influence is tremendous. For anyone even remotely associated with aviation, the FAA touches or intrudes upon their lives constantly. At the top of the FAA's organizational structure is the Administrator who presides over its headquarters office in Washington, D.C. Assisting him (or her) are numerous associate administrators who oversee the various functions of the FAA and have jurisdiction over air traffic and airway facilities, aviation standards, airports, policy and international aviation affairs, administration, and engineering and development.[2] Offices below the associate administrator level are shown in Figure 1.

FAA headquarters is represented by various regional offices within the United States which exercise jurisdiction over a multistate area and address problems that arise in the field. These regional offices carry out policies and enforce the rules and regulations developed in Washington.[3] The FAA also has international regional offices and an academy in Oklahoma City where FAA personnel are trained and records on aircraft and airmen are kept.[4] At an even more local level than the regional offices are the air carrier, general aviation, flight standard, and engineering and manufacturing district offices. Some regions have airport district offices to facilitate the administration of the airport improvement program.

Air Carrier District Offices (ACDOs) are responsible for assuring air carrier safety and grant certificates demonstrating compliance with the FARs. They are involved in approving air carrier operating procedures, monitoring airmen proficiency, and checking the adequacy of airports and aircraft used by the carriers. General Aviation District Offices (GADOs) promote general aviation safety by overseeing the conduct of airmen, checking the airworthiness of aircraft, monitoring air agencies, and initiating corrective action where aircraft accidents result from negligence or noncompliance with the FARs. These offices also hold clinics for the purpose of promoting safety. When an Air Carrier District Office is combined with a General Aviation District Office, it is known as a Flight Standards District Office (FSDO).[5] A fourth type of district office is involved in the certification of aircraft and related products. It is known as an Engineering and Manufacturing District Office or an Aircraft Engineering District Office. Other FAA offices are related to the air traffic control function. These include air route traffic control centers, flight service stations, and control towers.

The Federal Aviation Act of 1958 assigned to the FAA the following responsibilities: 1) the regulation of air commerce to promote its development and safety and to meet defense needs, 2) the promotion, encouragement, and development of civil aeronautics, 3) the control and use of navigable airspace and regulation of civil and military operations in such airspace in the interest of the efficiency and safety of both, 4) the consolidation of research and development with respect to air navigation facilities as well as their installation and operation, and 5) the development and operation of a common system of air traffic control and navigation for both military and civilian aircraft.[6] In summary then the FAA is charged with regulating safety and promoting aeronautics. All of its activities stem from or are consistent with one or both of these goals.

The FAA's major functions or activities can be divided into broad categories. These are:

1. Safety. This involves activities that relate directly to regulating and promoting aviation safety.

2. Air traffic control and air navigation. This involves the control of the use of navigable airspace and the regulation of civil and military operations in such airspace in the interest of the safety and efficiency of both.

3. Airports. The FAA is charged with administering a funding program

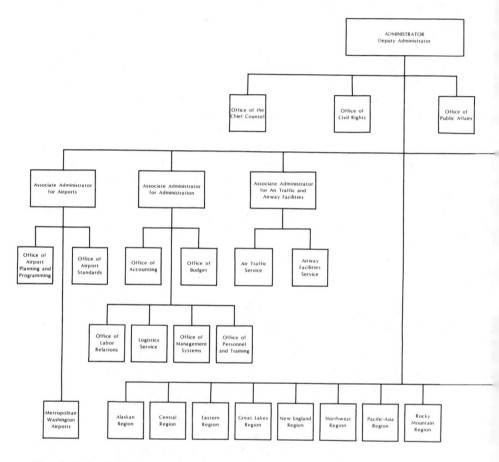

Fig. 1. Federal Aviation Administration organization chart. (From FAA Order 1100.1A, Jan. 19, 1981)

DEPARTMENT OF TRANSPORTATION
Federal Aviation Administration

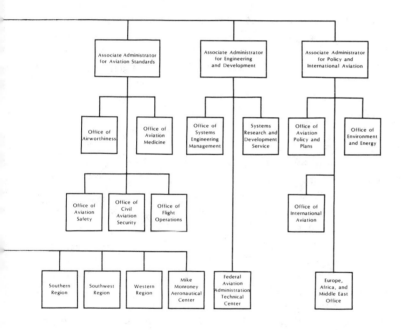

for the construction of airports and airway facilities in order to promote civil aviation.

4. Aviation policy and international aviation. The FAA is heavily involved in setting policies related to such items as airspace, the environment, energy, and so forth, in order to insure the safety and promotion of aeronautics. In the international sphere, the FAA has offices all over the world and works with other countries to insure that their aircraft meet FAA airworthiness standards.

Each of these functions will be discussed in greater detail in the following sections.

Aviation Safety

The FAA regulates aviation safety through the issuance of certificates demonstrating compliance with the Federal Aviation Regulations. These include certificates pertaining to airmen, aircraft, air carrier operations, air navigation facilities, air agencies, and airport operation. Each is discussed below.

1. Airmen Certificates. The FAA requires the certification of all airmen. Airmen include both pilots (student, private, commercial, air transport, flight instructor) and nonpilots (mechanics, repairmen, control tower operators, dispatchers, ground instructors, parachute riggers, flight navigators, and flight engineers). Airmen may have a rating which enables them to fly helicopters, gliders, or conduct instrument operations.

The certification process is designed to insure the competency of the applicant in his or her specialty and, where applicable, for his or her medical condition. Competency is gauged through the administration of written examinations and practical tests by the FAA or delegated representative. Medical condition is determined through physical examinations by a certified FAA physician.

Certificates are generally issued by the nearest FAA district office. This could be the general aviation, air carrier, or flight standards district office. Medical certificates are issued from the FAA Aeronautical Center in Oklahoma City. After a certificate is granted, the recipient is subject to periodic reviews and reassessment to insure that he has maintained his proficiency in his specialty. A person denied a medical certificate can write the Federal Air Surgeon asking reconsideration, petition the National Transportation Safety Board, or petition the FAA under the general rulemaking procedures of FAR Part 11[7] (See Chapter 5 for an explanation of the rulemaking process).

2. Aircraft Certificates. There are three categories of aircraft certificate: type, production, and airworthiness.[8]

The FAA issues type certificates for new models of aircraft, engines, propellers, and other applicances when they meet all applicable safety and noise standards. To determine whether prescribed standards are being met, an extensive, time-consuming, and costly battery of tests are carried out by the manufacturer under the supervision of the FAA. Any change in design of the aircraft or aircraft component requires a supplemental type certificate, or, if of large enough magnitude, a new certificate. No aircraft or part can be produced and sold to the public without a type certificate.

If an unsafe condition is discovered in an aircraft or aircraft component, the director of an FAA regional office can ensure corrective action by issuing an airworthiness directive in the case of an emergency or by working through the slower and more tedious rulemaking process.[9] A good example of an airworthiness directive was issued in 1975. It required that the floors in the crew and passenger areas of wide body aircraft be strengthened to prevent a collapse from a hole in the lower deck caused by depressurization.[10]

A production certificate is issued to those manufacturers who can meet the specifications prescribed in the type certificate of an aircraft or aircraft part. In essence, such a certificate is granted to manufacturers that the FAA deems qualified to produce a specific aircraft or aircraft part. Inspections are carried out to see the manufacturer continues to comply with the type certificate.[11]

Once the type design and production process have been certified, it is necessary to ensure that each aircraft (or aircraft component) meets all required specifications. This is done through the airworthinesss certificate, which indicates that a particular aircraft meets all airworthiness standards. This certificate must be in the aircraft and displayed at all times.[12]

3. Air Carrier Operating Certificate. An air carrier operating certificate is issued to all commercial carriers. It defines various operating criteria for ensuring safety and identifies the network over which the carrier is permitted to operate.[13] The certificate must be amended whenever a carrier alters its network or uses a new type of aircraft. This is an important point since it serves as a control over the indiscriminate entrance of carriers in new markets under deregulation.

The air carriers themselves are charged with operating their aircraft in a safe manner. Nevertheless, FAA Air Carrier District Offices are responsible for the certification and surveillance of air carrier operators. They must see to it that the air carrier complies with operational and maintenance requirements, as well as monitor the proficiency of commercial pilots through check rides.[14]

Air taxi operators (scheduled air taxis were known as commuters; unscheduled air taxis, as charter carriers with small aircraft) are certified by the appropriate General Aviation District Office.[15]

4. Air Navigation Facility Certificate. Section 606 of the Federal Aviation Act of 1958 (49 *United States Code* 1426) stipulates "the Administrator is empowered to inspect, classify, and rate any air navigation facility available for the use of civil aircraft, as to its suitability for such use. The Administrator is empowered to issue a certificate for any such air navigation facility."[16] Such certificates are required for nonfederal navigation aids, that is, navigation aids that are owned, operated, and maintained by local airport operators. These navaids must meet FAA standards as prescribed in FAR 171 to ensure their safe operation. They would include VHF omni-directional radio ranges (VORs), nondirectional beacons (NDBs), instrument landing systems (ILSs), various types of approach lighting, and so forth.[17]

5. Air Agency Rating Certificate. The FAA issues air agency rating certificates to flight and ground training schools as well as aircraft maintenance and repair facilities. To be certificated, a flight school must demonstrate that it has aircraft equipment available in good safe operating condition, the proper maintenance facilities and personnel, and certificated instructors. It must also possess adequate classrooms and teaching equipment and have an FAA approved curriculum.[18] A certificated aircraft repair agency must demonstrate that it has the proper tools, shop equipment, and personnel to repair adequately an aircraft or engine commensurate with the best practices of safety.[19]

6. Airport Operating Certificate. The Airport and Airway Development Act of 1970 as amended (superseded by the Airport and Airway Improvement Act of 1982) authorized the FAA to grant airport operating certificates to airports served by air carriers and to establish minimum safety standards for the operation of those airports. The airports are inspected periodically to insure compliance.[20] To receive a certificate, the airport must be adequately equipped to conduct a safe operation. This means that it should have fire/crash/rescue equipment, fencing, security facilities, and so forth. The airport design should also meet FAA standards and be consistent with the aircraft that is normally served.[21]

Examples of actions undertaken to meet certification requirements include the purchase of fire/crash/rescue vehicles, overlay and repair of runways, improving runway markings, clearing dangerous obstructions, installing fencing, upgrading lighting systems, and installing two-way radios in fire/crash/rescue vehicles.[22] The Administrator may use his or her discretion in exempting some airports from requirements which would impose an undue economic hardship upon them.[23]

There are also a number of safety enhancement programs undertaken by the FAA, which do not entail the imposition of regulations. In many instances, these are more successful than regulations which are difficult to enforce, rely on coercion, and may be out of date. The mechanic refresher and awards program ensures that mechanics receive the best possible training, that their skills keep pace with technological change, and that outstanding achievements are recognized and awarded. Similar programs are available for pilots.

Numerous safety clinics are also held. For example, the stall spin clinics have been offered to enhance instructor pilot skills. Various data collection programs are used to assemble information which have a bearing upon improving safety. This includes the service difficulty program, which spots aircraft maintenance problems; the aviation safety reporting system, which is used to help identify near misses or other dangerous actions by pilots; and the airport data program to spot airport safety problems.

Finally there are a number of research programs which look into ways of improving aviation safety. The medical safety research program attempts to eliminate physiological and psychological factors which jeopardize flight safety. Engineering development programs look into ways of preventing accidents during the various phases of flight and reduce their adverse effects when they do occur.[24]

Air Navigation and Air Traffic Control

The Federal Aviation Act of 1958 charges the FAA with operating and maintaining a common system of air navigation and air traffic control for civil and military aviation and managing the efficient use of the airspace.[25]

To accomplish these functions the Federal Aviation Administration is organized into three major groupings: (1) Air Traffic Service, which provides air traffic control services for civil and military aircraft, (2) Airway Facilities, which keeps air traffic control equipment and navigation aids in good working order (also installs federal navigation aids), and (3) Flight Inspection National Field Office, which checks the accuracy and effectiveness of navigation aids and communication systems using the FAA's own aircraft.

The air traffic control system consists of three types of facilities: 1) air traffic control towers for terminal operations, 2) air route traffic control centers for en route operations, and 3) flight service stations for flight planning and pilot briefing.

Air traffic control procedures hand off the pilot of the departing aircraft from ground control to tower control, to departure control, and then to the air route control center. All aircraft flying above the 18,000 foot level are in the positive control area. They must be transponder equipped, fly under instrument flight rules (IFR), and be under continuous air route traffic control center supervision. Aircraft flying IFR below this strata are given the same service but don't have to be transponder equipped unless they operate in a Terminal Control Area (TCA). Aircraft flying under visual flight rules (VFR) generally operate without air traffic service unless it is requested or when they operate at an airport with a control tower.

Backing up the air traffic control system is a wide variety of flight information services such as aeronautical charts, data banks, and Notices to Airmen (NOTAMs) indicating hazardous conditions.

The VHF omni-directional radio range with collocated tactical air navigation (VORTAC) is the principal navigation aid in use. It serves both civilian and military aircraft and provides the pilot with directional information in en route , transitional, or terminal airspace. Other navaids include the instrument landing system (ILS) and the nondirectional beacon (NDB).

The FAA is not only responsible for keeping the navigation aids in good working order, but often installs them with government funds. Airway Facilities is the FAA branch involved in purchasing equipment, undertaking site preparation activities, installing the navigation aids, and finally seeing to it that they are properly maintained. The FAA becomes heavily involved in installing those navigation aids which are not associated with an airport and are used for en route navigation (VOR or VORTAC).

Representative airspace management activities of the FAA include the following:

1. Terminal control area program. Terminal control areas generally extend from the surface to 7,000 feet with a radius of 20 nautical miles. Aircraft are closely controlled and monitored in this area.

2. Terminal Radar Service Area Program (TRSA). Within each TRSA, all aircraft on instrument flight plans are provided a standard separation from other aircraft on instrument flight plans and from VFR aircraft that voluntarily participate in the program.

3. Schedule restrictions. This involves establishing hourly operational quotas at the busiest airports in the country to prevent operations exceeding airport capacity, excessive landing delays, and provide an equitable distribution of air carrier, air taxi, general aviation, and military aircraft.

4. Air traffic control performance measurement system. This system compares airspace capacity with actual operations during peak hours to determine efficiency.

5. Area navigation (RNAV). The processing of data from VHF omni-directional radio range with distance measuring equipment (VOR/DME) stations by the airborne computer allows precise navigation along any route.

6. Obstruction evaluation and airports airspace analysis. These are undertaken to determine whether objects penetrate the airspace used by aircraft (especially VFR) in the vicinity of a given airport.[26]

Efforts to modernize the air traffic control system places greater reliance on automation, increasing capacity, positive aircraft identification, and reducing the probability of collisions. This subject will be treated further in Chapter 8.

Airports

The Federal Aviation Act of 1958 charges the Administrator with encouraging and fostering the development of civil aeronautics in the United States. Acting under this directive, the administration involves itself in the development of a national system of state and locally owned airports through a major federal funding program, the Airport and Airway Improvement Act of 1982.

This act authorizes specific levels of funding over a multiyear period for the development of airports and airways. The four major programs under the act are the Airport Improvement Program (AIP), Facilities and Equipment (F&E), Research and Development (R&D), and Operations and Maintenance (O&M). Funding authorizations for airport development under the act range from approximately $450 million in 1982 to $1 billion anticipated in 1987. Federal funds cover 90 percent of eligible project costs at most airports (75 percent at large and medium hub airports), with the remaining portion supplied by the state and/or local sponsor.[27]

The Airport and Airway Improvement Act of 1982 is financed through the federal Airport and Airway Trust Fund, the repository for federal aviation user taxes. (See Chapter 2 for a more detailed discussion of the act). Each year, based on the Department of Transportation's budget request, Congress appropriates money from the Trust Fund in an amount not to exceed the authorized funding levels specified in the act. The FAA then allocates these funds to airports and political jurisdictions around the country partly on the basis of prescribed formulas and partly at the discretion of the Secretary of the Untied States Department of Transportation.[28]

To understand the FAA's role in administering the program, it is necessary to take a brief look at the process by which construction projects are undertaken. The first step is to identify potential projects. Projects are normally identified through analysis undertaken in airport master plans, regional airport system plans, state airport system plans, or field inspections. Furthermore, no airport is eligible for federal funds unless it is identified in the National Plan of Integrated Airport Systems (NPIAS), the successor to the National Airport System Plan or NASP. This usually does not pose much of a problem since the NPIAS generally draws upon planning documents to determine which airports it should include. Project and sponsor eligibility criteria are contained in Federal Aviation Regulation Part 152.

Once projects are identified through the planning process, it is necessary to program them at the federal and generally the state level. This entails compiling a list of eligible projects to be funded during a single year or multiyear period, identifying when they should be constructed, the project scope and costs, and the sources of financing. The program listing is often prioritized, and projects are funded in accordance with the amount of money anticipated to be available.

Once there is some indication or feeling that the project has a high enough priority to be funded, the sponsor generally begins the arduous task of preparing the paper work to obtain a federal grant. This calls for the preparation of a preapplication, which if approved by the FAA, triggers the development of the final application for federal assistance. This must be accompanied by all the necessary project justification, plans and specifications (in most instances), and assurances that the sponsor will abide by all applicable federal laws and regulations.

Sometime during the course of the year, the FAA can make a grant offer to an airport sponsor in response to the application for federal funds. The amount of the grant, however, may be less than that requested by the sponsor, which often leads to cutting back on the scope of the project, or alternatively phasing construction. The sponsor executes (signs) the grant offer, returns it to the FAA, and awards a contract to the lowest "responsible" bidder. Once the contract is awarded, construction begins. Generally this construction is monitored to insure that it conforms to the standards prescribed in the plans and specifications. Payments are made to the contractor in installments as the work progresses. When the project is completed, a final audit is undertaken and the project is closed out.

The FAA plays a major role and is heavily involved in the process described above. Although any attempt to organize the FAA's activities into a simple sequence of events would be quite difficult, the following are examples of some of its airport activities: 1) funding and approving planning studies; 2) screening potential federal projects and ensuring that they meet all eligibility requirements; 3) establishing priorities for projects where needs exceed available revenues, which often entails meetings with the airport sponsor and sometimes the state; 4) reviewing project engineering, a function generally delegated to consultants who must certify the accuracy of their own work; 5) seeing to it that all preparations that are necessary to secure a grant are undertaken; 6) reviewing applications for federal assistance and making allocations of funds, allocation refering to the fact that money is earmarked for a potential project; 7) preparing grant offers which specify the amount of money to be allocated to a project and stipulate conditions which must be met; 8) issuing checks periodically to the contractor or airport sponsor as construction proceeds; 9) monitoring construction to ensure compliance with specifications; and 10) conducting final audits and closing out the project. Because of FAA staffing constraints, the last two activities have generally been delegated to other agencies.[29]

Aviation Policy and International Aviation

The FAA's role in aviation policy encompasses a wide variety of activities and in a sense is designed to coordinate the various functions of the agency. To achieve the FAA's basic goals, it is necessary to develop broad policies, objectives, and plans; prepare long-range forecasts; and conduct environmental studies and international aviation analysis.

Some of the activities that fall within the aviation policy area include: 1) conducting economic analysis relating to the function of the FAA—which involves assessing the allocation of costs among the users of the airport and airway system, undertaking forecasts to help determine staffing requirements, and making future preparations for accommodating growth in air commerce; 2) establishing goals, policies, and objectives for the national aviation system through the publication of various documents; 3) developing policy for the evaluation and control of aircraft noise; 4) recommending policy covering environmental and energy programs; and 5) coordinating and integrating FAA planning efforts with other levels of government and the private sector.

Because the Federal Aviation Act of 1958 directs the Administrator of the FAA to encourage the development of civil aeronautics abroad, the FAA is vested with responsibilities in international aviation. Its principal activities include:

1. Rulemaking. Because the FAA regulates the production of United States manufactured aircraft and monitors their airworthiness, and because United States manufactured aircraft dominate the world market, the FAA is heavily involved in regulating foreign air commerce. Foreign governments, nevertheless, are made a party to rulemaking procedures, and regulations are constantly being reviewed and upgraded.

2. Backing the export effort. Airline fleets of the world are predominantly made up of United States manufactured aircraft. This is due to an FAA aircraft certification system and its airworthiness directive backup afterward. The system ensures that United States manufactured aircraft shipped abroad are safe, airworthy, and advanced technologically.

The FAA also helps in the export of United States manufactured air traffic control systems including navigation aids, communication equipment, and airway facilities. It helps foreign governments establish safe air traffic control systems and assists United States manufacturers of this type of equipment in penetrating international markets.

3. Providing technical assistance to foreign governments in setting up their air traffic control systems; bringing foreign dignitaries to the United States to take a look at our systems.

4. Negotiating bilateral airworthiness agreements. The United States entered into bilateral agreements over airworthiness standards with Brazil and Poland. This involved certifying that foreign aircraft manufacturing industries can meet United States standards.

5. Playing a dominant role in International Civil Aviation Organization (ICAO) activities. The FAA is heavily represented on the ICAO council and works closely with ICAO to promote uniform safety and navigational aids.

6. Providing war risk insurance. United States carriers may be pressed into action in time of war. The FAA can provide war risk insurance in the event that the carriers cannot obtain it elsewhere.[30]

THE NATIONAL TRANSPORTATION SAFETY BOARD

The National Transportation Safety Board (NTSB) replaced the Air Safety Board which had operated under the auspices of the CAB. It was established by the Department of Transportation Act of 1966, and was placed within the United States Department of Transportation.[31] In 1974, an act was passed which severed the NTSB's ties to the Department of Transportation and made it a totally independent agency of the federal government.[32] The independent NTSB began operating on April 1, 1975. The primary function of the NTSB is to promote safety in transportation. Although the NTSB is involved in accident investigation and safety issues for all forms of transportation, this discussion will focus upon its role in aviation safety and aircraft accident investigation.

The NTSB has the authority to: 1) investigate, determine the facts, conditions, and circumstances and to determine the cause or probable cause of civil aircraft accidents in the United States and may participate in accident investigations abroad in concert with the International Civil Aviation Organization (ICAO); 2) issue safety recommendations, proposing corrective actions to reduce the likelihood of a similar accident; 3) conduct special studies and investigations on matters pertaining to air transportation safety; 4) assess techniques and methods of accident investigation; 5) evaluate the soundness of methods for transporting hazardous materials; 6) evaluate the adequacy of other government agencies with respect to transportation safety; and 7) review on appeal orders of the Administrator of the FAA, suspending, amending, modifying, or revoking operating certificates or licenses.[33]

Like the Federal Aviation Administration, the NTSB is headquartered in Washington, D.C., and has regional offices throughout the United States.

The board consists of five members appointed by the President and has a technical staff of more than 200 people. On the aviation side, only a part of the staff is devoted to accident investigation. Other people are involved in public affairs, technological advancements, and safety analysis.

Aircraft Accident Investigations

When an accident occurs, the operator of the aircraft is responsible for: 1) notifying the nearest NTSB office; 2) identifying himself, his aircraft, the place where the accident occurred, the result of the accident and the nature of the problem if known; 3) preserving the wreckage until the board arrives—common sense, however, dictating that the wreckage may be moved to help an injured person or to prevent a further hazard; and 4) filing a written report within 10 days.[34] If the pilot or passengers are taken to a hospital, an NTSB investigator usually makes a visit and conducts an interview.

How an investigation is undertaken depends upon the magnitude of the aircraft accident or incident. Major air carrier accidents are handled by the Washington office. It maintains a go-team on alert 24 hours a day, consisting of up to 10 experts in various aeronautical specialities. This go-team is composed of investigators who work at their regular jobs during the day and are on call, day and night, to fly to the scene of a major accident. On such operations, an NTSB member generally accompanies the go-team. At the accident site and related locations the investigators spend from 5 to 10 days collecting evidence which has a bearing on the cause of the accident for presentation at the subsequent public hearing.

General aviation fatal accidents are usually addressed by the NTSB's field office nearest the crash site. One investigator is in charge of each case and may be assisted as needed by specialists called in from Washington, D.C. The probable cause of general aviation accidents are generally determined by the NTSB without a public hearing after an evaluation of the investigator's findings.[35] The investigation of general aviation accidents involving no fatalities is generally delegated to the Federal Aviation Administration, although the NTSB retains the authority to determine the probable cause.[36]

In accidents between civil and military aircraft, the NTSB will work closely with military officials. In solely military aircraft accidents, where the FAA is involved, for example, through its air traffic control functions, FAA officials will generally be made a party to the investigation. In other military aircraft accidents, military officials undertaking the investigation may forward information to the FAA or NTSB, which would prevent a recurrence of the incident and enhance safety.[37]

Major accident investigations are managed by a representative of the NTSB. He or she creates and presides over numerous teams, each of which focuses on a particular aspect of the investigation. This includes areas such as maintenance, structures, systems, power plant operations, human factors, air traffic control, witnesses, and so forth. Each team is led by someone from the Federal Aviation Administration.[38]

Where significant safety issues arise in connection with an accident, the NTSB can create a three-man board of inquiry comprised of representatives from the NTSB, the public, and the President. The public representative must have aviation expertise.[39] Reports on the causes of civil aircraft accidents are made public. Records of major air carrier cases and other selected accidents are often issued as individual, narrative reports. In addition, computerized printouts of all accident reports appear in volumes issued several times a year.[40]

FAA and NTSB efforts have made the aviation safety record in the United States an impressive one. Flying by aircraft is much safer than driving. The safety record of commercial aviation is substantially better than that for general aviation. This probably relates to the fact that the larger commercial aircraft have more redundancy in their systems, have more warning devices, and have more experienced pilots. Within commercial aviation, the major airlines tend to have a much better safety record than the commuters or air taxi operators. Again this may be attributed to the type of equipment used and pilot proficiency.

Civil Aeronautics Board

Although the Civil Aeronautics Board (CAB) was terminated on January 1, 1985, its economic regulatory responsibilities before the passage of the Airline Deregulation Act of 1978 will be discussed to demonstrate how the CAB used to control the business practices of the airline industry. This will be followed by a discussion of the events precipitating airline deregulation, the deregulation act itself, and its impact.

The Rationale for Economic Regulation

Why should the airlines be treated differently than any other private industry and be subjected to government intervention in their day-to-day business practices? The basis of economic regulation of the industry rested upon two arguments. One was that the airline industry was in its infancy and needed protection to ensure safety and foster growth. The other, and more penetrating argument, was that the airlines were viewed as a public utility.

Airline service was "too important" to leave to the uncertainties of the marketplace and needed to be controlled by the government to insure the public interest. Airlines needed to be regulated to prevent monopoly abuses. It was argued that left unchecked, they would engage in cutthroat competition with the larger, stronger carriers forcing the smaller ones out of the market. The ultimate survivor of this competitive contest would then be in a position to charge whatever price it wanted and exact monopoly profits.

This scenario was predicated on the assumption that the airline industry was subject to economies of scale. In other words, larger carriers would have cost advantages enabling them to charge lower fares and force their competitors out of the market. The problem with that argument was that studies and historical experience had revealed that the airlines were not subject to economies of scale and that the larger carriers did not necessarily have lower cost structures nor earn a larger return on investment. Furthermore, even if a larger carrier could force a smaller one out of the market, under open competition, if the large carrier then raised its prices, it would induce new entrants into the market.

Another argument for economic regulation was that it was needed to ensure adequate service to the public. If there were open competition, carriers would only want to serve the largest markets and leave the small cities without service. It is true that under free market practices, service would only be provided where a return on investment comparable to or greater than an alternative use of those same resources would be received. This does not, however, rule out service to smaller cities with smaller aircraft more attuned to those markets.[41]

The economic arguments for regulation were supplemented by the rhetorical arguments of the airlines themselves, who found it in their interest to be shielded from competition. Since under the Civil Aeronautics Act carriers previously providing regular airmail service would be entitled to permanent certificates under the "Grandfather Clause," the act served as a barrier to new entrants.

The carriers through their lobbying organization, the Air Transport Association, contended that regulation was needed to ensure stability so that the carriers could obtain financing for their capital needs. Colonel Edgar S. Gorrell, president of the Air Transport Association, noted that:

> $120,000,000 of private capital has been invested in the present air transport system and that 50% of this investment has been lost. He further testified that unless legislation is enacted which would give the carriers the reasonable assurance of the permanency of their operation and would protect them from cutthroat competition, a number of airlines would soon be in serious financial trouble.[42]

The passage of the Civil Aeronautics Act of 1938 reflects concurrence with the arguments raised on behalf of economic regulation of the airline industry.

The Civil Aeronautics Board was the federal agency designated in the law to oversee the industry.

The Civil Aeronautics Board was an independent executive agency comprised of five members appointed by the President. Prior to deregulation, it exercised its authority by issuing economic regulations and rendering decisions, opinions, and orders on air carrier applications, and other matters that came before it for review.[43] CAB control over the industry was pervasive, but can be categorized into three major areas: fares, market entry, and other business practices. Other business practices included items such as airline mergers, intercarrier agreements, filing of reports and keeping of records, etc. Each of these areas of control will be discussed in the subsequent sections.

Control of Fares

Under the Civil Aeronautics Act of 1938, as amended by the Federal Aviation Act of 1958, air carriers were required to charge reasonable rates for the transportation of passengers and freight. These rates were published in its tariffs, along with other regulations and practices, and, in accordance with law, filed with the Civil Aeronautics Board. If the CAB found that a rate was unjust or unreasonable, it could suspend the tariff. After investigation, the CAB was authorized to determine and prescribe a different, or maximum or minimum charge, or both.[44]

Although the law charged the airlines with the responsibility for setting "reasonable" fares, it gave the CAB a tremendous amount of discretion over the fares an airline could levy. To ensure the establishment of reasonable fares, the CAB was empowered to prescribe rates and practices of air carriers to determine rate divisions, to establish through-air transportation service, and to suspend rates.[45]

The philosophy which guided the CAB's rate-making activites was that the fares established should be adequate to cover the air carrier's operating costs, assuming efficient management practices, and a reasonable return on investment. In determining what was an adequate fare, the CAB examined three factors—revenues, expenses, and rate of return. Revenues related to fare level and structure, demand responsiveness to fares, and load factors. Expenses included items such as depreciation, taxes, and cost allocation. Finally, rate of return focused upon the financial method that would be best for determining a fair return.

The determination of revenues, expenses, and rate of return was a complex task, and the CAB constantly battled with the airlines over rate-making standards. In order to address the myriad of rate-making issues and hopefully resolve differences in approach to the development of standards, the board instigated a series of fare investigations.[46] In the General Passenger Fare Investigation (GPFI), held between 1956 and 1960, the CAB decided to adopt standards which would provide the carriers with sufficient revenue to cover their operating expenses and realize a 10.5 percent return on investment. The CAB also established a general policy linking fare level to the cost of providing service but refrained from setting many specific standards.[47]

Approximately ten years later, the Domestic Passenger Fare Investigation (DPFI) established definite standards for setting fare levels and structure. This investigation was divided into nine phases which examined aircraft depreciation, leased aircraft, deferred federal income taxes, joint fares, discount fares, seating configuration and load factor, fare level, rate of return, and fare structure.[48] The standards which emanated from the DPFI virtually eliminated price competition in the airline industry. Airline fares were generally uniform in all markets of equal distance regardless of the costs, supply, seasonality, or traffic density. They tended to be based on average industry costs and an assumed inelasticity of demand which tended to lead to an upward bias in fare determination. Inelasticity of demand refers to the fact that the CAB operated on the assumption that a decrease in fare would result in a less than proportional increase in revenue.

While carriers were legally entitled to file tariffs that were different from their competitors, carriers that proposed moderate price decreases were forced to answer to competing carriers who complained that the rate reduction was unreasonably low and predatory. The extensive cost, uncertainty, and delay of CAB hearings generally discouraged the carriers from filing lower tariffs.[49]

Control of Market Entry

Another major area where the CAB controlled the airlines was through market entry. The Civil Aeronautics Act granted the board wide discretion in determining entry and route awards. Through the issuance of the Certificate of Public Convenience and Necessity (CPCN), the board was given the authority to determine which carriers might operate in scheduled interstate service and on which routes they operated. The applicant had to be found to be fit, willing, and able, and the transportation must be required by the public convenience and necessity.

Determination of whether a carrier was fit, willing, and able was based upon a carrier demonstrating that it had: 1) ample experience in the operation to be offered and satisfactory training and maintenance facilities, 2) proof that all necessary permits and licenses had been acquired, 3) evidence that adequate aircraft were available to provide service, 4) proof that the applicant had the necessary FAA operating certificates, and 5) evidence that the carrier had financial responsibility. In light of these criteria, it was very difficult for a new carrier to obtain a certificate.[50]

Determination of what constituted the public convenience and necessity was also the province of the CAB and was guided by the following considerations: 1. Was there a need for the new service? Need was assessed in terms of demand, distance between cities on the route, proximity of cities on the route to alternate air carrier airports, surface transportation between the points, capital outlay, and past service trends. 2. Could existing carriers provide the new service? 3. Could the applicant offer the new service without harming existing airlines? 4. Would the government bear any cost as a result of the new service, and, if so, did the benefits to the public outweigh those costs? To determine the answers to the above questions, a route case proceeding was necessary. Economic Regulations Part 302, "Rules of Practice in Economic Proceedings," set forth the rules and regulations governing cases involved in processing and acquiring a new route.

The phases in economic proceedings before the CAB usually included application, petitions to intervene by interested parties, prehearing conference, consolidation of similar cases, exhibits (written evidence), hearing, administrative law judge's initial decision, oral argument, final decision of the board, and judicial review.[51]

The CAB also had the power to place restrictions or conditions on certificates granted to carriers. Closed-door restrictions were used to prevent a carrier from transporting passengers between two points on a route that it was authorized to serve. For example, Ozark Airlines might be permitted to provide service from Chicago to St. Louis via Springfield and Champaign but could not provide nonstop service between Chicago and St. Louis. The reason for such a restriction was to protect competing carriers which provided direct nonstop service and to restrict the regional carrier's role to providing feeder sevice to the major hub.

Another CAB practice was to force carriers to serve points beyond their intended origin and/or destination to prevent them from a fast turn-around time and thus preclude their initiating shuttle service. The CAB also placed restrictions on American carriers providing international transportation. For example, Pan American World Airways flew from New York to Los Angeles and then on across the Pacific. A restriction on Pan American's certificate prevented the airline from carrying passengers between Los Angeles and New York because it would be competing with domestic carriers. Thus if a person wanted to fly from New York to Los Angeles and all the domestic carriers were full, he or she would be denied permission to board a Pan American flight even if seats were available.

Once granted, certificates could not be transferred between carriers without CAB permission. This resulted in situations in which a carrier was authorized to serve a point but did not use its authority. If another carrier wanted to come in and serve the point, it would either be prohibited or forced to go through lengthy proceedings.

Control of Business Practices

The CAB also played a major role in regulating the various business practices and operations of air carriers. This entailed regulatory supervision over accounts, records, and reports; consolidations, mergers, and other forms of control; interlocking corporate relationships, intercarrier agreements, and the classification of air carriers into groups with different rules and regulations for each. To aid the CAB in policing these business practices, it was empowered to require periodic and special reports from any air carrier and to require carriers to file copies of any agreement or contract it might have with another carrier. Carriers were also required to file a list (annually) showing the names of owners of more than 5 percent of the air carrier's stock.

With respect to mergers and acquisitions, the board was only permitted to approve consolidations which neither created a monopoly nor restrained competition or jeopardized another carrier. However, it circumvented this antimonopoly provision by approving mergers which prevented a carrier from failing. More recently the CAB has approved mergers which enhanced the financial viability of one or more the the carriers. Capital Airlines' merger with United in 1961 was one of the first mergers which substantially reduced competition. Competition was reduced in 19 markets including New York/Cleveland and Cleveland/Chicago. This merger was approved on the basis of the failing business doctrine, since Capital was on the brink of bankruptcy.

Local service carrier mergers in the 1960s were designed to reduce subsidy requirements (Frontier and Central; Bonanza, Pacific, and West Coast; Allegheny and Lake Central). Although the mergers did not substantially reduce competition, they did extend the carriers far beyond the "local" boundaries they were accustomed to serve. Ironically, as the local service carriers purchased jet aircraft to serve their more extensive system, subsidy requirements increased significantly.

In the 1970s the CAB once again resorted to the failing business doctrine to approve mergers between Northeast and Delta, Allegheny and Mohawk, and American and TCA. Although financial problems were a reason for approving mergers, there was nothing to preclude the merger of two financially viable carriers as long as it did not adversely restrain competition, jeopardize other carriers, and was not inconsistent with the public interest.[52]

The CAB exerted control over interlocking corporate directorships by examining annual reports which revealed individuals with more than a 5 percent interest in an airline. Individuals who held a corporate position with or had an interest in an airline were prohibited from becoming directly involved in or holding an interest in another aeronautics enterprise in order to avoid potential conflicts of interest.

Intercarrier agreements were also regulated by the Civil Aeronautics Board. These agreements related to items such as fares, baggage, ticketing, through service, aircraft leasing, maintenance, food service, and so forth. The board was empowered to approve intercarrier agreements if they were in the public interest, even if they violated antitrust laws. Thus the CAB was able to confer antitrust immunity upon airline agreements.

The CAB was also authorized to classify air carriers into different groups with rules and regulations for each. Under this authority, the CAB determined that small air carriers, those using aircraft less than 12,500 pounds that were not significantly involved in interstate commerce, were exempt from most economic regulations.[53]

Economic Regulation in Perspective

As a result of CAB control of the fares, market decisions, and miscellaneous other business practices of the airlines, the carriers were limited in the ways in which they could compete with one another. Airlines competed with one another chiefly in terms of service. They concentrated on providing frequent air service and offering attractive meals, hostesses, and other flashy gimmicks to enhance their image. Interest in frequency of service, however, increased costs and reduced load factors. It was also inefficient in terms of the amount of energy consumed.

In retrospect the CAB exercised direct control over the operation of the airline industry. A group of five individuals appointed by the President and supported by a relatively small technical staff was responsible for overseeing the fare structure and markets of the airline industry. Thousands of decisions were subject to CAB approval. As a result, the CAB was constantly showered with a barrage of applications and policy debates with the airlines who provided service and the local communities who demanded it.

A Multitiered Airline System

CAB regulation fostered a protected aviation industry and a multitiered airline system. Different classes of airlines evolved in accordance with their relationship to the issuance of certificates of public convenience and necessity.

The first category included those carriers which received certificates under the grandfather clause of the Civil Aeronautics Act and became known as the trunk carriers. They were the largest carriers that served major cities and traveled over extensive distances. The second class of carriers were certificated by the CAB under the "local service" experiment to provide feeder service from small and medium sized cities to large hubs. These were the local service carriers, sometimes known as regional carriers because they served a particular region of the country (Allegheny, Ozark, Southern, Piedmont, North Central, Hughes Airwest, and so forth). Because they served weak markets, the CAB granted them operating subsidies to sustain their operations. Later they granted them higher density markets as a means of offsetting losses on thin routes, especially since the local service carriers began converting their aircraft fleet to jets. The third class of carriers used small aircraft, that is aircraft under 12,500 pounds, in order to be exempt from CAB rate and market control. These were known as the scheduled air taxis or commuters.

Intrastate carriers, another class, operated large aircraft, but circumvented CAB regulations by operating wholly within a state. Thus they were not subject to interstate regulation. These carriers included Southwest Airlines in Texas and PSA in California in the early to mid 1970s. Other classes of carriers which arose were the all-cargo carriers Alaskan, Hawaiian, United States territorial and overseas flag carriers, and the supplemental carriers (which offered charter services through travel agents).

The Fall of the CAB

Disatisfaction with the regulatory system used to control the economic behavior of the airline industry led to the passage of the Airline Deregulation Act of 1978. This act called for the gradual phasing out of regulations and transition to an airline system governed by free-market forces. On January 1, 1985, the CAB was terminated. A discussion of the events leading up to the passage of the Deregulation Act and an assessment of its impact on the airline industry is presented in the following sections.

The Regulatory Debate

Beginning in the early 1970s, a debate arose over the merits of the airline regulatory system. Some contended that the United States airline system needed to be "liberated" from the constraints of CAB regulation; others argued that CAB regulation had produced the finest air transportation system in the world, and that it would be unwise to alter it. The principal arguments for and against airline deregulation that were presented at the height of the regulatory debate are summarized below.

Arguments for Deregulation

The move to deregulate the economic side of the airline industry was prompted by a perception that there were numerous flaws in the regulatory system that had evolved. Some of these flaws are described below.

1. CAB policy had become obsolete. The CAB's declaration of policy, written in 1938, was framed in the context of an infant industry in need of protection. The CAB had relied on this declaration of policy to limit competition. The airlines, however, had matured considerably and were capable of operating in a competitive environment.

2. Airline fares were unreasonable. Because carriers were only allowed to compete through frequency of service, overcapacity, leading to higher fares, resulted. By comparison, in markets served by scheduled intrastate carriers—PSA and Southwest Airlines—which were exempt from CAB regulation, fares were 40 percent below those offered by the regular carriers on the same routes. Efforts by some supplemental carriers to provide low fares were thwarted by the CAB. World Airways wanted to provide a $75 coast-to-coast fare, but the board refused to consider seriously the application.

3. Market entry and exit were difficult. The CAB refused to certify new carriers and in the early 1970s granted no new routes. Whenever a carrier wanted entry into a market, the existing carrier or carriers would object on the basis of traffic diversion. Hence larger communities were not getting the level of service that they needed or the additional service was unnecessarily delayed. Departing unprofitable routes was equally difficult. Carriers were forced to remain in markets that were economically nonviable longer than necessary because of local political pressures.

4. The regulatory system was highly inefficient. CAB protection of existing carriers from competition fostered inefficiency. Under a free-market system, if a business provides a service inefficiently and therefore at a high cost, a competitor can enter the market and using more efficient management techniques lower his or her price and drive the other out of business. But under CAB regulation an inefficient airline with high operating costs was protected from competition. Excessive costs were passed on to the rest of the industry and offset by fare increases. This inefficiency resulted in an inadequate return on investment for the airline industry as a whole. During a ten year period, the ROI reached 12 percent only two times.[54]

Arguments against Deregulation

While the arguments for the deregulation of the airline industry were compelling, an outpouring of criticism of the deregulation concept soon developed. In an effort to capture the strong sentiment that arose in opposition to deregulation, many of the lengthy arguments against deregulation are presented below. The sheer number of arguments, however, should not be viewed as an indictment of the deregulation concept.

1. Deregulation was too drastic a measure. Many contended that it would be unwise to discard the whole regulatory system because of a few defects. In general the system worked well, giving the United States the finest air transportation system in the world at a reasonable cost. The regulatory system could be improved upon by reform. There were some who even advocated tighter regulatory controls such as CAB regulation of airline flight frequency.

2. Air fares had increased at a lower rate than the Consumer Price Index. Under deregulation where free-market forces prevail, it was argued that air fares would increase at a rate commensurate with the Consumer Price Index. It was also argued that there were plenty of discount fares available without deregulation.

3. Safety would be jeopardized. The existence of cutthroat competition would force carriers, in order to reduce costs, to cut corners that would impair safety. Even though the FAA was responsible for seeing that safety standards were adhered to, the FAA was not adequately staffed to be able to police the entire industry.

4. Deregulation was theoretically valid, but wouldn't work in practice. Support for deregulation was based upon microeconomic theory and analytical models. The assumptions in those models, it was argued, were too weak to justify scrapping the entire regulatory system. In other words a theoretical model was being used to justify the elimination of regulation, and it was doubtful that it would work in practice.

5. Harm would be done to small community air service. Without regulation, the practice of using profits on lucrative routes to support service on unprofitable or marginally profitable ones would end. The elimination or reduction of air service at small and even medium size communities, because of the inability to generate a profit, would be detrimental to those regions' economic development. In many instances smaller aircraft would be substituted for the existing jet and turboprop equipment in smaller markets, reducing the level of service. These aircraft would be less comfortable, less safe, and without all-weather avionics.

6. The public would be inconvenienced. The trade-off between fares and frequency of service would be unacceptable to the public, especially business travelers. The only method of decreasing fares, given higher fuel and labor costs, would be to increase load factors. This would make air travel less convenient and less comfortable.

7. The viability of the airlines would be undermined. Under deregula-

tion it was argued that cutthroat competition would force weak carriers out of business, after which time existing carriers would raise their rates. It was contended further that new carriers could not easily reenter a market monopolized by a large carrier, since one does not start an airline overnight. Thus it was concluded that deregulation would result in market dominance by a few large carriers. Other problems that the airlines would face with deregulation included aircraft financing difficulties and a decrease in jobs. Airlines, it was argued, would have trouble securing financing to purchase equipment without the assurance of market protection, and the instability of the airline industry resulting from deregulation would contribute to a loss of jobs. (The latter argument was raised by airline employees rather than by management.)

8. Airports and airport operators would be adversely affected. Concentration of carriers in the most lucrative markets would intensify airport congestion problems at already overburdened facilities. Airport operators would have difficulty financing their operations because it would be difficult to sell long-term bonds without the assurance of which carriers would be serving the facility. Airport operators who expanded their facilities with the expectations of maintaining existing service or improving it might actually find themselves faced with a reduction in service.

The Push for Deregulation

The need for airline deregulation was highlighted by a General Accounting Office study which indicated that airfares could be reduced 20 to 25 percent if there were price competition in the airline industry. This study resulted in a vigorous debate on the advantages of an airline system governed by free-market forces, and contributed to the development of several legislative proposals to deregulate the industry. Proposals were submitted by the Gerald Ford administration, Senator Edward Kennedy (Massachusetts), Senator Howard Cannon (Nevada), and Congressman Glenn Anderson (California). All proposals sought to reform or eliminate regulations but in varying degrees. Most established a zone of reasonableness for fares, liberalized market entry criteria, and shortened the time requirements for CAB rulings. The Kennedy bill was the most extreme, advocating the transition to an almost completely competitive environment.

The Kennedy Hearings

Senator Edward Kennedy, chairman of the Senate Administrative Practices Committee, held hearings which looked into the way in which the airline industry was regulated. People from all sectors of the industry testified to the benefits and evils of deregulation. Airline officials, consumer advocates, airport operators, CAB officials, and representatives of various aviation interest groups all made their views known.

Frank Borman of Eastern Airlines was a particularly exciting witness. In order to demonstrate how deregulation would result in the overcrowding of aircraft, Borman brought with him models of airline seats which would be installed in newly configured aircraft. Newspaper accounts and pictures of a senator squeezed into a very narrow and uncomfortable seat dramatically put the point across. Other witnesses presented interesting arguments with a substantial amount of written exhibits and testimony provided to back them up. Copies of airline menus were included in the hearing report to demonstrate the lengths to which airlines competed with one another in terms of food and service rather than through price and market entry.

Vigorous debate on the deregulation issue continued. Lining up in favor of deregulation was a rather odd coalition of liberals and conservatives. Liberals supported the concept in the name of consumer advocacy, conservatives on the grounds that it would eliminate government interference in our lives. The specific groups advocating deregulation included Common Cause, the American Civil Liberties Union, certain economists, and air carriers who had generally been prevented from entering new markets.

Speaking against deregulation were many of the airlines, employee union representatives, chambers of commerce, airport operators, small communities, and some states.[55] The debate became rather intense with the Air Transport Association dispatching a "truth squad" around the country to warn of the evils of deregulation. This group came armed with facts and figures and a convincing list of cities that would lose service if deregulation occurred. The loss of service presumably would occur because traffic was insufficient to cover fully allocated costs on low density routes.

Supporters of deregulation raised a number of rather interesting counterarguments to the Air Transport Association claims. First, they pointed out that over the past 20 years the carriers had abandoned many markets even with the existence of regulations. Secondly, many low volume routes would not be eliminated because of the need to position aircraft at maintenance facilities at the end of the day. Finally the degree of cross-subsidy (using profits on lucrative routes to support service on financially marginal or unprofitable routes) had been exaggerated, since many passengers on low-volume segments fed and contributed to revenues on long-haul lucrative routes.[56]

The Appointment of Alfred Kahn to the CAB: Change of Policy

The appointment of Alfred Kahn to chair the Civil Aeronautics Board marked a significant change from previous CAB member efforts to defend the regulatory system. Kahn became an eloquent spokesman for deregulation and set in motion the dismantling of the agency over which he presided and the elimination of the regulations which it promulgated and enforced.

In recognition of the many valid arguments in support of deregulation, the CAB altered its philosophy even before the passage of the Deregulation Act. It began to encourage price competition through approval of numerous discount fares and liberalized market entry and exit procedures by granting more certificates and loosening certificate restrictions.

Many individuals, including the airlines, argued that given the reforms instituted, there was no need to deregulate the industry. What they overlooked, however, was the fact that changes in policy had been made at the discretion of the CAB and could easily be reversed at any time. The appointment of new board members with different philosophies could easily result in another policy shift, this time in favor of regulation.

The Airline Deregulation Act of 1978

The Airline Deregulation Act of 1978 prescribed by law what the CAB had begun to initiate at its own discretion, namely the gradual removal of economic control over the industry. The act, however, could never have been passed if not for a series of compromises reflected in the language of the final bill to appease those who expressed concerns over the consequences of deregulation. These included:

1. Emphasis on safety. Because many believed that deregulation would have an adverse effect on aviation safety, the act's declaration of policy contained a clause emphasizing the preeminence of safety; and another section called for a special study to monitor the effect of deregulation on safety, with corrective action to be taken as needed.

2. Gradual transition to deregulation. To allay the fears of those who believed the abrupt elimination of regulations was too drastic a measure, the act provided for a gradual phasing out of regulations over a five year period.

3. Assuring air service to small communities. To appease those communities and their political representatives who envisioned that deregulation would result in a loss of air service, the act guaranteed "essential levels" of air service for 10 years to all communities served at the time of its passage.

4. Labor protection provisions. To mollify the concern of the airline employees over job losses stemming from deregulation (due to airline bankruptcies or staff reductions), the act contained labor protection provisions.[57]

Table 14 itemizes the major provisions of the Deregulation Act, and contrasts them with they way in which the industry was regulated prior to its passage.[58]

The act was interpreted in a liberal fashion by the Civil Aeronautics Board and therefore implemented in an expedited fashion. For example, while the act provided for airlines to enter automatically one new market for each of the first several years, the CAB permitted the airlines to enter most new markets that they requested. In addition, although a zone of reasonableness for fares ranging from 50 percent downward to 5 percent upward was specified in the Act, the board granted many fares that were outside this range.

One of the more ambiguous and controversial features of the act pertained to the implementation of Section 419 which ordered the CAB to determine what constituted essential air transportation for each certificated point which received service from one or more certificated carriers on October 24, 1978.[59] Thus the CAB was placed in a precarious position of defining essential air service levels for each of the subject communities.

A definition of essential air service for each of the eligible points required answers to the following questions:

1. Where should service be provided to? The CAB usually designated a single hub based on historical travel patterns, although in some instances two hubs were designated. For example, in Arizona, Yuma had Los Angeles and Phoenix designated as hubs.

2. How many passengers would be boarding at the point daily? This was determined by looking at historical traffic levels. This figure would be used to determine passenger flows.

3. How many seats should be provided daily? The CAB determined this by taking its estimate of the number of boardings per day and, assuming a 50 percent load factor, multiplying by two.

4. How many round trips should be made daily? The board by law was directed to provide at least two round trips. In general the board prescribed such service at each point with minor adjustments for the weekend. It was decided that frequency of service should be left to the operator.

5. How many stops should be made? By looking at traffic levels, historic service patterns, and stage lengths, the board determined whether service to the hub should be direct or have stops.

The CAB shied away from designating aircraft to be used. The rationale was that the FAA regulations would ensure that safe equipment was used and the market would ensure that an adequate size and type of equipment would be employed. Nevertheless, the board did agree to consider aircraft types where it would be essential to ensure reliable service. The board's action was in reaction to requests by states and communities that it guarantee the use of 15-passenger aircraft that were pressurized and air conditioned.

The CAB also determined that no city should receive more than a guarantee of 80 seats in both directions or a total of 160 seats a day. It arrived

TABLE 14

A COMPARISON OF THE AIRLINE INDUSTRY BEFORE AND AFTER THE DEREGULATION ACT

Provision	Before the Deregulation Act	After the Deregulation Act
Policy	Competition is restrained. Airlines are regarded as an infant industry in need of protection.	The Civil Aeronautics Board (CAB) alters its policy to allow free market forces to govern the airline industry. It now emphasizes competition, new carriers, and market expansion by existing carriers. It also stresses safety, satellite airports, strengthening of small carriers, and preventing anticompetitive practices.
Market entry	Controlled through the issuance of the Certificate of Public Convenience and Necessity (CPCN). CAB slow and reluctant to grant new routes. Conditions placed on certificates to protect carriers from competition. (Examples: closed door restrictions, unused authority.)	Simplifies procedures and establishes time limits for granting certificates. Makes it easier to get a certificate and enter a new market. (Burden of proof falls upon opponent to show why the route should not be granted.) Gives carriers authority to enter and protect one market each of the first three years of the act without CAB approval. Grants unused authority to other carriers. Removes certificate restrictions. At the end of 1981 CAB control over market entry eliminated.

Rates	CAB has control over fares. Established based on industrywide average costs and rates of return; little price competition among carriers; prices are the same in markets of equal distance.	Carriers can vary their fares from the Standard Industry Fare Level downward 50 percent and upward 5 percent without CAB approval. Fare changes outside these limits are subject to CAB approval, but the CAB is directed to give emphasis to innovative and individual pricing. When a carrier changes its fare, competitors must be given notice via the tariffs.
Mergers and control	A person involved in any phase of aeronautics who wishes to gain control or merge with a carrier must secure CAB approval. CAB can approve mergers which reduce competition.	Narrows transactions subject to CAB approval to those undertaken by individuals substantially engaged in the business of aeronautics. The CAB can only approve mergers which reduce competition where the anticompetitive effects are outweighed by the transportation benefits and there are no alternatives.
Agreements	CAB can automatically approve agreements and confer antitrust immunity. All agreements must be filed with the CAB.	The CAB cannot approve agreements which substantially reduce competition unless the anticompetitive effects are outweighed by the benefits. Proponents of agreements must prove transportation need or public benefits; opponents must prove anticompetitive effects. The CAB is prohibited from the approval of capacity restrictions or rate fixing agreements. The filing of agreements is discretionary.

TABLE 14 (cont.)

Provision	Before the Deregulation Act	After the Deregulation Act
Subsidy	Subsidy granted to local service carriers to serve unprofitable markets.	Subsidy program is phased out in seven years.
Exemption	Carriers operating equipment less than 12,500 pounds and carrying fewer than 30 passengers are exempt from CAB regulations.	Exemption expanded to include carriers with aircraft of less than 56 passenger capacity or 18,000 pounds cargo capacity. Certificated carriers have a duty to enter into through service agreements with carriers operating under exemption. May also grant exemption if in the public interest.
Small community service	No communities are guaranteed service for a specific time interval.	Communities receiving service at the time the act is passed are guaranteed a minimum level of air service for 10 years. If subsidy is needed to retain service, it will be granted. Subsidies can be paid to commuters. Subsidies are based on carrier need but are subject to low bid.

Sunset provisions	Not applicable.	CAB terminated in 1985; CAB authority over markets terminated at the end of 1981; over fares January 1983.
		CAB authority over mergers, agreements, interlocks, transferred to Justice Department January 1, 1985.
		CAB authority regarding small community service transferred to the United States Department of Transportation.
		Domestic mail rate authority transferred to the Post Office.

Other minor provisions of the Act: Definitions, international route cases, employee protection, mutual aid pact, federal preemption, special studies, time limits on ruling on cases before the board.

at this conclusion because it contended that: 1) any community boarding 40 passengers per day (using a 50 percent assumed load factor this is equivalent to making 80 seats available each day) should be self-sufficient based on previous studies that were conducted, and 2) if the need for service were greater than the 80 seats in each direction, it would be taken care of by free-market forces. Thus the ruling was not designed to impose a limit on capacity in the market. While a great deal of controversy was generated by the CAB's Essential Air Determinations with many appeals made and suits filed, most of the board's decisions were upheld. Barring further legislative changes, in 1988 the Essential Air Service Program will be discontinued, and economic deregulation will be completed.[60]

Impacts of Deregulation

The passage of the Airline Deregulation Act of 1978 has had a significant impact on the functioning of the airline industry. While there is substantial debate over its impact, some of major effects experienced include:

1. Lowering fares in long-haul high density markets and increasing fares on short haul and low density markets. In general, a more rapid increase in average fare levels resulted because of rising fuel and labor costs and the removal of barriers to fare increases.

2. Increase of service levels in the high density markets including the introduction of new airlines and the lowering of service levels in the medium and low density markets. In some instances small communities have experienced increased service levels where a commuter airline using smaller equipment more attuned to the market replaced a carrier using high capacity jet aircraft.

3. More stringent standards for approvals of mergers and intercarrier agreements. This, however, did not preclude several mergers which occurred after the passage of the Deregulation Act.

4. Removal of protection from carriers. Airlines are no longer insulated from the swings of the business cycle, and experience the same problems as other businesses during unfavorable economic conditions.

5. The small community service subsidy program has reduced the overall subsidy need as a result of the use of smaller equipment with lower operating costs.

6. Airport congestion has resulted at airports inundated with new service after the Deregulation Act was passed.[61]

OTHER FEDERAL REGULATORS

The regulation of the aviation industry at the federal level is not confined to those agencies with "aviation," "aeronautics," or "transportation" in their titles. There is considerable regulation of the aviation industry by federal agencies which have little to do with aviation on a daily basis. The listing of other federal regulators, while somewhat incomplete, illustrates how difficult it would be truly to "deregulate" the aviation industry.

1. Department of Energy—responsible for the development of standby aviation fuel allocation and price control regulations.

2. United States Department of Labor, Occupational Safety and Health Administration—responsible for regulating the safety of the workplace.

3. Federal Communications Commission—issues licenses for radio operators, radio transmission equipment, avionics repair, and so forth.

4. Securities and Exchange Commission—regulates the reporting of financial interests in aviation companies through stock sales, reports, and so forth.

5. National Oceanic and Atmospheric Administration, United States Department of Commerce—responsible for the issuance of official air navigation charts, maps, and approach plates.

6. Environmental Protection Agency—responsible for protecting the quality of the human environment through the regulation of aircraft noise, and so forth.

7. National Labor Relations Board—responsible for assisting in achieving settlements of contract labor disputes.

8. Department of State and the President—responsible for negotiation and approval of bilateral agreements governing scheduled air service to other countries.

9. Department of Justice—enforces the antitrust rules for all industries, including aviation.

10. Department of the Treasury, Internal Revenue Service—enforces the corporate tax laws related to depreciation, business cost deductions, and so forth.

11. Civil Rights Commission—enforces minority hiring laws and minority business enterprise laws.

12. Department of Agriculture—enforces airline produce shipments and airport agricultural pest control laws.

13. Department of the Treasury, United States Customs Service—enforces the laws governing the importation of goods by air.

14. United States Immigration and Naturalization Service—enforces the laws related to illegal aliens.

15. United States Postal Service—develops and enforces regulations concerning the handling of the United States mail.

4

State and Local Regulators

STATE REGULATORS

Historical Perspective and Overview

Transportation regulation in America began at the state level with state charters for individual transportation companies. Later this original form of regulation was supplemented by the Grange Movement and the related "Granger Laws" passed by several midwestern states in the 1870s.[1] These laws were attempts by the states to regulate the railroads which, in their developmental stage, offered relatively poor service at high rates to rural midwestern states.[2]

The Granger Laws, however, were not enough to deal effectively with the *interstate* nature of the railroads. These laws were finally supplanted by federal regulation in 1877 with the passage of the Interstate Commerce Act.[3] This act, together with related Supreme Court rulings of this era, established the subservient state role in the regulation of transportation.[4] This role was focused on *intrastate* rather than *interstate* transportation.

The evolution of aviation regulation began in ways similar to the evolution of rail regulation. In fact, like the railroads, the first formal regulation of aviation (outside of Post Office regulations regarding the airmail) was established at the state level and not at the federal level. The state of Connecticut passed the first state aeronautics law in 1911. In 1921, Oregon became the first state to establish a state aeronautics agency. This occurred four years before the Kelly Act and five years before the Air Commerce Act of 1926.

In 1931 the National Association of State Aviation Officials (NASAO) was created to represent the interests of 25 states that had aeronautics agencies. Today 48 of the 50 states (all except Colorado and Nevada) have some form of aeronautics agency which administers state laws and regulations.[5] The organizational structure within which aviation is regulated at the state level varies. A total of 33 states have a division of aeronautics within a multimodal, state-level department of transportation. Most of the remaining 15 have an aeronautics commission with an aeronautics staff. A few have aeronautics units within a department of commerce or department of economic development.

Despite the dominance of the federal government in regulation of the aviation industry, the states have still established a significant role for themselves. For example, the states have established themselves in such areas as providing financial and technical assistance to airports, promoting air carrier service, conducting airport, airspace, and air service studies, owning/operating airports and maintaining aviation education programs for pilots, aircraft owners, airport managers, and the general public. Tables 15 and 16 illustrate the broad range of subjects covered in state aviation laws and regulations. Because of the diversity of these subjects, the remainder of this section will be divided into sections representing categories of regulatory function: economic, safety, environmental, airport development and operations, and aviation promotion.

TABLE 15
AVIATION LAWS AND REGULATIONS AT THE STATE LEVEL:
TOPIC AREAS COVERED BY MORE THAN 10 STATES

Areas of Coverage	Estimated Number of States[a]
Airport licensing, approval, etc.	39[b]
Aircraft licensing, registration	35
Airport zoning, obstruction limits	28
Airmen, pilot instruction	27
Handling of federal money, pass through, etc.	18
Liabilities (of aircraft operation, etc.)	15
Municipal airport operation	15
Heliports	12

[a]Estimates based on factored data from survey conducted by David A. NewMyer in 1981 of 50 states (with 26 responding), except "Airport licensing" category.
[b]Based on a 1978 survey conducted by the National Association of State Aviation Officials.

TABLE 16
AVIATION LAWS AND REGULATIONS AT THE STATE LEVEL:
TOPIC AREAS COVERED BY 10 STATES OR LESS

Areas of Coverage	Estimated Number of States*
Airport authorities, districts	10
State-owned airports	8
Accident reporting requirements	8
Airspace, air navigation facilities	8
Parachutes, parachute jumping	6
Airport managers/management	6
Aerial application/agricultural spraying	6
Environmental/noise control	5
Airports in border municipalities	5

*Estimates based on factored data from a survey conducted by David A. NewMyer in 1981 of 50 states (with 26 responding).

Economic Regulation

Prior to 1978, economic regulation of intrastate air transportation was one of the most visible regulatory efforts of the states. The development of *intrastate* air transportation was encouraged in the period from 1938 to 1978 because of the definition of the term *air commerce* contained in federal legislation. This term was defined as the carriage of passengers and freight between points in different states.[6] This language was interpreted to allow the carriage of passengers and freight by air between points within states to be regulated by the states. Thus, while the Civil Aeronautics Act of 1938 authorized the Civil Aeronautics Board to regulate the business practices of interstate carriers, carriers which operated entirely within a state or utilized aircraft weighing with cargo 12,500 pounds or less were generally exempt from federal control. To fill the void resulting from the federal government's lack of jurisdiction over these carriers, many states instituted their own economic regulations.

Several states, including California (through its Public Utilities Commission) and Texas (through its Aeronautics Commission) took advantage of this situation. These states were in the forefront of states which regulated passenger fares, routes, and freight tariffs for airlines flying between points within their respective boundaries. This regulatory action at the state level together with the lack of federal regulation of *intrastate* airlines, encouraged the development of a whole new class of airlines, the intrastate carriers. (PSA

Southwest and Air Florida are examples.) It was noted, however, in a study done by the National Association of Regulatory Utility Commissioners, that by 1976 all states were involved in some way or another in the regulation of intrastate air transportation.[7]

In 1978, with the passage of the 1978 Airline Deregulation Act, the state role in economic regulation was constrained by Section 105 of the act, which stated: "no state or political subdivision thereof and no interstate agency or other political agency of two or more states shall enact or enforce any law, rule, regulation standard or other provision having the force and effect of law relating to rates, routes, or services of any air carrier having authority under Title IV of this Act [the Federal Aviation Act of 1958] to provide interstate air transportation."[8]

This new section forbade the states to replace those regulations being dropped at the federal level. It also precluded two or more states from banding together to regulate interstate carriers with such "replacement" regulations. Additionally, following the lead set by the federal government, a number of states withdrew from the regulation of intrastate carriers and air taxi operators. For example, the Arizona Corporation Commission ended the practice of issuing certificates to carriers exempt from CAB regulation in 1978. This withdrawal from economic regulation of aviation at the state level was accompanied by an increasing emphasis on promotion of aviation and air service at the state level. This shift is described in more detail in the promotion portion of this section.

Safety Regulation

State safety regulations generally deal with airports, aircraft operations, and advisory airspace actions. Because of the strong federal government role in aviation safety regulation, the state role is limited to areas not preempted by federal regulations.

1. Airports. The leading topic area here is the airport licensure, approval, or site review function. The 39 states which have a role in this area function in several different ways. Alabama and Idaho, for example, relicense and inspect public-use airports annually but exempt personal-use airfields. Some states, such as Alaska, Hawaii, and Rhode Island, regulate through direct state ownership of most or all of the airports in their states.[9] States such as Illinois, Indiana, and New Jersey regulate all airports, public or private use. One state, Wyoming, has the power but does not use it.[10] Finally, 11 states do not have the power to regulate airports at all. These states include Texas,[11] which is in the top 10 listing of states having the most airports.[12] In a related area, it should be noted that heliport establishment is covered in 12 state laws.

In the airport zoning area, the states play an important role in helping to

protect airports from encroachment by obstructions. They do this by working with local governments, or sometimes directly with the airport itself, in
enacting a zoning ordinance which incorporates the language of FAR Part
77, "Objects Affecting Navigable Airspace." Many states created model
airport zoning ordinances based on FAA guidelines for use in creating local
ordinances.

2. Aircraft Operations. The regulation of the limits of the liabilities
related to aircraft operation are covered in the laws of 15 states. Also, the
regulation of aerial applications is an issue in a number of states, especially
those which have stronger agricultural economies. One of the issues in the
regulation of aerial applications is the problem of spraying near residential
areas. Another issue is the regulation, in cooperation with federal agencies, of
which chemicals can be used. Since aerial applications are crucial to expanding agricultural output, this will continue to be an important regulatory area
in many states. Finally, parachute operations are regulated by about 6 states.
This has been an area where, because of the high degree of visibility of such
operations—particularly near metropolitan areas—safety concerns have resulted.

3. Airspace. Operating requirements such as airspace definitions (in
conformance with and secondary to the appropriate FARs) and state navaid
operations are covered by approximately eight states. There is increasing
concern over airspace utilization on the part of states, particularly where
there is a high degree of air traffic congestion (such as in California, New
York, and Florida) or where Department of Defense (DOD) and FAA policy
conflicts concerning airspace use have remained unresolved (some western
states). While the state's role in airspace utilization and air traffic control is of
an advisory nature, many states are scrutinizing these issues more closely.
California and Arizona have formed airspace utilization committees comprised of representatives of all segments of the aviation industry to coordinate
airspace usage, and where feasible, resolve airspace conflicts. Florida has
undertaken a statewide airspace study.

Environmental Regulations

Related to airport and aircraft operations is the protection of the human
and natural environment from the impact of airports. Even though many
states have generic environmental laws (e.g., laws covering the broad areas
of environmental impact), only a handful of states, led by California, are
involved in the environmental/noise impact regulation of aviation at the state
level. California has detailed regulations which require implementation by
local governments and aircraft operators. As noted in Table 17, the key to the
California Noise Standards is the establishment of the Community Noise

Equivalent Level (CNEL). This method of evaluating airport noise in the community is based on actual noise measurements in the area around the airport. It is a "weighted" noise measure in that a penalty is established against evening and nighttime noise. Measurements must be taken 48 weeks out of each year at the noise measuring points around the airport.[13] Furthermore, certain noise limits or criteria must be met in certain years. These criteria were set with the idea of reducing noise around airports in California on a specific timetable. This timetable is targeted for an approximate reduction of 15 weighted CNELs between 1971 and 1985, with a final standard of 65 CNEL to be met by 1986.[14]

The California Noise Standards have had a significant impact on noise around California airports. However, there has also been an operational

TABLE 17

EXAMPLE OF STATE ENVIRONMENTAL REGULATIONS OF AVIATION:
THE CALIFORNIA NOISE STANDARDS

Key Features	Definition/Description
1. Community Noise Equivalent Level (CNEL)	The CNEL, measured in decibels, represents the average daytime noise level during a 24-hour day, adjusted to an equivalent level to account for the lower tolerance of people to noise during evening and nighttime hours.
2. Airport noise criteria for airports with turbojet and turbofan operations and 25,000 annual air carrier operations:	CNEL · · Effective Date 80 · · to 12-31-75 75 · · 1/76 through 12/80 70 · · 1/81 through 12/85 65 · · 1/86 and after
3. Designated compatible land uses	Agricultural, airport property, industrial, commercial, property subject to navigation easement, zoned open space, accoustically treated high rise apartments.
4. Noise measurement requirements	Measurement required for a minimum of 48 weeks per year on the centerline of landing and take-off flight tracks.

Source: California Statutes, Title 4, Department of Aeronautics, Subchapter 6, "Noise Standards" Register 70, No. 48, Nov. 28, 1970.

impact on some air carrier airports in California. One example is John Wayne/Orange County Airport. This airport has been constrained in terms of air carrier activity growth by the noise standards and by the Orange County Board's lack of agreement on terminal building expansion to meet growth. Recently developed aircraft with improved noise characteristics have helped meet the noise standards even though additional air carrier activity has been added.

Many states have not taken the action that California has in setting noise standards for airports because the states expected preemptive action at the federal level. However, this preemptive action has not been taken by the federal government. With the issuance of the *Aviation Noise Abatement Policy* in 1976, the United States Department of Transportation placed the responsibility squarely on state (and local) government:

> State and local governments are directly and uniquely responsible for ensuring that land use planning, zoning, and land development activities in areas surrounding airports is compatible with present and projected aircraft noise exposure in the area. They should work closely with airport proprietors in planning actions to be taken in confining serious aircraft noise exposure to within the airport boundary and reducing the number of people seriously affected by airport noise.[15]

Since this policy has been issued, there has not been a flood of state regulatory actions in this area. For the most part, the states have seemed to defer to local governments on this issue.

Airport Development and Operations

One of the states' strongest areas of involvement in aviation regulation lies in their contribution to airport development and airport operations. The states have legislation which enables them to create special airport authorities or airport districts, own or operate their own airports, and play a dominant role in the collection and distribution of revenues earmarked for airport development.

Of interest in Table 16, is the relatively large number (10) of states which have airport authority or airport district laws. These laws create a special unit of local government, which exists separately from general purpose governments such as counties or cities, for the purpose of operating an airport. These special districts or authorities usually have taxing authority separate from the general purpose governments. This is advantageous to the airport operator and, in some cases, to the city or county. An interesting note in Table 16 related to airport operations is that several states mention airport managers in their state laws and regulations. Mostly, the laws require designation of someone to act as airport manager. However, it is a little known fact that even this much regulation of airport managers exists at the state level.

Many states are legislatively allowed or required to own and operate airports. An estimated 8 states have specific legislation covering this. However, as shown in Table 18, a total of 595 airports are owned by 34 states. This is a heavy direct involvement in aviation by the states. But it should be noted that a majority of these 595 airports are landing areas operated for recreation purposes in remote areas or in state and federal parks.

A final area of state interest in airport development and operation is in the area of aviation facility support. For example, many states give technical advice regarding airports. Others give direct aid for airport planning done within their states. States also collect and distribute funds for airport development. Table 19 reveals that a total of $283,507,641 in state funding of airport related programs was achieved in 1981–82.

The major state sources of funds for airport development include, but are not limited to, taxes and fees on: 1) aviation gasoline, 2) jet fuel, 3) aircraft and pilot registration, 4) state-owned airports, and 5) airline flight property.

TABLE 18
STATE-OWNED AIRPORTS AND LANDING AREAS*

Alabama	2	Nebraska	3
Alaska	411	New Hampshire	1
Arizona	1	New Jersey	2
Arkansas	1	New Mexico	4
Connecticut	6	North Carolina	7
Florida	4	North Dakota	2
Hawaii	14	Oklahoma	5
Idaho	31	Oregon	36
Indiana	1	Pennsylvania	5
Kentucky	3	Rhode Island	6
Louisiana	4	South Dakota	1
Maine	1	Tennessee	1
Maryland	1	Texas	5
Minnesota	1	Utah	2
Mississippi	1	Vermont	10
Missouri	2	Virginia	1
Montana	1	Washington	19

Total 595

Source: National Association of State Aviation Officials, NASAO Databank (Washington, D.C., Mar. 1982), 8–12.
*Not counted in this table are "special case" airports such as the University of Illinois-owned Champaign-Urbana Airport, Illinois.

TABLE 19
STATE FUNDING OF AIRPORT AND AIRPORT-RELATED PROGRAMS, 1981–82

State	Amount	State	Amount
Alabama	$ 379,000	Montana	$ 293,000
Alaska	67,841,410	Nebraska	1,533,462
Arizona	3,684,000	Nevada	—
Arkansas	850,000	New Hampshire	211,607
California	5,517,000	New Jersey	—
Colorado	—	New Mexico	203,000
Connecticut	9,005,000	New York	1,733,000
Delaware	300,000	North Carolina	7,000,000
Florida	4,500,000	North Dakota	2,750,000
Georgia	2,000,000	Ohio	550,000
Hawaii	86,276,614	Oklahoma	615,000
Idaho	733,400	Oregon	802,721
Illinois	7,469,087	Pennsylvania	6,015,036
Indiana	1,757,445	Rhode Island	2,063,696
Iowa	1,152,500	South Carolina	1,612,211
Kansas	—	South Dakota	324,500
Kentucky	610,000	Tennessee	1,569,490
Louisiana	5,422,000	Texas	5,000,000
Maine	2,243,193	Utah	275,000
Maryland	23,232,902	Vermont	578,700
Massachusetts	346,894	Virginia	1,280,700
Michigan	2,852,000	Washington	825,392
Minnesota	10,064,354	West Virginia	500,000
Mississippi	75,582	Wisconsin	863,943
Missouri	373,530	Wyoming	9,320,274

Total $283,507,641

Source: National Association of State Aviation Officials, *NASAO Databank* (Washington, D.C., Mar. 1982).

Some states supplement these user taxes with revenues drawn from the general fund.

Handling of federal grants is mentioned by an estimated 18 state laws and/or regulations. Most require such funds to be "passed through" the state government. This pass-through requirement allows the states to influence airport investments at the local level. The procedures for distributing federal and state airport funds varies from state to state, but generally involves the preparation of an annual listing of projects earmarked for funding. Where the number of project requests exceeds the amount of available revenues, most states employ some sort of priority rating system with the objective of channeling funds to projects that offer the greatest benefits to the state.

Some states have specific legislation which defines a process to select projects for state funding. Arizona's legislation (ARS 28-111), for example, states that the following factors must be assessed in developing priority ranking of projects: sufficiency rating, user benefits, economic factors, continuity of improvement factors, social factors, land use aesthetic and environmental factors, conservation factors, safety, life expectancy of project, recreational factors, and the availability of state and federal funds. California has much more precise regulations which specify exactly how a program of airport projects is assembled. These regulations define eligibility criteria for sponsors and projects, funding priorities and application procedures, and an evaluation process to be undertaken by the state.

Aviation Promotion

Aviation-related promotional activities undertaken by the states cover a wide range of subjects. Some are related to aviation safety promotion, others are related to airport or air service promotion. For example, promotional activities undertaken by states include the preparation of technical reports written to encourage air service to small communities within individual states or regions. Examples of these promotional reports are: 1) Kentucky's *Air Commuter System Study*, December 1974; 2) Oregon's Commuter Air Service Project *Summary Report*, May 1975; 3) Illinois' *Illinois Essential Air Service Study*, August 1979; and 4) North Carolina's *Small Community Air Service Route and Marketing Study*, February 1980. These studies are used as a basis to provide state subsidies for air service or to provide state testimony on behalf of essential air service.

Another promotional function is aircraft and pilot licensing and registration and the aircraft inspections and pilot clinics supported by the revenues gained from licensing and registration.

Finally, aviation education is a key promotional responsibility of the states. Several states provide aviation eduation seminars for local civic leaders, airport managers, and airport commissioners. Other states support summer aviation education programs for elementary and secondary teachers.

Conclusions

At times the states have been criticized because their regulations add another layer of red tape and, in some cases, seem to overlap federal regulations. On the other hand, the relatively small size of state aviation regulatory bodies as compared with federal agencies allows many states to be more responsive than the federal agencies. States agencies are also closer to and more familiar with some local problems. This fact has allowed most states to defend themselves against the criticisms of overlap and red tape. In fact, many state aviation agencies serve in the role of finding the way through federal red tape.

Local Regulators

Local regulators of aviation can be defined as associations or local governments below the state level. This includes regional councils of government (COGs), regional planning agencies, counties, cities, towns, airport authorities and special districts.

Regional Associations

Regional councils of government or regional planning agencies are associations of the various political subdivisions within a single or multi-county area. Such associations exist for the purpose of coordinating development within specified regions and serve as forums for exchanging information, airing grievances, and arbitrating disputes.

Although regional associations have no true regulatory authority, they are eligible to receive federal funds for undertaking regional airport system planning. Through system plans, COGs and regional planning bodies play a role in identifying potential new airport sites and determining the proper level of development for existing airports. They also become involved in addressing airport noise and airspace issues, which, because they effect many political jurisdictions, require a regional perspective.

Regional associations in large metropolitan areas tend to be most active in airport planning and development matters. The North Central Texas Council of Governments played a major role in coordinating airport development in the Dallas–Fort Worth area, and lent support to the establishment of a regional air carrier airport to serve the two cities. The Southern California Association of Governments (SCAG) has become heavily involved in locating new airport sites and dealing with sensitive airspace and noise issues in the multicounty Los Angeles metropolitan area. The San Diego Association of Governments has jurisdiction only over political subdivisions in San Diego County.

Regional associations of government often serve as a liason between individual political subdivisions and the state. For example, in California, when the state prepares to assemble its annual program of airport projects, it consults with and obtains suggestions from the 18 or so regional planning agencies, rather than dealing directly with each individual airport sponsor. This saves time and allows for more local input in setting funding priorities.

Local Governments

As can be seen in Table 20, a total of 4,201 airports are owned by local governments (e.g., cities, towns, villages, counties, park districts, port authorities, airport authorities, special districts, and so forth). As owners of the airports which handle the vast majority of civilian aviation activity, local governments have had to establish regulations which provide guidance for aviation activity in areas of local jurisidiction. Generally these regulations have been established in the following key areas: 1) tenant agreements and obligations, 2) aircraft operating rules/traffic patterns, 3) environmentally related rules (usually related to aircraft rules), 4) zoning/compatible land use development ordinances, 5) parking and other ground vehicle regulations, 6) public conduct, 7) emergency, 8) safety and security, and 9) Miscellaneous rules (liability limits, smoking areas, and so forth).

A sample outline of a local airport ordinance is contained in Table 21. As can be seen, the Phoenix example covers a broad range of topics affecting the daily operations of the airport. Omitted from this version of the Phoenix ordinance, however, is the issue of airport noise regulation. Airport noise can be regulated by local governments in a number of ways. As is illustrated in Table 22, airports have implemented time-limited curfews, aircraft type-related curfews, noise monitoring (with limits and set fines), and other methods. Also, there are limits on ground run-up of aircraft engines, departure and arrival paths, altitudes, and so forth. One airport (Teterboro in New Jersey) has implemented a preregistration program for corporate jet aircraft operators wishing to use the facility. This preregistration program is used as a way to inform airport users of the environmental regulations as well as alert them to noise-sensitive areas around the airport.

One example of a local airport noise regulation is that passed by the City of Los Angeles for Los Angeles International Airport in 1978. It says, in part:

> The purpose of this regulation is to reduce aircraft noise in the communities surrounding Los Angeles International Airport by (a) the establishment of an aircraft noise mitigation limit for new types and classes of aircraft which seek to commence operations at Los Angeles International Airport; (b) the implementation of a three-phase compliance program with FAR Part 36 noise criteria to be completed by January 1, 1985; and (c) the assurance that all affected aircraft shall conform to FAR Part 36 noise criteria by January 1, 1985.[16]

Of course, an immediate purpose of this ordinance was to provide a local restriction on operations by the Anglo-French Concorde Supersonic jet aircraft. This noisy aircraft was being flown by British Airways and Air France who were attempting to gain operating rights into American airports. However, the ultimate purpose of the ordinance was to restrict aircraft noise in the vicinity of the airport in compliance with state law.

TABLE 20

THE MAGNITUDE OF LOCAL GOVERNMENT OWNERSHIP OF AIRPORTS

	Number	Percent of Publicly Owned	Percent of Total
Local government-owned airports	4,201	87.6	27.2
State government-owned airports	595	12.4	3.9
Federal* government-owned airports	2	Insignificant	Insignificant
Total publicly owned airports	4,798	100.0	31.0
Total privately owned airports	10,678	—	68.9
Grand total	15,476	—	100.0

Source: National Association of State Aviation Officials *NASAO Databank* (Washington, D.C., Mar. 1982). Calculations were made based on 1982 figures for total airports in the nation to arrive at the "local government-owned airports" figure.

*Civilian only.

TABLE 21
LOCAL AIRPORT ORDINANCE EXAMPLE:
CITY OF PHOENIX, ARIZONA, AVIATION DEPARTMENT

Article I—In General
    Division 1—Definitions and General Rules and Regulations
    Division 2—Tenant Obligations
    Division 3—Miscellaneous Provisions
    Division 4—Aircraft Rules
    Division 5—Motor Vehicle, Bicycle and Pedestrian Traffic and
        Parking
    Division 6—Emergencies
    Division 7—Conduct of the Public
    Division 8—Safety
    Division 9—Aircraft Traffic and Taxi Patterns

Article II—Airport Business and Industry
    Division 1—Use and Operation of City-Owned Buildings,
        Hangar Sites, Light and Heavy Industrial Leases,
        the Leasing of Land

Source: "Airport Field Rules and Regulations," Ordinance G-969, City of Phoenix, Arizona, Aviation Department, Mar. 1970.

Another example of local government involvement in aviation-related regulations is in the area of land use planning and zoning. Where airports are located on unincorporated land, or have impacts on unincorporated areas, the county can play an important role in developing zoning to promote compatible land use. In the state of California, counties are delegated the responsibility for determining airport noise problems, conducting noise monitoring, and developing noise abatement programs. This responsibility is described in the *California Administrative Code*, Title 21, Section 5050. Finally, many counties throughout the United States own and operate airports. Los Angeles County owns five airports; Cuyahoga County owns several general aviation airports in the Cleveland area; Mohave County in Arizona owns the Kingman Airport; and Williamson County in Illinois owns the Williamson County/Marion-Herrin Airport.

TABLE 22
EXAMPLES OF LOCAL GOVERNMENT ENVIRONMENTAL
REGULATIONS AFFECTING AIRPORTS

Airport	Type of Regulation
Los Angeles International, California	FAR 36 limits on fleets of aircraft operated at airport
Van Nuys (operated by the City of Los Angeles)	FAR 36 limits; 11:00 P.M.– 7:00 A.M. limited curfew
Ontario, California (operated by the City of Los Angeles)	Community Noise Equivalent Level goals
Santa Monica, California	Jet ban
John Wayne/Orange County Airport, California	Specific limits on the number of air carrier movements (related to state laws)
San Diego/Lindbergh Field, California	FAR Part 36 curfews★
Boston-Logan International	FAR Part 36 curfews★
La Guardia Airport, New York	Noise monitoring FAR Part 36 limits
John F. Kennedy International Airport, New York	Noise monitoring FAR Part 36 limits
Newark International Airport, New Jersey	Noise monitoring FAR Part 36 limits

Source: Department of Transportation, Office of the Secretary, and the Federal Aviation Administration, *Aviation Noise Abatement Policy* (Washington, D.C., Nov. 18, 1976), 21.
★A FAR Part 36 curfew is one which restricts jet aircraft from operation during certain hours unless they meet FAR Part 36 noise standards. This involves the early application of FAR Part 36, even though not required until 1985.

Conclusions

While the purview of local aviation regulation is narrow, this form of regulation is still very important. Local government regulation has been shown to be strong in three key areas: 1) those affecting airport-tenant relationships, 2) those affecting airport noise, and 3) compatible land use zoning and planning.

5

The Regulatory Framework

THIS CHAPTER DESCRIBES THE RULEMAKING process and discusses the "instruments" of regulation that the federal government uses to control the aviation industry.

THE RULE-MAKING PROCESS

The rulemaking process is described in Part 11 of the Federal Aviation Regulations; and FAA rulemaking policies are elaborated upon in Order 2100.13.[1] There are two categories of rulemaking procedures. The first deals with airspace and airworthiness,[2] the second with all other categories.[3] Because of the highly technical nature of airspace and airworthiness regulations, the following discussion will be confined to the rulemaking procedures for the more general "all other categories." The Administrator of the Federal Aviation Administration initiates rulemaking procedures at his own volition, but may be influenced to do so by petitions from interested parties.[4]

Any individual may petition the Administrator (or in some cases a delegated official) to issue, amend, or repeal a rule—or to be made exempt from a rule. In most instances the petition is submitted to the Rules Docket (AGC-204), Federal Aviation Administration, 800 Independence Avenue, Washington, D.C. 20591. The petition must explain what type of action is sought (issue, amend, repeal, make exempt); the petitioner's interest in the action requested (in the case of exemption, the petitioner must explain the nature of the relief sought and the person and equipment covered by the exemption); and the justification in support of the petitioner's request.[5]

After receipt of a valid petition for rulemaking, the FAA publishes a summary of the petition in the *Federal Register*.[6] Appendix 1 depicts a petition for rulemaking from an airline captain.[7] Note that the captain complies with the requirements of filing a petition by: 1) stating what he wants—amendment of FAR 121.587; 2) declaring his interest in the case—he is an airline captain who finds that the cockpit becomes uncomfortably warm during flight with the cabin door closed; 3) giving reasons to support his request—locking the cabin door is not a deterrent to hijacking; in the event of an accident on take-off and landing, the locked door has interfered with safe evacuation by crew members; and high temperatures in the cockpit can impair the pilot's performance.

If the petition submitted is not justifiable, the Administrator will notify the petitioner of this fact in writing and explain the reasons for denying it.[8] If, on the other hand, the petition discloses adequate reasons for undertaking a rulemaking proceeding or granting an exemption, then the Administrator may: 1) issue a Notice of Proposed Rulemaking (NPRM), or, if there is not enough information to draft a rule, issue an advance NPRM; 2) adopt a final rule; or 3) grant an exemption to a rule.[9]

Preparing an NPRM is not an easy task. The FAA must identify the problem and draft a rule which provides a solution to the problem that is clearly understood, does not conflict with other regulations, is placed in the FARs so that it can be found, and is enforceable.[10] Each NPRM must contain the following information: 1) the time, place, location, and nature of the rulemaking proceeding; 2) the authority under which it is issued; 3) a description of the issues involved or the substance of the rule; 4) a period for written comments; and 5) a statement of how and to what extent interested persons may participate.[11]

The NPRM in Appendix 2 illustrates how a regulation, no matter how well-intentioned, can have undesirable and unexpected consequences.[12] FAR 121.391 requires a minimum complement of flight attendants (roughly one for each 50 seats or fraction above) on airlines for the purpose of assuring safety during flight. However, it also had been interpreted to apply during intermediate stops when passengers remain on board the aircraft. Thus if a flight attendant were to leave the aircraft to assist a handicapped passenger to the gate area (assuming the minimum complement was on duty), the subject airline would violate FAR 121.391. The rule as interpreted obviously interferes with the ability of the flight attendant to carry out his or her responsibilities and ultimately undermines safety. The proposed rule would amend FAR 121.391 to reduce the number of flight attendants who must remain on board during stops to one-half the required complement. Note that the NPRM, as published in the *Federal Register* includes a summary of the issue, background information, and, at the end, the proposed rule itself. It also provides for a

60-day comment period ("Comments must be received on or before March 22, 1982").

Public participation is a key element in the rulemaking process and may be accomplished by: 1) submitting written comments reflecting personal views or commenting upon the views of others, 2) presenting oral arguments at a conference with the Administrator of the FAA or delegated official, 3) appearing at an informal hearing presided over by an FAA official, 4) requesting an informal appearance before the appropriate federal official to state a case or argument, or 5) any other procedure deemed appropriate.[13] An NPRM may be modified or withdrawn as a result of the comments received. After the comment period expires, the Administrator may adopt a final rule, which is then published in the *Federal Register*.[14]

INSTRUMENTS OF REGULATION

The previous section discussed the process by which a rule or regulation is issued, amended, repealed, or an exemption from a rule obtained. A regulation, however, is only one of the many instruments that the federal government uses to assert its control over the aviation industry. The "instruments" of regulation that the government normally employs include laws, regulations, certificates, orders, airworthiness directives, and Federal Aviation Administration Advisory Airculars.

Laws

Aviation laws are passed by the legislative branch of the federal government and are generally authored by congressional staff members. All United States laws can be found in the *United States Code* and are grouped by subject matter into titles. Title 49, for example, is labeled "Transportation" and contains the Federal Aviation Act of 1958 (referred to as the Federal Aviation Program).[15] Laws can also be located in *Statutes at Large* where they are arranged in chronological order.[16] This document, however, presents laws in their original form and does not reflect subsequent amendments.

Some of the more prominent aviation laws which have had a significant effect upon the industry include: 1) the Federal Aviation Act of 1958,[17] 2) the Airport and Airway Development Act of 1970,[18] 3) the Airline Deregulation Act of 1978,[19] 4) the Aviation Safety and Noise Abatement Act of 1979,[20] and 5) the International Air Transportation Competition Act of 1979.[21] In some instances a law will be passed which amends a portion of a preexisting piece of legislation. For example, the Airline Deregulation Act of 1978 eliminates most of Titles II and IV of the Federal Aviation Act which deal with economic regulation and adds a new Title XVI to the act which specifies when the Civil Aeronautics Board will be terminated.

Certain laws which are not directly related to aviation nevertheless have a profound impact on the industry. The National Environmental Policy Act of 1969 (NEPA), which required that an environmental impact statement accompany major Federal projects,[22] prompted provisions in the Airport and Airway Development Act of 1970. These provisions required that an Environmental Impact Statement (EIS) be prepared for federal airport projects which significantly affect the human environment (for example, new runways, new airports, runway extensions, and so forth). In a similar fashion, as a result of civil rights legislation, all applications for federal airport assistance must include assurances that the airport sponsor will not discriminate against anyone on the basis of race, color, or creed. Failure to adhere to these assurances can result in the forfeiture of federal funds received.

Regulations

While laws are passed by the legislative branch of government, regulations are issued or promulgated by the executive branch. Regulations are generally issued to comply with the policies, goals and objectives, and the general direction set forth in laws. For example, Federal Aviation Regulation Part 36,[23] dealing with aircraft noise standards, was developed in response to Section 611 of the Federal Aviation Act of 1958. Section 611 specified that the Federal Aviation Administration prescribe and amend standards for the measurement of aircraft noise.[24]

The majority of aviation regulations are contained in Title 14 (Aeronautics and Space) of the *Code of Federal Regulations*.[25] The code is found in any public library, published annually, and updated daily in the *Federal Register*. Title 14 is divided into three chapters which deal with safety regulations (FARs), economic regulations (ERs) and NASA regulations. Once the Airline Deregulation Act of 1978 is fully implemented, many of the economic regulations will either be eliminated or placed under the jurisdiction of other executive departments.

Other important aviation regulations are contained in Title 49 (Transportation) of the *Code of Federal Regulations*.[26] These pertain to nondiscrimination and minority business enterprise participation in transportation programs, relocation assistance, international air transportation rulings, aircraft allocation (airline) for civil defense, the carriage of hazardous materials, and National Transportation Safety Board practices. These regulations as well as the others cited above are discussed in greater depth in Chapter 6. There are also nonaviation regulations which have an impact on the industry. These regulations relate to the environment (CFR, Title 40),[27] Housing and Urban Development (CFR, Title 24), and so forth.[28] Special Federal Aviation Regulations (SFARs) are issued in response to a special set of conditions and generally expire when those conditions no longer exist. For example, the air traffic controllers' strike precipitated the issuance of several SFARs because of the reduced number of controllers available to handle the traffic. Once the capacity of the air traffic control system had returned to prestrike levels, those SFARs were rescinded.

Certificates

To demonstrate compliance with the FARs, the Federal Aviation Administration issues six different types of certificates. These were discussed at length in Chapter 3 as they related to the FAA's regulatory reponsibilities, and are summarized below.

1. Airmen Certificates. These certificates are issued to pilots, mechanics, control tower operators, ground instructors, and parachute riggers. They demonstrate compliance with the appropriate FARs and insure the competency of the applicant in his or her specialty. Certificates are obtained through written and practical examinations.[29]

2. Aircraft Certificates. The three categories of aircraft certificates are type, production, and airworthiness. The FAA issues type certificates for new models of aircraft, engines, propellers, and other appliances when they meet airworthiness standards, noise requirements, and are believed to be safe. A production certificate is issued to the manufacturers who are capable of meeting the specifications in the type certificate of an aircraft or aircraft part. An airworthiness certificate is issued for each aircraft, and indicates that it complies with the standards of its type certificate and is maintained in safe operating condition.[30]

3. Air Carrier Operating Certificates. These are issued to commercial passenger carriers. The certificate identifies the various requirements needed to ensure safe air carrier operations. These include aircraft weight and balance, crew hours, crew proficiency as exhibited during en route inspections, and so forth. The certificate also identifies the route network over which the carrier is allowed to operate.[31]

4. Air Agency Rating Certificates. These are issued to flight and ground training schools as well as aircraft maintenance and repair facilities. The certificates assure that the "air agency" has adequate facilities, competent instructors, and a sound curriculum.[32]

5. Airport Operating Certificates. The Airport and Airway Development Act of 1970 authorized the FAA to grant airport operating certificates to airports served by air carriers and to establish minimum standards for the operation of those airports. The FAA inspects the airport periodically to ensure compliance.[33]

6. Air Navigation Facility Certificates. These are issued by the FAA to

ensure that air navigation facilities are maintained in proper operating condition. Examples of such facilities include VHF omni-directional ranges, non-directional beacons, instrument landing systems, and so forth. When these facilities are maintained and owned by entities other than the federal government, they must be certified.[34]

Orders

Orders are issued by executive agencies and in general prescribe the rules, policies, and procedures that the particular executive agency must adhere to in carrying out its responsibilities. While orders are issued by all executive departments, FAA Orders are those which have the greatest impact on the aviation industry, and therefore will be the focal point of this discussion.

FAA Orders are not as accessible as regulations. They are not found in most libraries and generally must be acquired from the FAA itself. Some of them contain classified information and thus are not available for distribution. The best method for identifying relevant orders is to consult the FAA Directives Checklist[35] and then write to the appropriate FAA region requesting a copy of the orders needed. A list of FAA Orders by identification number and category is contained in Appendix 3.[36]

Some orders are an outgrowth of and related to specific Federal Aviation Regulations. For example, FAR Part 11 outlines the general rulemaking process,[37] and FAA Order 2100.13 identifies the procedures that must be followed by FAA personnel in preparing a rule.[38] FAR Part 152 requires that an EIS accompany all project applications involving a major federal action,[39] while FAA Order 1050.1C describes the requirements for and contents of the EIS.[40] FAR Part 36 prescribes aircraft noise standards,[41] and FAA Order 1100.128 implements those noise standards.[42]

Other FAA Orders are issued in response to directives from the United States Department of Transportation and are designed to implement those directives. For example, DOT Orders 5600.1 and 5610.1C relate to procedures for considering environmental impacts and preparing environmental impact statements for transportation facilities. These DOT Orders prompted the development of FAA Order 1050.1C, *Policies and Procedures for Considering Environmental Impacts.*[43]

Other categories of FAA Orders are those which describe internal procedures that must be followed by FAA employees (travel and transportation, employee health and safety, training, administration and management policies); technical standard orders (minimum performance standards for specific materials, parts, processes, or appliances used on civil aircraft); and those which are issued strictly for informational purposes (list of joint use airports, FAA glossary, and so forth).

FAA Orders are very difficult to keep abreast of for a number of reasons:

1. There are so many of them. There are hundreds of FAA Orders which either directly or indirectly affect the industry. In many instances individuals are not even aware of the existence of these orders, let alone understand their content.

2. Orders are issued, updated, and rescinded on a continual basis. Thus it is difficult to be sure that the procedures followed are still in effect or are the most current.

3. The availability of orders are restricted, and/or many contain classified information which prevents their distribution.

4. Many of the orders are lengthy and contain highly technical information which discourage reading.

Executive Orders

Executive Orders are issued by the Executive Office of the President. Their issuance is based upon powers vested in the President by statute and the Constitution of the United States. A listing of executive orders can be found in Title 3 of the *Code of Federal Regulations*. "A Codification of Presidential Proclamations and Executive Orders,"[44] January 20, 1961–January 20, 1981, itemizes the Executive Orders by subject headings including "Aeronautics and Space." Listed below are the Executive Orders which were issued that pertain to aeronautics during those years.

Executive Order No.	*Description*
10840	Designating the Federal Aviation Administration as an agency to have certain contractual authority under the Assignment of Claims Act of 1940, as amended.[45]
11047	Delegating certain authority to the Secretary of Defense and the Administrator of the Federal Aviation Administration.[46]
11920	Establishing executive branch procedures solely for the purpose of facilitating presidential review of decisions submitted to the President by the Civil Aeronautics Board.[47]
12079	Authorizing certain functions of the heads of departments and agencies under the Airport and Airway Development Act to be performed without the approval of the President.[48]

A recent Executive Order which is not directly related to aviation has, nevertheless, had an impact on the aviation industry. Executive Order No. 12291 was issued for the purpose of improving government regulations by eliminating unnecessary paper work and requirements that do not fulfill their intended purpose.[49] In response to this order the FAA reviewed its present and proposed rules to determine whether any economic or other burdens may be reduced without compromising safety.

Airworthiness Directives

The FAA may issue an "Airworthiness Directive" with respect to aircraft, aircraft engines, propellers, or appliances when unsafe conditions exist in a product and those conditions are likely to exist or develop in other products of the same type of design. The directive is designed to correct the unsafe condition. Airworthiness Directives are actually considered amend- ments to FAR part 39,[50] and failure to comply with them is a violation of the FARs. They are published in the *Federal Register*. Airworthiness Directives have been issued with respect to correcting the cargo door on the DC-10, eliminating the deployment of the spoiler (used to slow down aircraft during landing) during flight, modifying the fuel intake port on selected Beeach aircraft, and so forth.

Advisory Circulars

Advisory Circulars are prepared by the FAA and provide information and guidance on complying with FAA regulations. The advisory Circular numbering system corresponds to the numerical arrangement of the FARs. Thus, for example, while FARs in the 150 category pertain to airports, related Advisory Circulars are denoted: AC-150/ . . . Appendix 4 contains a list of Advisory Circulars by category.[51] When an Advisory Circular is referenced in a regulation, it becomes a part of the regulation and is legally binding. FAR Part 152, for example, references 65 Advisory Circulars which prescribe standards for airport construction and equipment. These Advisory Circulars are listed in Appendix 5.[52]

Advisory Circulars which are not cited in a regulation provide guidance, but their use is not mandatory. Nevertheless, the FAA often expects the aviation community to use these circulars for needed direction. While the subjects covered in the Advisory Circulars are too numerous to elaborate on, the FAA publishes an Index (AC 00-2TT) which is updated annually.[53] This index lists all the circulars and provides a brief summary of the contents of each.

Conclusions

This chapter has described the rulemaking process and the miscellaneous "instruments" of regulation that the federal government uses to control the aviation industry. While some level of regulation will probably always be necessary, care should be taken to avoid some of the problems that undermine the effectiveness of regulations and the regulatory system. These include:

1. Regulatory proliferation. This is the tendency of a law or regulation to instigate the creation of other "instruments" of regulation in a chain reactionlike manner. The result is a complex and unwieldy regulatory system.

2. Regulatory conflicts. Numerous regulations overlap and sometimes, depending on their interpretation, conflict with one another. This makes compliance and enforcement quite difficult.

3. Regulatory obsolescence. The tedious nature of the rulemaking process together with the sheer volume of regulatory "instruments" makes it very difficult to update regulations in a timely fashion. As a result regulations may be out-of-date and inapplicable.

4. Regulatory obstructionism. Regulations in an attempt to ensure conformity with a specific set of standards stifle innovation. While the innovation may not actually conflict with the intent of the law, because it is something new and different it may not readily be accepted.

With the above reservations, the regulatory system, when kept under control, can be a sound mechanism for assuring the safety of the aviation network. The next chapter will describe in detail the specific regulations which form the basis for federal control of the aviation industry.

6

The Regulations

INTRODUCTION

Aviation regulations have been in existence for many years. As early as 1920, the United States Air Service issued regulations for the operation of aircraft. Some of these regulations are cited as follows: 1) "Don't take the machine into the air unless you are satisfied it will fly." 2) "Pilots should carry hankies in a handy position to wipe off goggles." 3) "Riding on the steps, wings or tail of a machine is prohibited." 4) "No machine must taxi faster than a man can walk." 5) "Do not trust altitude instruments." 6) "If you see another machine near you, get out of its way." 7) "Pilots will not wear spurs while flying."[1] While humorous by today's standards, these regulations were considered essential to ensure safety and taken very seriously more than 60 years ago.

As the aviation industry has advanced technologically, the body of regulations which constitutes the foundation of today's regulatory system has become more extensive and complex. In order to assist the reader in disentangling the myriad of aviation regulations and in obtaining a better understanding of their content, this chapter will discuss and describe them in three major categories: economic and related, safety/environmental, and miscellaneous. These three categories roughly correspond to the groupings contained in the *Code of Federal Regulations* as follows: Title 14, Chapter 1, Title 14, Chapter 2, and Title 49. Environmental regulations are treated separately from but are closely related to the safety regulations since the protection of the environment and its inhabitants from the adverse environmental impact of aircraft operations have safety implications.

ECONOMIC AND RELATED REGULATIONS

With the implementation of the Airline Deregulation Act of 1978 and the return of the airline industry to virtually free-market principles, the economic and related regulations contained in Chapter II of Title 14 of the *Code of Federal Regulations* will become for the most part obsolete. Appendix 6 lists the contents of Chapter II, the regulations listed being divided into three parts: economic, procedural, and special.[2] Because these regulations will either be deleted or transferred to the jurisdiction of other executive agencies in the near future, there is little need to summarize their content. Nevertheless, a brief description of the types of regulations may be instructive to understand how the Civil Aeronautics Board once exercised total control over the economic practices of the airline industry. The Civil Aeronautics Board's control of the industry prior to deregulation is discussed in some detail in Chapter 3.

Economic Regulations

The economic regulations can be categorized into seven major groupings as follows: 1) certificates of public convenience and necessity in domestic air transportation (Parts 201–4, 206, 207–8); 2) foreign air carriers and foreign transportation (Title 14, Parts, 211–18, 262, 297); 3) Air fares and rates (Title 14, Parts 221, 221a, 222–23); 4) Carriage of airmail (Title 14, Parts 231–32); 5) Airline business practices such as accounts, stock ownership, record keeping, data reporting, and so forth (Title 14, Parts 235, 240–41, 245–47, 249–51, 261–62); 6) Air cargo (Title 14, parts 222, 291, 296–97); and 7) exemptions from regulations (Title 14, Parts 287–89, 292, 298–99).[3] While the future status of these regulations, given deregulation, is uncertain, some general observations and conclusions can certainly be made.

1. Since airlines have the discretion to set fares and choose markets, regulations pertaining to Certificates of Public Convenience and Necessity, and air fares and rates, will be deleted. This also applies to air cargo carriers.

2. Regulations pertaining to airline business practices will be reduced substantially. Nevertheless, some of them dealing with filing certain data may be retained.

3. Regulations concerning the carriage of airmail will be deleted and future policies and agreements will be negotiated between the Post Office and the airlines.

4. Since many regulations are being deleted, the category dealing with exemptions from those regulations will become mostly obsolete.

5. Regulations pertaining to foreign air transportation will remain in some form and be transferred to the United States Department of Transportation. This is due to the fact that economic regulations in foreign air transportation has not been entirely eliminated because of the protectionist policies of many foreign countries.

Procedural Regulations

Closely related to economic regulations are procedural ones which prescribe how matters are to be brought before and handled by the Civil Aeronautics Board.

Parts 300 and 302 cover the rules of conduct and practice respectively in CAB proceedings. Procedural rules categorized in Part 302 relate to general cases, enforcement, mail rates, exemptions, rates and fares, adequacy of service, route proceedings, standardized methods for calculating cost estimates, agreements, airmail contracts, and expedited procedures for processing licensing cases.[4]

There are also procedural rules regarding the inspection and reproduction of CAB rulings and access to records and board meetings. Two economic regulations, Part 312 and 313, implement two federal laws—the National Environmental Policy Act and the Energy Policy Conservation Act.[5]

The last four regulations in this subpart ironically were prompted by deregulation. They relate to CAB procedures governing unused authority, downgrading air service levels, compensating carriers for losses, and Essential Air Service Determinations. After the elimination of the CAB, the United States Department of Transportation will handle the Essential Air Service Determinations and either adopt the procedures set forth in Part 325 or develop new ones.[6]

Most of these procedural rules will become obsolete since deregulation obviates route cases, fare determinations, and miscellaneous other airline business practices formerly subject to CAB review. Furthermore, the CAB itself was terminated on January 1, 1985. Nevertheless some of the general rulemaking authority and procedures held by the board have been transferred to the United States Department of Transportation to enable it to fulfill its responsibilities in the area of air transportation.

Other Regulations

The other regulations in Chapter II deal with highly specialized issues, organization, and CAB policy. The special regulations are so specific, and cover such a narrow section of the industry, that there is little need to elaborate upon them. One example of special regulation is "Overseas Military Personnel Charters."[7] Others are listed in Appendix 6. Organization regulations specify matters pertaining to the organization, delegation of authority, fees and charges for special services performed by the board, and guidelines for individual essential air service determinations.[8] The final part of Chapter II, Part 399, deals with statements of general policy of the CAB;[9] while Parts 400–1199 are reserved for future regulations.

SAFETY REGULATIONS

The Federal Aviation Regulations (FARs) contained in Chapter I of Title 14 of the *Code of Federal Regulations* are commonly brought to mind when any discussion of aviation regulation is undertaken. The subject matter treated in each FAR is logically organized into subparts and sections which are identified in a table of contents placed directly after the title of the FAR. A review of the table of contents in itself reveals a great deal about the FAR. Each individual FAR contains sections which explain its scope, to whom or what it applies, its general nature, and its more specific provisions. Other related FARs may also be referenced. Although regulations are often criticized as ambiguous, the FARs are written in a clear and concise fashion. Nevertheless, because of the imprecise nature of language, these regulations are subject to different interpretations.

It should be emphasized that the FAR summaries that follow are designed to give the reader an idea of the regulations' contents but are no substitute for a complete reading of the FARs. If the reader is interested in a particular FAR or a set of them applies to his or her area of specialty, those regulations should be read in their entirety. The following sections will discuss the FARs by categories which group similar FARs together. They include general, procedural rules, aircraft, airmen, airspace, air traffic and general operating rules, air passenger carriers, certification and operations, schools and other certificated agencies, airports, navigational facilities, administrative regulations, and withholding security information.

General

FAR Part 1 covers definitions and abbreviations. Definitions are important because they avoid confusion as to whom and to what the various regulations apply. For example, certain regulations (Part 121) govern the activities of flight crew members. Therefore it is essential to know what the FAA means by the term "flight crew member." Other important definitions include aircraft, flight plan, and so forth.[10] Abbreviations are important because aviation terms are lengthy and cumbersome to repeat continuously. This is particularly crucial as a time-saving device during communication between pilots and controllers.

Procedural Rules

FAR Part 11 deals with "General Rule Making Procedures," and is divided into two categories—rules other than airspace assignment and use, and rules and procedures for airspace assignment and use.

The FAA Administrator initiates the rulemaking process but may be encouraged to do so by petitions from interested parties. The major steps in formulating a rule (regulation) are the receipt and review of a petition for rulemaking, the preparation of a Notice of Proposed Rulemaking (NPRM) by the FAA, the publication of the NPRM in the *Federal Register* for public comment, the review and analysis of comments, possible revisions to the proposed rule in response to comments, and the publication of the final rule in the *Federal Register*.[11]

FAR Part 13 is entitled "Investigative and Enforcement Procedures." This regulation explains how to file a complaint against any person who violates a regulation, prescribes civil penalties for violating aviation regulations, explains circumstances under which an aircraft may be seized by the federal government, identifies how to request a hearing, and explains how an investigation is to be carried out by order of the Administrator.[12]

Aircraft

There are airworthiness standards established for different categories of aircraft and aircraft components. These are generally engineering standards defined by a given numerical threshold. Included in this category are also standards related to aircraft noise, aircraft maintenance, rebuilding, and alteration, and identifying, registering, and recording the titles of aircraft. A description of some of the specific FARs in this category is presented below.

FAR Part 21 covers procedures for the FAA certification of aircraft and related appliances, in particular, type, production, and airworthiness. Type certificates are required for new aircraft, engines, and propellers, and signify that they meet applicable airworthiness and noise standards. Changes to an existing product, if of a large enough magnitude, also require a type certificate while minor changes are accommodated through a supplemental certificate.

Any individual may apply for a type certificate by forwarding the proper forms, drawings, and basic data to the appropriate FAA regional office. To determine whether the product is safe and worthy of a certificate, it is subjected to an extensive battery of tests, under FAA scrutiny, which establish the operating limits and stresses that it can withstand. Each type certificate includes the product's type design, operating limitations, certificate data sheet, applicable regulations, and any other conditions. The type certificate can be transferred to a third party through a licensing agreement and by notifying the FAA.

A production certificate must be held by a manufacturer that produces aircraft and related items. Anyone may apply for a production certificate for a product if he or she holds a type certificate, the rights to a type certificate, or a supplemental type certificate. The requirements that the manufacturer must adhere to include, but are not limited to, adequate quality control systems, inspection test procedures, and product assembling processes.

An airworthiness certificate signifies that an aircraft meets all prescribed FAA standards. Any owner of an aircraft (or agent of the owner) may apply for such a certificate. Standard airworthiness certificates are issued for normal, utility, acrobatic, or transport category aircraft; special airworthiness certificates are issued with conditions attached or apply to special situations. To receive an airworthiness certificate, an aircraft must be properly marked and identified in accordance with FAA regulations, and either be manufactured under a production or type certificate or alternatively conform to the type design approved under a type certificate or supplemental certificate and applicable Airworthiness Directives, and pass an inspection. An airworthiness certificate may be amended with the approval of the FAA, is transferred with the aircraft it covers, and remains in effect unless suspended, revoked, or otherwise terminated. For the certificate to remain in effect the aircraft must be subjected to periodic maintenance and inspections.[13]

FAR Part 23 prescribes airworthiness standards for normal, utility, and acrobatic category airplanes. These standards relate to flight, structure, design and construction, powerplant, equipment, and operating limitations and information. Examples of standards contained in this part include but are not limited to the presence of an audible stall warning, the availability of structures that can withstand specified inertial forces and give aircraft passengers a reasonable chance of escaping injury in emergency landing conditions, fabrication methods that produce consistently sound structures, control systems that can be operated smoothly and are arranged and identified conveniently, the isolation of the engine from the rest of the airplane by a firewall or related structure, the availability of a current maintenance manual, and so forth.[14]

FAR Part 25 establishes airworthiness standards for transport category aircraft. Because of higher performance characteristics, as well as the fact that these aircraft transport the public for hire on a more frequent basis, these standards are more stringent than those included under Part 23.[15]

FAR Part 36 establishes maximum permissible noise levels for most aircraft types. Different thresholds are established for each model of aircraft and included in that model's type certificate. Turbojet and large transport category aircraft must have their noise levels reported in units of Effective Perceived Noise Level (EPNdB) in decibels.[16]

FAR Part 43 describes "Maintenance, Preventive Maintenance, Rebuilding and Alteration" standards. It describes who is authorized to perform maintenance and repair work, how to return an aircraft to service after maintenance, how to keep maintenance records, and the work performance rules that must be adhered to in working on aircraft.[17]

FAR Part 45 explains the standards for the identification and registration marking of aircraft. Each aircraft and many of its components must be marked in a prescribed fashion and the markings must be visible. The markings must contain certain information related to the builder's name, model designation, builder's serial number, type certificate number, production certificate number, and so forth. All United States registered aircraft must have nationality and registration marks of prescribed specifications. There are rules for how markings are to be displayed, where they are to be located and what size they should be.[18]

FAR Part 47 explains when aircraft registration is required and how to register the aircraft. The purpose of registration is that it provides evidence of ownership or interest, controls transfer from one individual to another, helps establish the location of the owner in the event of problems, and helps to identify the number of civil aircraft in the United States.[19]

FAR Part 49 deals with the "Recording of Aircraft Titles and Security Documents." It explains procedures to be followed, fees charged, and defines encumbrances against aircraft or aircraft parts.[20]

Airmen

The series of FARs designated by parts 61, 63, 65, and 67 deal with the certification of airmen. Airmen include both pilots and nonpilots whose work is closely associated with commanding an aircraft or other object of flight. These regulations describe the requirements necessary to demonstrate technical proficiency and in some instances medical adequacy. Depending on the nature and complexity of airmen operations, the requirements vary in terms of stringency.

Part 61 describes the requirements for pilots and flight instructors.[21] Part 63 identifies the standards for flight crew members other than pilots such as "flight engineers and navigators."[22] Part 65 prescribes certification requirements for nonpilot airmen including air traffic control operators, aircraft dispatchers, mechanics, repairmen, and parachute riggers.[23]

Part 67 establishes medical standards for the different classes of pilot. The first, second, and third class medicals have progressively lower physical requirements. These requirements relate to: vision, ear, nose, throat, and equilibrium; mental condition, blood pressure, and general medical condition. A certificate may be issued with operating limitations for those who don't meet medical standards.[24]

Airspace

FARs in the 70s category deal with airspace designation and usage.

FAR Part 71 designates federal airways, area low routes, controlled airspace, and reporting points,[25] while FAR Part 73 defines special use airspace. Special use airspace is airspace of defined dimensions identified by an area on the surface of the earth where limitations are imposed on aircraft operations. Typical examples include military operations areas, military restricted areas, and the airspace over the White House.[26]

FAR Part 75 covers jet routes and area high routes which pertain to routes generally between 18,000 feet and 45,000 feet.[27]

FAR Part 77 sets standards for determining obstructions in navigable airspace, provides for studies of and hearings on the impact of obstructions, and sets requirements for notifying the Administrator of the FAA of construction which might pose a hazard to flight.[28] The most prominent feature of this regulation is the definition of five types of geometrical planes (known as civil imaginary surfaces) in three-dimensional space around an airport and its runways. If an object penetrates the geometrical plane, it is considered an obstruction.[29]

Air Traffic and General Operating Rules

FAR Part 91 specifies general operating and flight rules and is a particularly important regulation for pilots to be thoroughly familiar with. General operating rules relate to preflight actions, the position of flight crew members during takeoff and landing, fuel requirements, limitations on alcohol consumption, dropping objects from aircraft, VHF omni-directional radio range (VOR) equipment check, and so forth. Flight rules pertain to altimeter settings, operations at airports with control towers, VFR minimums, and so forth. Other important sections of FAR Part 91 cover maintenance requirements, large and turbine powered multiengine requirements, and operating noise limits.[30]

FAR Parts 93, 95, 97, and 99 are highly specialized and relate to special procedures to be followed for takeoff and landings, especially under instrument flight conditions.

FAR Part 93 details special air traffic control rules and airport traffic patterns. These special procedures are arranged by airport or airway. For example, Subpart D prescribes traffic patterns for Anchorage, Alaska. Part 93 also contains rules for high density airports.[31]

FAR Part 95 prescribes the altitudes governing the operation of aircraft under IFR conditions on federal airways, jet routes, and so forth. It has one section dealing with mountainous areas.[32]

FAR Part 97 specifies "Standard Instrument Approach Procedures," while Part 99 sets rules for the operation of aircraft in the Air Defense Indentification Zone (ADIZ).[33]

FAR Part 101 prescribes rules governing the operations of moored balloons, kites, unmanned rockets, and free balloons.[34]

FAR Part 103 prescribes operating rules for ultralights. An ultralight is a "vehicle" which is manned by a single operator for recreational or sport purposes, does not carry an airworthiness certificate, weighs less than 155 pounds if unpowered, or weighs less than 254 pounds empty weight if powered, and has specific operating and structural characteristics.

This regulation stops short of certificating operators or the vehicles they use but does impose operating rules on ultralights to ensure their safe usage. The following are examples of these operating rules: no person may operate an ultralight in a hazardous manner, nor during hours of darkness; aircraft right-of-way rules must be respected; no person may operate an ultralight over a congested area or in certain types of controlled or restricted airspace without prior permission; no person may operate an ultralight vehicle when the flight visibility or distance from the clouds is less than prescribed minimums (identified in the regulation).[35]

FAR Part 105 establishes various standards governing parachute jumping.[36]

FAR Part 107 provides for passenger security rules as documented in a security program and applies to air carrier airports.[37] Security requirements for airports served by small air carrier aircraft are defined in FAR Part 108.[38] The security program is designed to protect passengers from acts of violence and aircraft piracy.

Air Passenger Carriers, Certification and Operations

This category of regulation prescribes the rules and standards which govern the operation of air carriers. The types of air carrier included within this category include major domestic and flag carriers, charter carriers, air travel clubs, helicopter carriers, foreign air carriers, rotorcraft external-load operators, and agricultural aircraft operations. One of the regulations in this category also prescribes standards for airports that are served by air carriers.

Principal regulations in this category which will be described in greater detail are FAR Part 121 (certification and operations for larger air carriers), FAR Part 135 (certification and operations for air taxis and commercial operators of small aircraft), FAR Part 137 (agricultural aircraft operations), and FAR part 139, (the certification and operation of air carrier airports).

FAR Part 121 governs the certification and operation of major air carriers using larger aircraft. This rather lengthy regulation contains 23 subparts which explore the many facets of air carrier operation. Topics covered in the subparts include but are not limited to:

1. Certification rules. These explain how to apply for a certificate, the contents of a certificate, and operating specifications.[39]

2. Approval of routes. Each carrier must demonstrate the ability to conduct operations over a route and that adequate facilities and services are available for the proposed operations.[40]

3. Manual. This subpart describes the procedures for preparing and maintaining a manual for the use and guidance of flight and ground operations personnel in conducting operations.[41]

4. Aircraft requirements. Certain older models of aircraft cannot be operated in Part 121 operations. For example, aircraft type certificated prior to 1942 cannot be utilized unless they meet certain requirements and conditions.[42]

5. Airplane performance operating limits. These define operating limits for one-engine inoperative and takeoff and landing limitations.[43]

6. Special airworthiness requirements. These pertain to ventilation, the location of fuel tanks, fire extinguishing systems, and so forth.[44]

7. Instrument and equipment requirements. These explain the types of equipment that aircraft must contain as well as the cockpit check procedures.[45]

8. Flight operations. These requirements prescribe standards for air carrier flight operations including but not limited to crew-member responsibilities, appropriate equipment, emergency procedures, takeoff and landing procedures under normal and engine inoperative conditions, passenger briefings, the provision of inflight services, and airplane security.[46]

9. Airman and crew member requirements. These specify acceptable ages for pilots, appropriate crew complement, and other miscellaneous requirements.[47]

10. Training program. This identifies the proper training program for crew members, aircraft dispatchers, and other personnel.[48]

11. Flight time limitations. These define flight time limitations per day, week, month, and year for pilots and crew members.[49]

FAR Part 121 also has sections dealing with maintenance, preventive maintenance and alterations, dispatching and flight release rules, and records and reports.

FAR Part 135 applies to air taxi operators and commercial operators of small aircraft. These are aircraft that have a maximum capacity of 30 seats or less or a maximum payload capacity of 7,500 pounds or less. There is also a special provision, however, that covers air taxi operations with large aircraft. FAR Part 135 is less stringent than Part 121, but similar in nature. The principal sections of this regulation govern:

1. Flight operations. This governs administrative procedures, airworthiness checks, operating information, informing personnel of operational information, the carriage of cargo, pilots, and flight crew members.[50]

2. Aircraft and equipment. This governs aircraft proving tests, requirement for dual controls, equipment such as voice recorders, fire extinguishers, oxygen, radio and navaid equipment, emergency equipment over water, radar, and so forth.[51]

3. VFR/IFR operating limitations. VFR limitations pertain to minimum altitudes and visibility, fuel supply, and "over-the-top" (flying above the clouds) carrying of passengers. IFR limitations pertain to destination airport weather minimums, alternate airports, takeoff, approach and landing minimums, and so forth. This part of the regulation also specifies operation limitations during icing conditions for both IFR and VFR flight as well as airport requirements.[52]

4. Flight crew members. Requirements are set forth in four subparts pertaining to the qualifications and operating experience of the pilot and second in command, flight and duty time limitations, testing requirements, and training.

5. Airplane performance operating limitations applicable to operators of large aircraft similar to FAR Part 121 in nature.[53]

6. Maintenance, preventive maintenance, and alterations. This specifies standards governing responsibility for airworthiness, inspection programs, maintenance procedures, manual requirements, authority to perform maintenance, personnel, and so forth.[54]

FAR Part 137 governs agricultural aircraft operations. These operations are unique because they occur at low altitudes and involve the dispensing of pesticides and/or other substances. Anyone engaging in agricultural operations must hold a certificate demonstrating that he or she has proper pilot credentials, specially equipped and airworthy aircraft, and knowledge and skills regarding agricultural type aircraft operations. The operating rules applicable to agricultural aircraft include, but are not limited to permission to deviate from FAR Part 91 general flight rules, the requirement to carry a certificate during flight operations, the availability of properly equipped and airworthy aircraft (for example, pilot shoulder harnesses are required), prohibition of dispensing substances in a way that is hazardous to persons or property, and the availability of adequate personnel.[55]

FAR Part 139 covers the certification and operation of airports served by air carriers. The Airport and Airway Development Act of 1970 as amended, mandated the certification of all airports served by CAB certificated carriers. This regulation then, implements portions of that act. Airports served by air carriers using small aircraft receive a limited certificate.

To receive and maintain a certificate, the airport operator must keep an airport operations manual. This manual documents compliance with relevant regulations, includes instructions for airport personnel in carrying out their responsibilities, includes operational lines of succession, includes maps or charts to familiarize the individual with the airport, contains provisions for the avoidance of interruption or failure of utility facilities or navaids during construction work, and shows operating approval by the Administrator of the FAA as well as any restrictions.[56]

To be eligible for certification, the airport must meet numerous construction and safety standards. Some of the more important requirements are cited below:

1. Pavement areas. No more than three inches difference between the elevation of the pavement and shoulders are allowed.

2. Safety areas. These are the areas adjacent to the runways and taxiways. They should not have any potentially hazardous ruts or other surface deviations and should be clear of objects, and have an adequate sewer system for drainage.

3. Marking and lighting runways, thresholds, and taxiways. Elevated taxiway and runway lights, obstruction lights, taxiway centerline lights, and approach aid lighting must all be in operable condition. Airport markings must be visible (runway centerline, threshold, and touchdown zone).

4. Fire/crash/rescue equipment. The airport must have a fire/crash/rescue vehicle of a certain weight and capacity to hold chemical extinguishing agents.

5. Hazardous materials. The airport must have adequate controls and procedures for handling hazardous materials.

6. Traffic and wind direction indicators. The airport must have wind direction indicators of some type and a segmented circle.

7. Emergency plan for response to all emergency conditions. This plan relates to procedures to be followed in the event of aircraft accidents, bomb threats, natural disasters, structural fires, and so forth.

8. Ground vehicles. Procedures for safe operation of ground vehicles on the airport environs must be followed. Such vehicles should generally be equipped with a two-way radio.

9. Obstructions. Obstructions must be lighted.

10. Navaids. Construction of facilities on the airport should not interfere with navaid usage.

11. Public protection. Caution must be exercised to ensure safeguards against inadvertent entry of persons or animals onto any airport operations area.

12. Bird hazard reduction. Instructions for the removal of factors that attract birds are needed where applicable.

13. Procedures for reporting information to air carriers and other airport users. These pertain to conditions on and in the vicinity of the airport that affect the safe operation of aircraft such as a rough runway or the presence of snow.[57]

Among some of the more important operating requirements that the airport must comply with under this regulation are the prompt repair and clearance of airport pavement areas, snow removal where applicable, the cleaning and replacement of lighting, and efforts to control obstructions.[58]

Schools and Other Certificated Agencies

This category of FARs covers pilot schools, ground instructors, repair stations, and aviation maintenance technical schools.

FAR Part 141 sets forth the requirements for issuing pilot school certificates and associated ratings and the operating rules for the holders of those certificates. In order to receive a certificate, a school must demonstrate that it has adequately trained personnel, acceptable aircraft and facilities, and a sound curriculum. Schools may be granted examining authority, enabling them to grant pilot certificates to graduates of its program, without the student taking FAA examinations.[59]

FAR Part 143 identifies the requirements for issuing ground instructor certificates and the general operating rules for the holders of those certificates. A ground instructor must demonstrate his or her practical and theoretical knowledge of the subject for which he or she seeks a rating by passing a written test on the subject. Acceptable performance on the test entitles him or her to a certificate which should be kept readily available for inspection.[60]

FAR Part 145 covers the requirements for issuing repair station certificates and associated ratings and the operating rules for the holders of those certificates. Specific ratings issued include airframes, engines, propellers, radios, instrument and other accessories. The holder of the certificate must demonstrate that it has adequate space for storing equipment and materials, adequate work and assembly space, and proper ventilation, lighting, and temperature to assure that the quality of work is not impaired. Individuals working in the station must have adequate training and proper supervision.[61]

FAR Part 147 establishes the requirements for issuing aviation maintenance technician school certificates and associated ratings and the rules governing the holders of those certificates. The three types of rating issued under this part are airframe, powerplant, and airframe and powerplant. The requirements in this regulation cover facilities, equipment and materials, instructional equipment, tool and shop equipment, general curriculum and instructors.[62]

Airports

FARs in the 150 series deal with airports.

FAR Part 150 is a relatively new regulation which took effect (in interim form) on February 28, 1981. It prescribes requirements for airport operators who choose to develop an airport noise compatibility planning program under the federal program. The rule implements portions of the Aviation Safety and Noise Abatement Act of 1979, which adopts a modified version of rules recommended by the EPA, and establishes the administrative procedures to be followed by the FAA in fulfilling its responsibilities under the act.

This regulation establishes a single airport noise measuring technique and a single system for determining human response to airport noise. It also prescribes a standardized airport noise compatibility program, including: 1) development of noise contours and noise compatibility programs by airport operators, 2) standard noise methodologies and units for use in airport assessments, 3) identification of land uses compatible or incompatible with various levels of noise around the airport, and 4) FAA procedures for evaluation and approval or disapproval of noise compatibility programs by the Administrator.[63]

FAR Part 152 implements the Airport Improvement Program of the Airport and Airway Improvement Act of 1982. It describes the procedures that applicants for federal funds for airport construction must follow. The first part of the regulation defines sponsors and projects eligible for federal assistance, procedures for applying for federal funds (preapplication, allocation of funds, application), standards for offering, accepting, and amending a grant agreement, circumstances under which it is necessary to provide an opportunity for a public hearing, and the nature of that hearing.[64] With respect to project funding, the regulation specifies allowable project costs, the federal share of project costs, land acquisition procedures, and rules for grant payments and project close out.[65] The final section of this regulation, "Energy Conservation in the Airport Aid Program," implements Section

403 of the Powerplant and Industrial Fuel Use Act of 1978 in order to encourage the conservation of petroleum and natural gas.[66]

FAR Part 154 pertains to the acquisition of federal land to undertake a federally funded airport project or operate a public airport. If necessary to carry out the project or efficiently operate the airport, the Administrator may request the federal agency in control of the property to convey it to the airport sponsor. The head of the department or agency may convey it, if he or she determines that it is not inconsistent with the needs of his or her department or agency. Where the airport property is conveyed, the recipient must agree to comply with certain conditions set by the FAA related to continued airport use, nondiscrimination, and so forth, and comply with all relevant legislation.[67]

FAR Part 155 covers the "Release of Airport Property from Surplus Property Disposal Restrictions." This regulation establishes procedures for releasing federally owned property to a nonfederal airport sponsor for public use. This is particularly applicable where the use of a military airport is discontinued and a local sponsor wishes to operate it as a civilian facility.[68]

FAR Part 157 prescribes that any individual who plans to construct, alter, activate, or deactivate an airport must notify the Administrator. Projects for which federal aid has been requested or those involving a temporary airport whose use is limited to VFR need not be reported.[69]

FAR Part 159 prescribes the rules and regulations for the operation of the two federally owned airports serving Washington, D.C. (Washington National and Dulles). These rules cover items such as user charges, curfews, noise restrictions, operating procedures, and so forth.[70]

Navigational Facilities

FAR Part 171 prescribes the standards governing the installation, operation, and maintenance of navaids which are not owned by the federal government. These navaids include but are not limited to the VOR, NDB, and ILS. Each navaid must meet minimum performance requirements. The owner of the facility must make periodic reports on its operational characteristics and any malfunctions that happen to occur.[71]

Administrative Regulations

Four regulations—FAR 183, 185, 187, and 189—cover administrative requirements.

FAR Part 183 "describes the requirements for designating private persons to act as representatives of the Administrator in examining, inspecting, and testing persons and aircraft for the purpose of issuing airman and aircraft certificates." In addition it states "the privileges of those representatives and prescribes rules for their exercising of those privileges." Examples of recipients of delegated authority are aviation medical examiners, pilot examiners, designated engineering representatives, designated manufacturing inspection representatives, and air traffic control tower operator examiners.[72]

FAR Part 185 covers testimony by employees and the production of records in legal proceedings. It also deals with service of the legal process and pleadings. In short, this rule names the FAA officials who become a party to legal proceedings and have the authority to take further action.[73]

FAR Part 187 prescribes fees for FAA services not covered in other FARs. These services pertain to providing duplicates or certificates, and copies of documents with affixation of a seal for validation purposes.[74]

FAR Part 189 describes the types of messages that may be transmitted by FAA communications stations and prescribes the charges therefor. The messages relating to flight safety, air traffic control instructions, weather, administrative messages, notices to airmen, and so forth, are transmitted without charge. However, messages originated by and addressed to aircraft operating agencies or their representatives (such as airlines) relevant to necessary day to day operations are issued at a charge of $.25 for each 10 words.[75]

Withholding Security Information; War Risk Insurance; Aircraft Loan Guarantee Program

FAR Part 191 governs the release of any records or any information contained therein in the possession of the FAA which has been obtained or developed in the conduct of research and development activities. Some records are not to be released for public inspection or copying. These relate to hijacker profiles, profiles for baggage screening, an airport or airline security program, detection devices for explosives, threats of sabotage, and so forth.[76]

FAR Part 198 specifies aircraft that are eligible for insurance in the event of war, procedures for applications for insurance, premiums and payment thereof, and war risk insurance underwriting. Insurance can be acquired for aircraft and passenger and cargo liability.[77]

FAR Part 199 prescribes the conditions under which loan guarantees can be made to air carriers for the purchase of aircraft, who is eligible for loan guarantees, priorities, and so forth.[78]

ENVIRONMENTAL REGULATIONS

Airport noise was not a major environmental issue until the development of the jet engine and its widespread use in commercial aviation in the early 1960s. The advent of the jet age unfortunately coincided with the rapid growth of suburban areas around major airline airports. Airports, particularly in urban areas, had to be expanded to meet increasing demands and to serve larger aircraft, while suburban areas were growing to serve increasing and/or migrant populations. This simultaneous growth resulted in environmental conflicts and problems for the airlines, airports, and people living around them.

While only two FARs (FAR Parts 36 and 150), summarized in the preceding section, are directly related to minimizing the adverse environmental impact of aircraft and airport operations, the federal government's role in environmental regulation is substantial. In addition to promulgating regulations, it has exercised its authority through the passage of laws, the issuance of orders, and the formulation of policy. This section thus defines environmental "regulations" in the broader context of regulatory instruments covered in Chapter 5.

The following subsections examine five aspects of federal environmental regulation, particularly as it relates to the aviation industry. These include: 1) environmental impact statement requirements, 2) FAR Part 36, 3) the Noise Control Act of 1972, 4) aviation noise abatement policy, and 5) FAR Part 150 (Interim Rule).

Environmental Impact Statement Requirements

National Environmental Policy Act
On January 1, 1970, the National Environmental Policy Act of 1969, or NEPA, (PL 91-190) was enacted. This act was the landmark piece of legislation in the field because it contained requirements for environmental review. Section 102 of NEPA required the preparation of Environmental Impact Statements (EIS) by federal agencies on proposals for legislation and other major federal actions that would significantly affect the quality of the human environment. Before preparing the EIS, the responsible federal agency was required by NEPA to consult with and obtain comments from any other federal agency with legal jurisdiction related to, or special expertise in, any of the environmental impacts being studied. Another major provision of NEPA is that it created the Council on Environmental Quality (CEQ).[79]

The CEQ and EPA
The Council on Environmental Quality (CEQ) was created to monitor overall environmental conditions in the nation and to supervise the environmental review procedures employed by the various federal funding agencies under the legislative requirements of NEPA. In this effort, the CEQ issued preliminary guidelines for the preparation of EISs in April 1970. Later that

same year, the Environmental Protection Agency (EPA) was formed out of a hodgepodge of federal offices and bureaus.

The Clean Air Act of 1970 (PL 91-604) was passed in late December 1970 and clarified the relationship between the CEQ and EPA. Section 231 of the act gave the EPA the legal mandate to review and comment on the environmental impact of any project, legislation, or regulations proposed by any other federal agency. Section 231 further stated that any of these matters found unsatisfactory by the EPA with regard to public health and environmental quality was to be referred to the CEQ by the EPA Administrator. In a sense the EPA is the "staff" to the CEQ which carries out the legislated environmental review functions dictated by NEPA. The CEQ retains an overview role.[80]

CEQ Guidelines

Important among the evolving environmental regulations and legislation are the final guidelines issued by the CEQ on August 1, 1973, with regard to the preparation of the EISs. This document, entitled Guidelines for the Preparation of Environmental Impact Statements (40 CFR Part 1500) contains the original outline of an EIS. The environmental impact assessments prepared today have many of the features recommended then. The CEQ guidelines from 1973 recommended that the following eight items be included in the EIS: 1) a description of the proposed action, including a statement of its purposes and a description of the environment affected; 2) the relationship of the proposed action to land use plans, policies, and controls for the affected area; 3) the probable impact of the proposed action on the environment, including the positive and negative effects, as well as the primary and secondary effects; 4) alternatives to the proposed action on the environment, including the positive and negative effects, as well as the primary and secondary effects; 5) any probable adverse environmental effects that cannot be avoided; 6) the relationship between local short-term uses of man's environment and the maintenance and enhancement of long-term productivity; 7) any irreversible and irretrievable commitments of resources that would be involved in the proposed action should it be implemented; and 8) any indication of what other interests and considerations of federal policy are thought to offset the adverse environmental effects of the proposed action identified in items 3 and 5, above.[81]

As implementation of the guidelines commenced, the EPA found that the paper work generated would be formidable. The unexpected volume of statements forced the EPA to a regional, decentralized review concept. It also forced the EPA to ask the funding agencies for more screening of the projects to be reviewed under the NEPA law and the CEQ guidelines. This additional screening resulted in individual funding agencies issuing their own guidelines for environmental review.

Federal Aviation Administration Guidelines

Since the federal agency which controls the funds for a particular project is required to prepare an Environmental Impact Statement (EIS) on any "major" action, the federal agency must assemble information for the preparation of the EIS. Over the years several different guidelines have been issued, culminating in FAA's Order 1050.1C *Policies and Procedures for Considering Environmental Impacts* (January 10, 1980, *Federal Register*). These most recent guidelines are less stringent in terms of data/information requirements than prior FAA Orders.

The FAA specifies that the initial assessment of airport environmental impact should fall on the sponsor (e.g., the airport owner). In preparing such Environmental [Impact] Assessment Reports, or EIARs, it should be kept in mind that the primary purpose of an EIAR is to determine whether an EIS is needed from the federal agency involved in the project (in this case the FAA). The FAA outlines the following general purposes for EIARs: 1) to determine whether any potential impact is "significant, which would trigger the environmental impact *statement* process; 2) to understand the problem (if any) and identify reasonable alternative solutions, including the proposed action; 3) to provide the basis for the FAA's finding of no significant impact if the proposed action has no significant impacts; 4) to identify and satisfy special purpose federal laws, regulations, and executive orders (e.g., the NEPA guidelines, CEQ guidelines, state guidelines, and so forth); 5) to identify and satisfy state and local laws and regulations applicable to the proposal; and 6) in completing the above, to indicate agencies consulted and to identify cooperating agencies for environmental impact statement preparation purposes.

Pursuant to the key purpose of the EIAR—to determine the need for an EIS—FAA guidelines note that if one or more of the following types of impact is identified in an EIAR, an EIS must be prepared:

1. Historic preservation—if the proposed action has an effect that is not minimal on properties protected under Section 4(f) of the DOT Act or Section 106 of the Historic Preservation Act.

2. Natural, ecological, cultural, or scenic resources—if the proposed action has a significant impact on natural ecological, cultural, or scenic resources of a national, state, or local significance, including endangered species, wetlands, floodplains, and coastal zones.

3. Adequate relocation—if the proposed action is highly controversial (excluding disagreements over relocation payment levels) with respect to the availability of adequate relocation housing.

4. Community disruption, community plans—if the proposed project causes substantial division or disruption of an established community, or disrupts orderly, planned development, or is determined not to be reasonably consistent with plans or goals that have been adopted by the community in which the project is located.

5. Surface traffic—if the proposed action causes a significant increase in surface traffic congestion.

6. Noise levels—if the proposed action has a significant impact on noise levels of noise sensitive areas.

7. Air quality—if the proposed action has a significant impact on air quality or violates the standards for air quality of the Environmental Protection Agency or an affected locality or state.

8. Water quality—if the proposed action has a significant impact on water quality or may contaminate a public water supply system.

9. Environmental laws—if the proposed action is inconsistent with any federal, state, or local law or administrative determination relating to the environment.

10. Effects on people—if the proposed action directly or indirectly affects human beings by creating a significant impact on the environment.

11. Prime and unique—if the proposed action has a significant impact on prime and unique farmlands.[82]

Notwithstanding the above circumstances, airport improvements which typically require the preparation of an EIS include new airport development, new runways, extended runways, expanded apron areas, pavement strengthening, and land acquisition associated with future airport expansion.

Federal Aviation Regulation Part 36

This FAR was published in the *Federal Register* on November 18, 1969, and became effective on December 1, 1969. This is essentially a noise certification standard for aircraft. It sets noise limits and dates for the achievement of the prescribed limits with classifications by aircraft weight and speed (subsonic or supersonic). It also describes methods for measuring noise from aircraft going through certification tests.

FAR Part 36 has been amended 10 times through 1980. Each amendment has, in some way, tightened the original regulation. The *original* regulation exempted those aircraft certificated to fly prior to the creation of FAR Part 36. This included aircraft such as the Boeing 707, 727, and 737, as well as the McDonnell Douglas DC-8 and DC-9. On the other hand, the Boeing 747 (first flown in 1969), the McDonnell Douglas DC-10 (first flown in 1971), and the Lockheed TriStar L-1011 (first flown in 1972) were all affected by the original regulation.

The various amendments added throughout the 1970s began retroactively to add exempted aircraft to the coverage of the regulation. For example, versions of the Boeing 707 produced *after* December 31, 1975, were required to meet the provisions of FAR Part 36. This effectively shut down the 707 production line, except for those aircraft being sold to foreign buyers. The same fate was met by the Douglas DC-8 a year earlier. Other narrow-bodied aircraft that the manufacturers wanted to retain in production had to be re-engined or otherwise modified to meet FAR Part 36 requirements.[83]

The actual FAR Part 36 certification measurements were conducted as follows:

1. Takeoff measurements were made 3.5 nautical miles from the start of the takeoff roll on the extended runway centerline. On takeoff measurements, aircraft of 600,000 pounds or more had to emit no more than 108 Effective Perceived Noise Decibels (EPNdBs). The EPNdB is a quantity that is calculated from actual noise measurements and adjusted by weighting for those frequencies that are perceived to be more annoying to the human listener. There is also an adjustment for the duration of the sound measurement and the presence of "pure tones" in the measurements. For aircraft at 300,000 pounds, 5 EPNdBs are subtracted to reach the maximum allowed, and so forth down to 93 EPNdB for 75,000-pound aircraft.

2. Approach measurements are taken one nautical mile from the landing threshold on the extended runway centerline. Again, 108 EPNdB is the maximum noise limits for 600,000-pound aircraft, 103 EPNdB for 300,000-pound aircraft, down to 93 EPNdB for 75,000-pound aircraft.

3. "Sideline" measurements are taken parallel to the runway centerline 0.25 nautical miles away for three engine (or less) aircraft and 0.35 nautical miles away for four engine (or more) aircraft. The maximum noise limits for sideline are the same at each measuring point as for the approach category.

4. Overall FAR Part 36 noise levels can be met for each aircraft being tested and still have the maximum limits exceeded in one or two of the three categories. This occurs when the sum of the EPNdBs by which two categories are exceeded is no more than three EPNdBs and, for one category, when it is no more than two EPNdB. Finally, tests should be done at or near sea level, at 77°F, 70 percent relative humidity, and zero wind.[84]

The Noise Control Act of 1972

This act is particularly significant because it formally involved the Environmental Protection Agency in the Federal Aviation Administration's regulatory responsibilities regarding aviation noise. It did this by specifically amending Section 611 of the Federal Aviation Act of 1958, and renaming it "Control and Abatement of Aircraft Noise and Sonic Boom." The new wording requires the Federal Aviation Administrator to consult with the EPA in a review of all existing noise-related regulations and in the promulgating of new regulations. It also mandates the EPA to review regularly the FAA's regulatory effort related to aircraft noise control. It notes that, if the EPA has reason to believe that the FAA's action with respect to aircraft noise regulations "does not protect the public health and welfare," then the EPA can request that the FAA continue to review and take steps to resolve the problem area.

The immediate effect of this legislation was to involve directly the EPA in aviation noise regulation at the national level. Over the remaining years of the 1970s, the EPA suggested aircraft noise regulatory changes to the FAA. It was especially influential in the areas of: 1) suggesting deadlines for meeting FAR Part 36 standards for the older narrow-bodied jets already in fleets; and 2) suggesting noise regulations applicable to general aviation aircraft under 75,000 pounds.[85]

Aviation Noise Abatement Policy

The Aviation Noise Abatement Policy was issued jointly by the Federal Aviation Administrator and the Secretary of Transportation on November 18, 1976. It was issued neither as a regulation nor law by the United States Department of Transportation but as a departmental statement regarding the control of aviation noise. It did, however, announce some regulatory steps to be taken by the FAA in order to implement the policy. Key among the regulatory actions announced in the policy was a compliance schedule for all those aircraft not already meeting FAR Part 36. This compliance schedule noted that all four-engine aircraft (707s, DC-8s, and so forth) must be retired or retrofited within eight years (with one-quarter of the fleet completed in four years and one-half in six years). The earliest 747-100s that did not meet FAR Part 36 standards had to comply within six years, with one-half within four years. Finally, the two- and three-engine narrow-bodied jets (727s, DC-9s, and so forth) also had to comply within six years with one-half in four years. At the latest, FAR Part 36 compliance is assured by late 1984.

The policy included many other things aside from the compliance deadline announcement. The policy suggested a broad-ranging "attack" on the noise problem, with airport proprietors, (mainly local governments), the airlines, aviation consumers, airport area residents, planning agencies, as well as the federal government, all involved in the "attack."

The policy focuses on federal actions in four key areas: 1) source regulation for present and future aircraft (FAR Part 36), 2) retrofit/modification, 3) aircraft operating procedures, and 4) federal research and development. It is interesting to note that the policy focuses considerable attention on the airport proprietor as well as state/local government responsibilities in the generation of solutions to the airport area noise problem. The policy notes that the airport proprietor is "closest" to the noise problem with the best understanding of local conditions and problems. Also, the policy notes that state and local governments are "directly and uniquely responsible" for ensuring that land use planning and zoning actions are taken in areas around airports.[86] The problem with the policy is that it has not been supported with regulatory or legislative action in these important areas. Therefore, aside from source-related actions announced in the policy, it has been an academic exercise.

Federal Aviation Regulation Part 150 (Interim Rule)

The history of events leading to the promulgation of Interim Rule FAR Part 150 is perhaps as important as the actual content of the regulation. It is important because it demonstrates: 1) the relationship between two federal agencies with overlapping authority in promulgating a rule, 2) the differences in perspective between the FAA and EPA, and 3) the lengthy and complex nature of the rulemaking process. The origins of this FAR date back to October 1976, when the Environmental Protection Agency (EPA) submitted to the FAA a recommended regulation concerning an airport noise regulatory process. This was done in accordance with the authority granted the EPA by the Noise Control Act of 1972. This same act required the FAA to review any proposed rules, and to adopt, modify, or deny them with good reason.[87]

On November 2, 1976, the FAA published Notice No. 76-14 containing the EPA recommended regulation (FAR 140) prescribing "procedures for the development, approval, and implementation of an airport noise abatement plan, for airports required to be certificated under FAR Part 139." Of the 73 comments received in response to Notice No. 76-14 (published in the *Federal Register*), 63 opposed the EPA proposed rule. The objections were based on the following arguments: 1) the economic burdens imposed by the rule would be too great, 2) a noise plan should not be a condition for airport certification, 3) the rule imposes responsibilities on the airport operator (controlling adjacent land uses, for example) that may be beyond his or her control, and 4) the airport noise evaluation process methodology (ANEP) included in the proposed rule is too difficult and complex to explain to laymen.[88] As a result of the comments received, no immediate action was taken on the proposal.

In January 1979, the Air Transport Association (ATA) submitted a petition for rulemaking to the FAA dealing with "Airport Noise Abatement Plans: Regulatory Process." The ATA's proposal was much less stringent that that submitted by the EPA. It provided for a 90 day grace period between the time of the plan's submission and its implementation. If negative comments were received on the plan after its publication in the *Federal Register*, its implementation could be delayed for 180 days. During that period interested parties could present arguments on behalf of or in opposition to the plan. The ultimate decision on the plan would rest with the Administrator of the FAA through a formal administrative process.

An interesting feature of the ATA petition is that the Administrator of the FAA would not be required to approve each airport noise plan, but he or she would be required to terminate existing plans or disapprove proposed plans that have an adverse effect on aviation safety, airspace utilization, air commerce, or that were unjustly discriminatory. In other words an "acceptably" prepared plan would not require approval, but an "unacceptably" prepared plan would require disapproval.[89]

Two years later the FAA published an interim rule FAR Part 150 covering the submission of airport noise abatement plans. Part 150 is a modification of the original rule submitted by the EPA and represents somewhat of a compromise between the disparate views of the EPA and ATA. The real impetus to the promulgation of this rule, however, was the passage of the Aviation Safety and Noise Abatement Act of 1979 (ASNA) (PL 96-193). Title I of the ASNA Act required that the Secretary of the United States Department of Transportation, in consultation with the EPA, promulgate a rule establishing a single noise measurement system and a system for gauging human response to noise, and define land uses incompatible with airport development. Following the standards and criteria contained in that rule, certificated airport operators were also encouraged to submit noise abatement plans for which federal funding was to be made available.[90]

The legislative guidance provided in Title I of the ASNA Act established the basic principles upon which FAR 150 was developed. These principles are itemized below: 1) The federal government (FAA) must set uniform noise standards. 2) The federal government (FAA) must identify land uses compatible with different levels of noise exposure. 3) Local officials should be free to undertake land use compatibility planning without fear of preempting federal authority. 4) The development of noise compatibility programs should be voluntary and should not be a condition for airport certification. 5) The FAA will approve a plan if it does not place an undue burden on interstate commerce, foreign commerce, and aviation safety and if it offers a reasonable means for reducing incompatible land uses. 6) The plan should not require flight procedures that interfere with aircraft safety. 7) A single system of measuring noise is necessary, encompassing A-weighted decibels for single events and Ldn for cumulative noise measurement.[91] The major provisions of FAR Part 150 are listed in Table 23 and compared with EPA's original proposal.

A unique aspect of FAR 150 is the administrative process that it defines for reviewing and approving an airport noise plan. Plans are submitted simultaneously to the Director of the Office of Energy and the Environment (FAA, Washington) and to the appropriate FAA Regional Director. Following submission, a 180 day review period is initiated, with notice of the plan given to the public through its publication in the *Federal Register*. The review period does not require formal proceedings but, rather, dictates an informal administrative process with final approval authority resting on the Administrator of the FAA.[92]

MISCELLANEOUS REGULATIONS

While the majority of aviation regulations are located in Title 14 of the *Code of Federal Regulations*, others which directly or indirectly impact the industry are contained in Title 49. These regulations are briefly summarized below.

Part 21, "Nondiscrimination in Federally-assisted Programs of the Department of Transportation—Effectuation of the Civil Rights Act of 1964." This requires that recipients of federal funds *not* discriminate on the basis of a person's race, color, or creed in their hiring practices.[93]

Part 23, "Participation by Minority Business Enterprises in Department of Transportation Programs." This requires that recipients of federal funds make maximum efforts to use minority businesses when awarding contracts or purchasing materials and supplies.[94]

Part 25, "Relocation Assistance and Land Acquisition for Federal and Federally-assisted Programs." This provides that individuals whose residences or business properties must be relocated as a result of federal projects be fairly compensated for equivalent housing or the loss of business proceeds.[95]

Part 27, "Nondiscrimination on the Basis of Handicap in Programs and Activities Receiving or Benefitting from Federal Financial Assistance." This prohibits recipients of federal funds from discriminating against the handicapped. For example, airport sponsors must take steps to make their facilities accessible to the handicapped.[96]

Part 81, "Recommendations to the President Under Section 801 of the Federal Aviation Act of 1958." This establishes procedures for individuals to forward comments to the United States Department of Transportation regarding DOT's recommendations to the president relating to CAB decisions on overseas and international transporation.[97]

Part 91, "International Air Transportation Fair Competitive Practices." This prescribes the Secretary of the United States Department of Transportation's role in protecting United States flag carriers from all forms of discrimination or unfair competitive practices by foreign entities, and in compensating them for excessive charges levied by foreign governments for the use of airport or airway property.[98]

Part 93, "Aircraft Allocation." This notes that the United States Department of Transportation allocates aircraft to the Department of Defense for use in the Civil Reserve Air Fleet Program under certain contingencies and identifies where lists of those aircraft can be found.[99]

Part 175, "Hazardous Materials Regulation: Carriage by Aircraft." This sets forth requirements for aircraft operators transporting hazardous materials. Among its general rules are notifying passengers about hazardous materials restrictions, notifying the pilot in command of the presence of hazardous materials, marking hazardous materials and assuring that they are accompanied with the appropriate paper work, and reporting hazardous materials incidents. More specific rules govern the loading, unloading, and handling of hazardous materials, and the classification of hazardous materials so that the conditions under which they may be carried can be clearly defined.[100]

Part 821, "Rules of Practice in Air Safety Proceedings." This governs all air safety enforcement proceedings before a law judge, involving a review or appeal of an action by the FAA Administrator and upon appeal to the board (NTSB) from any order or decision of a law judge.[101]

Part 830, "Notification and Reporting of Aircraft Accidents or Incidents and Overdue Aircraft, and the Preservation of Aircraft Wreckage, Mail, Cargo, and Records."[102] This is self-explanatory.

Part 831, "Aircraft Accident/Incident Investigation Procedures."[103] See Chapter 3 in which the accident investigative procedures of the NTSB are explained.

TABLE 23

COMPARISON OF PROPOSED EPA RULE (FAR 140) WITH THE ADOPTED RULE (FAR 150)

EPA Proposed Rule (FAR 140)	FAA Modification of Rule (FAR 150)
All airports that hold operating certificates in accordance with FAR Part 139, *must* submit a noise plan.	Airports that hold operating certificates in accordance with FAR Part 139, may voluntarily submit a noise plan. Other public use airports that wish to participate in the program may also submit plans.
Noise contours must be expressed in terms of day-night average sound level (Ldn).	Noise contours are to be expressed in terms of Ldn and the A-weighted decibel scale for single events.
An airport noise evaluation process (ANEP) is to be used for identifying non-aircraft noise levels.	The methodology for accounting for non-aircraft noise is to be left to the discretion of the airport operator.
Government entities having authority over land uses subject to noise levels exceeding 55 Ldn must be identified.	Government entities having authority over land uses subject to noise levels exceeding 65 Ldn must be identified.

A public hearing must be held prior to the submission of the plan.	Opportunities for public participation must be afforded prior to submission of the plan, but the method of public participation is not limited to a public hearing.
An assessment of the plan for reducing noise impact for 2, 5, and 10 year intervals following submission of the plan must be undertaken.	Assessment of the plan for reducing noise impact at the time of submission and 1985 must be undertaken. If the plan is submitted after December 31, 1982, an assessment will be made for five years after submission.
The noise plan is to be updated within four years of its initial preparation.	The noise plan is to be updated on an as-needed basis.
Administratively, the review of the noise plan is to be undertaken as a part of the airport certification process.	Administratively, a separate process is to be developed by the FAA for reviewing noise plans.

Conclusions

This chapter has presented an overview of aviation related regulations. Because the implementation of the Airline Deregulation Act will obviate many of the economic regulations, this category of regulations was very briefly described. The summary of the FARs provides the reader with basic guidance on the content of key safety regulations. Those regulations which are of greatest interest or particularly applicable to the reader should be read in their entirety. The section on environmental regulations provides insight into the legislative basis for environmental rules, the respective responsibilities of the FAA and EPA, and a review of some key environmental regulations. The chapter concludes with a brief summary of miscellaneous other regulations which have an impact on the aviation industry.

7

The Regulated: How the Major Segments of the Aviation Industry Are Regulated

INTRODUCTION

This chapter traces, through two methods, the regulation of the various parts of the aviation industry. The segments of the industry to be reviewed will include: 1) commercial aircraft/airframe manufacturers, 2) major/national airlines, 3) commuter/regional airlines, 4) airports, 5) fixed base operators, 6) corporate flight departments, and 7) airmen.

Two methods of review will be utilized when examining each industry part. They are:

1. The overview method. An overview or summary of the major regulations affecting each industry segment will be presented.

2. The case study method. Following the overview of each segment will be a case study of that industry segment. The case studies will illustrate the application of major regulations to the segments. The case studies to be included are: a) commercial aircraft/airframe manufacturers: "Evolution of Transport Aircraft Certification"; b) major/national airlines: "New Entrants"; c) commuter/regional airlines: "Starting a Commuter Airline"; d) airports: "State Regulation of Airport Safety"; e) fixed base operators: "Regulations Affecting Fixed Base Operators' Leases and Operations"; f) corporate flight departments: "Regulations Affecting the Expansion of the Reliever Airport System"; and g) airmen: "Credentialing for Student and Private Pilots."

COMMERCIAL AIRCRAFT/AIRFRAME MANUFACTURERS

Overview

Table 24 illustrates the range of regulations affecting the commercial manufacturers. Aside from the business and industry regulations which affect companies in and out of aviation and aerospace, there are extensive regulations of manufacturers from the Federal Aviation Administration. These regulations are focused primarily on the safety-related aspects of aircraft manufacturing. FAR Parts 23 and 25 contain construction standards which guide the building of safe and airworthy aircraft. FAR Part 21, "Certification Procedures for Products and Parts," specifies the processes by which the aircraft manufacturer works toward Type, Production, and Airworthiness Certificates on new or remanufactured aircraft. These three separate certificates are all required before an aircraft can be built and flown in mass produced quantities. In conjunction with the Type and Airworthiness Certificates, aircraft must meet the noise standards identified in FAR Part 36, "Noise Standards: Aircraft Type and Airworthiness Certification." Finally, almost all aircraft are subject to the Airworthiness Directives issued through FAR Part 39 by the appropriate FAA regional director. These directives are issued directly to aircraft owners and manufacturers to provide emergency notification of any modifications or special maintenance steps required to correct an aircraft airworthiness problem. These directives can also be found in the *Federal Register*.

In addition to the FAA, a wide range of federal agencies affect aircraft manufacturers with their regulations, guidelines, and recommendations as shown in Table 24. These regulations include the Occupational Safety and Health Administration regulations concerning the safety of the industrial workplace, Security and Exchange Commission guidelines concerning stock offerings, Department of Labor/National Labor Relations Board regulations concerning negotiations with unions, Environmental Protection Agency regulations regarding pollution (air, water, and noise) and solid waste disposal, and National Transportation Safety Board recommendations to the FAA concerning aircraft airworthiness or safety.

In addition to federal-level requirements, there are several state-level requirements including but not limited to obtaining the necessary licensure to do business, conforming to the state tax laws, and meeting the environmental regulations of the state. There are also some miscellaneous regulations or requirements placed on aircraft manufacturers through the World Bank/Export-Import Bank, which finances sales to foreign countries; local governments, which regulate land use zoning affecting plant location and/or expansion; and industry associations, which issue voluntary guidelines to be followed such as flight or maintenance manual formats, and so forth.

Case Study: Evolution of Transport Aircraft Certification.
The Case of the Boeing 767

The Boeing 767 is the first all-new large transport aircraft built in the
United States since the late 1960s. The certification challenges it presented,
together with its sister aircraft, the Boeing 757, were difficult. This case
study will outline the certification process, especially as it relates to the flight
test component.

The Boeing 767 entered production in July 1978 with the announcement
of 30 orders for the new aircraft by United Airlines. Deliveries to United
began in August 1982, a little over four years later.[1] The four year period of
initial production and certification of the aircraft presents an interesting
chronology.[2] What makes this process even more interesting, however, is
that the Federal Aviation Administration's administrative structure for handling new aircraft certification began to change during the initial production
and certification of the 767.[3]

The certification of a new transport aircraft requires a large commitment
of resources and time. The company is responsible for providing airworthy
aircraft for use in FAA certification tests. In the case of the 767, five aircraft
were used in the flight test phase. Each of the aircraft was assigned specific
test assignments, as shown in Table 25.[4]

The flight test phase of the 767 certification began in December 1981 and
concluded with basic certification in July 1982. In addition to the basic
certification, a special certification program involving a two person crew
(rather than three person) was undertaken. The original flight-test program
leading to original certification required 1,350 flight hours, while the additional certification involved 200 more flight hours. Finally the flight test
program for the 767 required a substantial investment by Boeing in equipment and facilities to provide state of the art response to the regulatory
requirements of certification.[5]

All of this flight time and all of these tests have a bearing on three
important areas of certification performed by FAA: 1) airworthiness, 2) type
(including noise), and 3) production. These certificates allow the 767 to fly
and be mass produced in America. Noise certification assures that the aircraft
will meet minimum noise standards, which are intended to help make airport
environs quieter.

The administration of the certification process is an interesting combination of federal government and company responsibilities. As noted in earlier
chapters, responsibilities delegated by the FAA to the aviation industry are
key to the functioning of federal regulation of aviation. For example, the 767
was certificated to a large extent by designated engineering representatives or
DERs.[6] These DERs are Boeing employees who were chosen by the Federal
Aviation Administration for roles in the certification of the 767. The DERs

TABLE 24
OVERVIEW REGULATORY CHART FOR A MAJOR AIRCRAFT/AIRFRAME MANUFACTURER

Federal Aviation Administration	Other Federal	State	Other
A. FAR Part 21, Certification Procedures for Products and Parts 1. Subpart B—Type Certificate	A. Occupational Safety and Health Administration—Workplace safety	A. Licensure to do business	A. World Bank/Export-Import Bank—Financing of foreign sales
2. Subpart G—Production Certificate	B. Securities and Exchange Commission—Stock offerings rules	B. Tax laws	B. Local government—Land use zoning and laws affecting plant locations
3. Subpart H—Airworthiness Certificate	C. Department of Labor/National Labor Relations Board—Union relationships/negotiations	C. State environmental and pollution control regulations	

B. FAR Part 23—Airworthiness Standards: Normal, Utility and Acrobatic Category Airplanes

C. FAR Part 25—Airworthiness Standards: Transport Category Airplanes

D. FAR Part 36—Noise Standards: Aircraft Type and Airworthiness Certification

E. FAR Part 39—Airworthiness Directives

D. Environmental Protection Agency—Federal-level pollution/waste control

E. National Transportation Safety Board—Safety recommendations to FAA concerning aircraft and airworthiness of aircraft

F. Department of the Treasury/Internal Revenue Service—Tax laws affecting aircraft leases and purchases

C. Voluntary Associations—The Air Transport Association of America, for example, publishes standard formats for aircraft flight and maintenance manuals. The Aerospace Industries Association of America represents manufacturer interests.

TABLE 25
BOEING 767 FLIGHT TEST PROGRAM AIRCRAFT ASSIGNMENTS

1. *Aircraft One:* Flutter, aerodynamics, stability/control, take-off performance, high-speed characteristics, landing gear, buffet boundary, simu-
   lated icing, control system, flaps and spoilers.

2. *Aircraft Two:* Engine calibration, nacelle cooling, thrust management
   computer, brake and antiskid, refused take-offs, flight management
   system, inlet pressure tests, fuel vent system, fuel tank calibration, thrust
   reverse calibration, stability/control tests, avionics system and electrical
   system tests.

3. *Aircraft Three:* Flight loads, landing performance, flight management
   system, landing gear system, pneumatic system, anti-ice system tests,
   ram air turbine operation cabin pressurization review, and auxiliary
   power unit tests.

4. *Aircraft Four:* Overall function and reliability tests, noise measurements,
   engine calibration, high-speed characteristics, low-speed performance,
   aerodynamic certification, flight deck layout review, environmental control system tests, and electrical system tests.

5. *Aircraft Five:* Backup airplane and test aircraft for the General Electric
   CF6-80A engine (rather than the Pratt and Whitney JT9D-7R4 engines
   on the first four aircraft).

Source: Boeing Commercial Airplane Company, 1982.

are trained and licensed by the FAA after their selection. This training and
licensing is focused on giving the DERs the necessary skills to approve
detailed aspects of the 767 design. The FAA takes care in DER selection to
assure that most DERs testing Boeing aircraft come from the production and
flight test parts of Boeing rather than the design section. This, according to
the FAA, avoids the problem of putting a DER in the position of reviewing
his or her own previously accomplished design work.[7]

The DER also provides a significant resource advantage to the FAA.
The federal government can maintain a direct role in transport aircraft
certification without having to pay DER salaries. As it is, the FAA has been
faced with major hiring problems because of the need to replace personnel
fired during the air traffic controllers strike in August 1981. Also, the federal
government in general can not be as responsive to dramatic changes in the
workload of its employees. Therefore, the DER is a compromise which
maintains the certification process under federal control.

Also of note is the fact that the 767 (and sister aircraft 757) did force the
FAA to review its overall approach to transport aircraft certification. Prior to

the Boeing 767 and 757 certification, each of the FAA regions theoretically had a staff to handle such certification functions. However, it was realized that such duplication of effort was not affordable with the federal budget deficits growing every year. Therefore, a process was initiated during the Carter administration to concentrate transport aircraft certification in a particular region of the FAA. The initial descriptive title for this proposal was the "lead region" concept. Because of the concentration of FAA effort on the Boeing 767/757 programs, the logical choice for a transport aircraft "lead region" was the Northwest Mountain Region of the FAA in Seattle. Also, the large transport aircraft manufacturers in America are concentrated on the West Coast. The result of the deliberations concerning the lead region concept was the creation of a "Transport Aircraft Directorate," including offices in both Seattle and Southern California. In addition to the Transport Aircraft Directorate, other directorates are being formed for utility aircraft and engines.

In conclusion, the certification of an all-new transport aircraft is a complex task employing several different FARs and requiring extensive government/industry cooperation on technical issues. The 767 certification played a role in encouraging the FAA to revise its role in certificating transport aircraft. However, some have criticized the hastiness of the certification process for the 767 and the practice of delegating regulatory authority to employees of aircraft manufacturers.[8] Therefore, the 767 will be a carefully watched aircraft as it operates in its first years in airline service.

MAJOR/NATIONAL AIRLINES

Overview

The major and national airlines (see Table 26) are all regulated by FAR Part 121, "Certification and Operations: Domestic, Flag and Supplemental [now Charter] Air Carriers and Commercial Operators of Large Aircraft." This regulation specifies standards for everything ranging from flight and maintenance standards in airline operations to the number of flight attendants (and their training) needed for each size of aircraft. It is a very comprehensive regulation including coverage of: 1) flight crew complement and qualifications (including methods of training), 2) security of aircraft, 3) maintenance of aircraft, including manuals, 4) hazardous material, 5) aircraft operations manuals, and 6) passenger safety and safety procedures.

Major and national airlines also have to respond to the requirements of FAR Part 25, "Airworthiness Standards: Transport, Category Aircraft." This regulation, in addition to manufacturing standards, provides coverage of the standards to which transport aircraft (such as the Boeing 727 or the

TABLE 26
OVERVIEW REGULATORY CHART FOR THE MAJOR/NATIONAL AIRLINES

Federal Aviation Administration	Other Federal

A. FAR Part 121—Certification and Operations: Domestic, Flag, and Supplemental Air Carriers and Commercial Operators of Large Aircraft	A. Civil Aeronautics Board (until sunset)
	
	  1. Sec. 401 Certificate (prior to Jan. 1, 1982)
	
	  2. Merger applications
	
	  3. Essential air service
	
	  4. Reporting requirements

B. FAR Part 25—Airworthiness Standards: Transport Category Airplanes	
C. FAR Part 36—Noise Standards: Aircraft Type and Airworthiness Certification	B. National Transportation Safety Board—Safety recommendations to FAA concerning airlines and airline operations
D. Slots at busy terminal airports	
E. Post–air traffic controller strike rules (slots, flow control, general aviation, reservations, etc.)	C. OSHA—Workplace safety D. Department of Labor/National Labor Relations Board—Union negotiations
F. SFAR 38—Air Carrier Operating Certificate	E. Department of Justice—Antitrust rules F. Department of the Treasury/IRS—Tax law a. Securities and Exchange Commission—Stock offerings H. Department of Energy standby fuel allocation rules I. Environmental Protection Agency—Aircraft noise emissions and other pollution control rules

McDonnell Douglas DC-9) must be maintained by the airlines. Another major regulation faced by the airlines flying large aircraft is FAR Part 36, "Noise Standards: Aircraft Type and Airworthiness Certification." This regulation, as noted in Chapter 6, covers noise standards for transport aircraft, which must be met by 1985.

States	Airports	Other
A. Licensure to do business	A. Terminal space (access leases)	A. Voluntary associations Air Transport Association technical manuals, etc.
B. Tax laws	B. Curfews	B. Airlines with international routes:
C. State Environmental laws	C. Noise restrictions	1. Must gain route approval through Department of State and the President
		2. Must file fares through International Air Transport Association
		3. Must meet International Civil Aeronautics Association safety rules
		4. Its passengers must be screened by the U.S. Customs, Immigration and Naturalization Services, and the Department of Agriculture.

The Federal Aviation Administration is also responsible for the major regulatory changes that have been put into effect since the August 3, 1981, air traffic controllers' strike. These "temporary" regulations—called Special FARs or SFARs—have focused on slots for airlines using major air carrier airports, flow control rules for en route airspace, and a general aviation reservation system for small aircraft operators' use of major airports. They have placed a significant operations burden on the major and national carriers.

Other federal agencies regulating the major and national airlines are also shown in Table 26. They included the Civil Aeronautics Board, until the agency "sunset" (was closed down) in 1985. The CAB maintained a significant role with regard to the issuance of Part 401, "Certificates of Public Convenience and Necessity," until December 31, 1981. In addition, the CAB formerly reviewed merger applications and monitored the Section 419 Essential Air Service Program. The Essential Air Service Program affects both major and national carriers but generally affects national carriers more heavily since many national airlines are former regional/local service carriers which formerly provided significant service to small communities.

The National Transportation Safety Board has a direct regulatory influence over the airlines and airline operations through its review of aviation safety matters. For example, when there is a major accident such as the crash of the Air Florida 737 near National Airport, Washington, D.C., in January 1982, the NTSB sometimes issues immediate safety recommendations. Of course, these regulatory recommendations go to the FAA first. The FAA then issues the necessary regulatory change proposals via the applicable procedure (Notice of Proposed Rulemaking, Airworthiness Directive, and so forth).

The Occupational Safety and Health Administration regulates workplace safety in all businesses, including the airline business. OSHA regulations affect working environments such as airline maintenance and overall facilities, but generally not the flight or ramp areas (which are the responsibility of the FAA).

The Department of Labor affects the airline industry through work rules, labor protection rules, labor negotiations, and labor mediation requirements administered through the National Labor Relations Board. Crucial to the application of these regulations is the ability of each airline to meet the financial challenges of the 1980s without being significantly constrained by labor problems or laws.

The Department of Justice will be increasingly involved in the regulation of the airline industry as the CAB sunset begins to take effect. Generally its involvement will focus on the review of the antitrust aspects of merger applications and intercarrier agreement discussions in the airline industry. These subjects were reviewed through the CAB.

The Department of the Treasury has a regulatory impact upon the major and national carriers through the Internal Revenue Service (IRS). The IRS regulates the larger airlines in the way that they regulate most businesses— through corporate tax laws and limits on business deductions and credits.

The Securities and Exchange Commission has an important approval role in the transfer of ownership of stock—which can be a crucial factor in the take-over of one company by another. The role played by the SEC together with the CAB delayed the take-over of Continental Airlines by Texas International Airlines. In this case, the delay was caused by the process involved in Continental's attempts to gain approval of an employee stock ownership plan by the SEC.

The Department of Energy has a minor regulatory effect on the airlines through its "standby" or emergency fuel allocation controls. These regulations played a crucial role in the operation of the airlines during the 1979 energy crisis.

The Environmental Protection Agency (EPA) is involved together with the FAA in regulating noise emissions from airline aircraft. The EPA's role is to propose the engine noise emission standards which are, in turn, translated into changes in the Federal Aviation Regulations (FARs)—usually FAR Part 36, in the case of noise standards. Presently, airline aircraft are facing a January 1, 1985, deadline for conformance to FAR Part 36. For some airlines, there will be difficulties in meeting this deadline because of the nation's economic difficulties and the resultant impact upon the airline's recapitalization plans.

State regulatory bodies have less to do with major and national airlines than they once did. As a result of the Airline Deregulation Act of 1978, the states no longer require airlines to file for fares and routes—as some required prior to the 1978 act. However, the airlines must still conform to state tax, licensure, and environmental laws. An example of how state law affects airlines is the reincorporation of Ozark Airlines in the state of Delaware in 1974 (it was originally incorporated in Missouri). This allowed Ozark to benefit from Delaware's more liberal corporate laws. On the negative side (from the airlines viewpoint) are the variations in state law related to the environmental impact of airport operations. These state laws—which in some cases can restrict overall airline operations at an airport or may indirectly restrict operations—can have a severe impact upon airline scheduling and marketing functions.

Individual airport sponsors are having a critical regulatory impact on airlines. For example, airlines must work closely with airports concerning access to the airport's terminal buildings. At the larger airports around the country, most airlines have long-term lease or bond commitments regarding terminal space. At some airports, these long-term commitments have presented flexibility problems to airlines now that the Airline Deregulation Act of 1978 has begun to give airlines increased entry/exit freedom. In addition to terminal building access-related regulations, many airports also have curfews on airport activity. These restrictions have come about in recent years due to noise sensitive land uses being developed near major airports. Aside from curfews, there are other noise-related restrictions (such as bans on engine run-ups for maintenance, runway closures, noise abatement procedures on takeoff and landing, and so forth) which have significantly affected airline operations.

A significant aspect of regulation for major and national airlines is self-regulation through the voluntary association which represents larger airlines. The organization which represents most major and national airlines is the Air Transport Association of America (ATA). The ATA provides a forum for the major and national airlines to discuss common problems. The ATA has, for example, issued standard technical manuals depicting the formats for aircraft flight and maintenance manuals used by the airlines.

Finally, major and national airlines that operate or intend to operate international routes are regulated in several ways. For example, these carriers must first obtain route approval through the President of the United States, the Department of State, and (until 1985) the Civil Aeronautics Board. New routes to international points also must be included in bilateral treaties governing air service between the United States and many other countries. Aside from route approval, each international airline must conform to safety regulations issued by the International Civil Aviation Organization. Also, fares for international flights may be filed through the International Air Transport Association. Finally, passengers (and their baggage) on international routes are subject to screening by the United States Customs Service, the Immigration and Naturalization Service, and the Department of Agriculture. The purpose of these screenings is to regulate entry into the United States of illegal goods, illegal aliens, and illegal produce/agricultural pests.

Case Study: New Entrants

As noted in Chapter 1, there are several airlines (see Table 7) which have begun operations since 1979 with transport-sized aircraft over a limited number of short haul, medium/high density markets. There are also more waiting to begin operations pending improvement in economic trends (see Table 27). Most observers credit deregulation for the "flood" of new large aircraft operators, even though Midway Airlines, among others, was planning to begin operations prior to deregulation.

In any case, the "new entrants" have begun operations at a turbulent time for airlines operating large aircraft. Fuel costs have risen dramatically, the market for air transportation has slackened due to the economy, and the new carriers have not necessarily experienced an easy time from a regulatory perspective. These are some of the regulatory problems encountered by the new entrants since beginning operations in 1979:

1. The regulatory aftermath of the Professional Air Traffic Controllers (PATCO) strike, including increased air traffic control restrictions and a reduced number of available "slots" at major hubs, was a major setback for new entrants. Nearly all of the new entrants are focusing their new route structures on a small number of markets serving one or two major hubs. Some, such as Midway Airlines, have elected to operate out of alternate air carrier airports within the hub. The airspace restrictions put into effect after the PATCO strike affected everyone, including the new entrants. The president of Midway Airlines, Gordon Linkon, noted: "If there had been no air traffic controllers strike . . . I think we would not be precisely situated as we are. We would have done some things differently."[9] Linkon continued: "the new carriers and those that are standing outside the ballpark trying to get in have suffered considerably more than those that are on the playing field with

TABLE 27
PROPOSED NEW ENTRANTS

Name	Company Location
Air Chicago	Western Spring, IL (Chicago-Midway Airport)
Aircore Aviation	Teterboro, NJ
Air International	Erie, PA
Air Nevada	Las Vegas, NV
Air United States	Pasadena, CA
Arizona Pacific Airlines	Las Vegas, NV
Best Airlines	Florence, KY
Cal-Coast Airlines	San Luis Obispo, CA
1st Cooperative Airline	Santa Monica, CA
Freedom Airlines	Johnson City, NY (Broome County Airport, NY)
Great American Airways	Reno, NV
Houston Airlines	Houston, TX
Jetwest International	Phoenix, AZ
Northeast Sunrise Airlines	Ontario, CA
Texasamerican Airways	Jamaica, NY (JFK International, NY)
Transwestern Airlines of Utah	Logan, Utah
Trenton Hub Express Airline	Flemington, NJ
Westair Jet	Burlingame, CA

Source: "Carriers Newly Certificated or with Pending Applications," *Aviation Daily*, Jan. 29, 1982.

enough service to enough places that they have the flexibility of trading off."[10]

Lamar Muse, chairman of Muse Air Corporation and also former head of one of the "original" new entrant intrastate airlines, Southwest, was even more direct in his criticism of poststrike rules: "The industry is going down the drain. This is regulation in the worst form you could conceive. The Civil Aeronautics Board never said how many trips you could make or at what time of day. And the FAA doesn't know what they are doing."[11] So, Mr. Muse argued that the FAA had slipped back into prederegulation government involvement in establishing industry controls.

The lack of flexibility allowed to new entrants mentioned above by Gordon Linkon of Midway Airlines also makes it difficult for new entrants to deal with the problem of slot negotiations. This problem, an outgrowth of the situation brought on by the PATCO strike and related controller firings, places new entrants at a distinct disadvantage. In essence, they have few, or no, slots with which to negotiate because they are so small and so new.

2. Airport access. New entrants, because of their size and because they are directly competitive with the major and national airlines, have found it difficult to gain gates at some hub airports. The reason for this is the existence of long-standing financial arrangements at many hub airports which have given the older airlines considerable control over gate access. The entire question of gate subleasing, discrimination against smaller carriers, and related issues has been of concern to airport managers and to the FAA.[12]

3. Airport noise rules. Individual airport noise rules and deadlines for complying with federal noise standards (1985 for FAR Part 36) have affected the airlines' selection of aircraft. As established carriers replaced older models of noncomplying aircraft with new, quiet equipment, a strong market for used aircraft was created. New entrants without much capital could purchase or lease these used aircraft for a relatively low price to inaugurate service and generate needed revenues. These carriers, however, were gambling that they would be financially capable of modifying existing aircraft or purchasing new ones before the 1985 federally mandated noise standards took effect.[13]

Because of circumstances, then, the government approval process required to attain operational status is not nearly the problem for new entrants that the economy and obtaining financial backing pose. While it is true that slot, gate acquisition, and noise approval problems are serious regulatory issues, they are minor compared to the lengthy CAB proceedings which preceded approval of only a handful of new trunk and local service carriers in over thirty years. In perspective, then, the regulatory problems of new entrants in the 1980s have shifted away from overall economic regulatory issues (such as competition on routes, and so forth) to operational considerations based on limits on the air transport system.

Commuter/Regional Airlines

Overview

Like the major and national airlines, the commuter/regional airlines are regulated in important ways by the Federal Aviation Administration (FAA). As noted in Table 28, commuter airlines must be certified by the FAA. They also must operate in compliance with those flight and safety regulations appropriate to the size of aircraft operated. Commuter air carriers operate under the provisions of Part 135 of the Federal Aviation Regulations (FARs). This FAR outlines rules regarding general operations, crew member qualifications, and aircraft equipment maintenance requirements. It should be noted that commuter airlines operating large transport category aircraft (over 30 passengers) must comply with Part 121 of the FARs.

The FAA implemented major revisions to its carrier regulations in the late 1970s. One of these revisions was the establishment of a new Part 135 rule which moves toward an equivalent level of operational safety between large and small aircraft used in airline service. Under this revised rule, *all* aircraft flown by United States air carriers (CAB certificated or not) operate at a common regulatory standard.

The Revised FAR 135 now includes:

1. Aircraft maintenance. The FAA requires that a "continuous airworthiness maintenance program" be established for all commuter aircraft with over 10 passenger seats. Also, smaller aircraft must be maintained under a more strict maintenance program than under prior regulations.

2. Crew requirements. Multiengine commuter aircraft are required to be operated by crews holding airline transport pilot certificates. Also, the new FAR Part 135 specifies flight crew training, proficiency, and testing programs which are similar to those used by the major and national airlines.

3. Aircraft equipment and performance. Equivalency of all aircraft manuals with FAR Part 121 manuals for larger aircraft has been mandated.

Another revision to air carrier regulations in 1978 was the FAA's issuance of Special Federal Aviation Regulation (SFAR) 38. This new regulation established a single FAA air carrier operating certificate for all scheduled airline operations, regardless of the type of CAB authority held. This revision simplified FAA certification of commuters and larger airlines while assuring that *all* carriers meet the operating rules appropriate to the size of aircraft they have in service.[14]

It is clear that there are some key similarities in the regulation of major/national airlines and commuter/regional airlines. For example, all airlines must receive an air carrier operating certificate under Special Federal Aviation Regulation Part 38. Also, the general operating, airworthiness, and

TABLE 28
OVERVIEW REGULATORY CHART FOR A COMMUTER/REGIONAL AIRLINE

Federal Aviation Administration*	Civil Aeronautics Board (until January 1, 1985)
A. FAR Part 135—Operating Rules for airlines operating aircraft up to 18,000 pounds gross weight (30 passengers)	A. Part 298—Operating Requirements
	B. Fitness Requirements (including reporting requirements)
B. FAR Part 121—Operating Rules for airlines operating large aircraft (over 18,000 pounds/30 passengers)	C. Essential Service Requirements
	D. Uniform System of Accounts
C. FAR Parts 23, 25—Aircraft Airworthiness Requirements	
D. Slots and other post–air traffic controller strike requirements	**Department of Transportation (USDOT)**
E. SFAR 38—Air Carrier Operating Certificate	A. Fitness requirements (after Jan. 1, 1985)
	B. Handling of hazardous materials

*See Appendix 4 for the complete titles of the FARs cited here.

airspace regulations are similar. Finally, the general business regulations from IRS, FCC, the Postal Service, Agriculture, and DOT are much the same among all airlines.

The commuter airlines, however, because of their size and because of the nature of their operations are in some respects different from their larger airline "cousins." Commuters benefit from their small size because they are not as strongly affected by EPA noise regulations and by state environmental regulations as are the major and national carriers. Furthermore, because of the size of commuter airlines, general business regulations from the SEC and NLRB have minimal impact on this segment of the industry.

Commuters are affected in different ways by some of the regulations. For example, some FAR part 135 all-cargo commuter airlines are in business primarily to fly mail for the United States Postal Service (USPS). Thus, USPS regulations are crucial to those carriers. Also, airport access regulations are critical to the commuters. None of these carriers were in existence

Other Federal Regulations	State	Airports	Other
A. Federal Communications Commission—Certification of communications equipment and operators B. Department of Agriculture—Control of agricultural shipments C. United States Postal Service—Regulation of carriage of mail D. Department of the Treasury, Internal Revenue Service—Tax laws	A. Fare filings (not necessary in every state) B. Licensure to do business	A. Terminal use (LAX example) B. Operating rules (airport authority) C. Tax laws	The Regional Airline Association and the National Air Transportation Association represent the interests of commuter airlines.

prior to the early 1960s and were, therefore, not present to participate in the original use agreements at most airports. Yet, the scale of the operations of most commuter airlines is so small that the terminal use and operating rules of one or two key airports can make a substantial difference in the operating success of many commuter/regional carriers.

Case Study: Starting a Commuter Airline

The purpose of this case study is to describe some of the regulatory problems in establishing a commuter airline. There are many problems involved in launching *any* new business. The objective of this portion of the book is to outline the regulatory peculiarities of starting new commuter airline companies.

Since the passage of the 1978 Deregulation Act the interest in air transportation has increased considerably. The changes brought about by the

Deregulation Act focus on the major airlines' freedom to serve any markets and set any fares they wish. Some points previously served by larger carriers were quickly abandoned after the 1978 act was passed. Coupled with this newfound freedom is the provision in the Deregulation Act that specifically recognizes commuters as a potential source of replacement services for abandoned routes. This recognition is contained in the new Section 419 and elsewhere in the act. Additionally, the act makes commuters eligible for possible feaeral subsidies and for guaranteed loans from the federal government. Establishing a small airline has always been, and will continue to be, a high risk business. It is possible, however, to bring many of the risks under control by mastering the regulatory steps that must be taken to establish a successful commuter airline.

Commuter carriers usually have had operating characteristics significantly different from the other segments of the airline industry. A reason for the differing characteristics of commuters was that they were historically limited to operating aircraft with a gross weight not exceeding 12,500 pounds. This limitation affected the size of aircraft used by the commuters until the late 1970s. Under the 1978 act, the limit on commuter aircraft was raised to permit operations with aircraft not exceeding 60 seats. This recent trend, brought about by the 1978 act and the subsequent revision of the classifications among the various types of airlines, means that it is no longer easy to identify a commuter airline strictly by the type of aircraft flown.

Until 1978, it was virtually impossible for a new airline operator to obtain a Section 401 certificate of public convenience and necessity from the CAB, while a CAB Part 298 commuter airline certificate could be obtained for $15.00 and proof of the required liability insurance. Now, the so-called fitness determination is the crucial first regulatory step for all commuters. This is a determination made by the USDOT that the company meets minimum financial criteria. Liability insurance must still be acquired.

Commuters must also meet the safety requirements of the Federal Aviation Administration. As noted earlier, the FAA requirements affect safety, while the CAB (until its termination) affects economics. The airlines using large transport aircraft operate under FAR 121, while commuters generally operate under FAR 135. The FAR 121 requirements are still more strenuous than the 135; however, since deregulation, the FAA has set new standards for commuters operating aircraft with more than nine passenger seats. This new rule, Part 135.2, as mentioned earlier, raised the standards for commuter airlines almost to the level of 121 operators.

Next, interline agreements—which are approved through the Air Transport Association (ATA)—must be obtained. The following items must be submitted to ATA by the new carrier in order to receive consideration for interlining: 1) a recent financial statement, 2) a copy of the 298 certificate, 3) a list of locations the airline proposes to serve, 4) a general description of the airline and its purposes, and 5) a sample of the baggage tag and ticket coupon which the airline plans to use and a sample of any other items, such as miscellaneous charge orders or airway bills, which are planned for use. Additionally an Airline Clearing House number must be obtained before ticket stock can be printed. The Airline Clearing House is similar to a bank clearing house, and it is the means whereby all airline tickets that are sold by one airline for another are exchanged for cash or credits for equivalent sales.

All the previously mentioned material is gathered together and sent to the Air Transport Association of America (ATA). The ATA, in turn, forwards it to each of the airlines. Under their rules, the ATA must forward the request for interline agreements within 10 days after it receives an application. As the agreements are returned to the ATA, notification of concurrence or nonconcurrence is received from each of the carriers. Without securing an interline agreement, and notifying the publishers of the *Official Airline Guide* (OAG) of an agreement, commuter connections cannot be shown in the OAG.

Once the interline agreements are obtained, the new carrier must then make sure that the new commuter's schedules are shown in the OAG with connections to other carriers. This is *not* an automatic step and requires analysis of historic market data to make sure that the new commuter's connections meet minimum traffic requirements to be listed in the OAG. If this minimum traffic level is not fully established, then the OAG has what is called the "paid connection" service which allows for below-minimum connections to be listed in the OAG.

Joint fares are also crucial to the new commuter because, if no joint fare exists for connecting carriers, then the two single fares are simply added together. Joint fares, then, are a form of discounting which must be approved in advance to make the new commuter's services attractive. These joint fares must be established through the Airline Tariff Publishing Company, which usually requires a four- to five-month lead-time allowance.

It is important to recognize that a new airline must display its schedules in the *Official Airline Guide* approximately 30 days prior to beginning operations. This means that schedules must be in place and sent to the OAG approximately 45 days before the OAG publication date. The OAG will not accept an airline's schedules until the necessary federal approvals have been acquired. Also, the other airlines cannot approve interline agreements until these approvals have been acquired. The lead time is, therefore, significant. To illustrate the lead time required, assume that the new airline is to begin services on June 1. The following dates then serve to illustrate the point:

	Minimum time prior to operation
1. Start-up of operations, June 1	
2. Schedules printed in the OAG, May 1	1 month
3. Schedules to be sent to the OAG for publication, March 15	2½ months
4. Interline agreements approved, March 10	3 months
5. Interline agreements applied for, February 1	4 months
6. Joint fares applied for, January 1	5 months
7. All federal requirements met, December 1	6 months

As the above timetable illustrates, federal requirements must be completed a minimum of six months before the first date of operating an airline. Logically, therefore, the necessary aircraft must be acquired and the proper insurance obtained some time before the sixth month, so that there is enough time for the remaining steps to be completed.[15]

It should be noted that federal economic regulation is not as time-consuming a requirement in the creation of a commuter airline as the various requirements that the industry imposes on itself (interline agreements, joint fares, OAG listings, and so forth). In summary, there are many regulatory requirements when setting up a new commuter airline. Today the industry's own self-regulatory standards are as demanding or more demanding than the federal requirements faced by a new commuter airline. However, one thing has not changed over the years: The major stumbling block for most new commuter carriers is not the regulations but obtaining the start-up financing.

AIRPORTS

Overview

As is shown in Table 29, a large number of Federal Aviation Regulations, including all those in the 150 series, apply to airports. For example, FAR Part 157 requires that an airport operator notify the appropriate FAA office of airport alterations (e.g., runway opening/closing), openings, closings, and any other airfield facility changes. Also, FAR Part 152 details some of the requirements to be followed in obtaining money from the Airport Improvement Program (AIP) under the 1982 Airport and Airway Improvement Act. Supporting orders and advisory circulars further delineate how the money is to be accounted for and which items are eligible for AIP money and which are not. FAR Part 159 is interesting in that it details the operating structure for the FAA owned airports (e.g., National and Dulles International, serving Washington, D.C.). The newest FAR in the 150 series—FAR Part 150—contains guidelines for airport noise compatibility planning undertaken with federal money. This regulation is important as it places responsibility (albeit voluntary at this point) for noise compatibility planning at the local level.

Outside the 150 series are two key airport-related FARs. The first is FAR Part 107 (and 108 for commuters) which details federal requirements for airport security at airports servicing scheduled air carriers. The security requirements require that all passengers boarding scheduled flights be screened for weapons as an antihijack measure. Furthermore, "sterilized" concourses beyond the security screening points are required to be maintained. Finally, security screening for the airfield itself is required at these airports to restrict unauthorized access to ramp, taxiway, and runway areas. The second important FAR is Part 139 which specifies crash-fire-rescue (CFR) facilities, equipment, and emergency/disaster plans, and other airfield standards needed to obtain an airport operating certificate. While these requirements are presently not applicable to commuter air service airports, there are proposals to extend FAR Part 139 requirements to commuter airports.

The FAA's special FARs put into effect since the air traffic controllers strike in August 1981 have had a significant impact on airport traffic. These regulations effect usage through "slot" controls. A slot is a period of time within a day that a particular airline or general aviation aircraft operator can conduct a flight at a particular airport. The FAA's allocation of slots actually preceded the controllers strike at four airports—O'Hare (Chicago), Los Angeles International, La Guardia (New York), and National (Washington, D.C.). However, the earlier slot allocations were geared more to airport capacity restrictions while the current slot allocations are tied to the capacity of the air traffic control system with a reduced controller staff.

Other federal agencies also have a regulatory impact on airports. For example, the National Transportation Safety Board (NTSB) can make regulatory recommendations to the FAA concerning airports or support facilities on an airport. This can occur when an airport facility problem is considered by the NTSB to be a contributing factor in an aircraft accident. The Environmental Protection Agency (EPA) has a more direct regulatory effect upon airports through its administration of the nation's environmental laws and regulations. The EPA is responsible for the administration of the provisions of the National Environmental Policy Act of 1969. As noted earlier, this includes the review of environmental impact statements prepared by the FAA and other federal agencies concerning actions which have a significant impact on the quality of the human or natural environment. The EPA is also jointly responsible with the FAA for the proposal of regulations to control aircraft noise emissions.

TABLE 29
OVERVIEW REGULATORY CHART
FOR A PUBLICLY OWNED, PUBLIC USE AIRPORT

Federal Aviation Administration*	Other Federal Regulations
A. Airports are established under FAR Part 157	A. National Transportation Safety Board recommendations concerning airports
B. Certificated under FAR Part 139 (large aircraft flown by CAB certificated airlines)	B. Environmental Protection Agency 1. Noise regulations 2. Administration of environmental impact assessment requirements under the 1969 NEPA Act
C. FAR Parts 107–8—Security	
D. FAR Part 152—Federal Airport Improvement Program	C. Department of Transportation administration of 1. Uniform relocation & real properties acquisitions 2. Minority business enterprise regulations 3. Affirmative action requirements
E. FAR Part 150—Environmental Planning	
F. FAR Part 77—Objects Affecting Navigable Airspace	
G. Post–air traffic controller strike requirements (slots, flow control, etc.)	

*See Appendix 4 for the complete titles of the FARs cited here.

The Department of Transportation, the FAA's parent agency, is responsible for the oversight of all transportation related projects to ensure that these projects conform to minority business enterprise, affirmative action, and uniform relocation and real property acquisition requirements. These requirements assure the protection of individual rights in the completion of federally funded airport projects.

State regulations of airports usually focus on the site/location approval process. Also included in many states are minimum facility standards for airports—minimum runway lengths, runway widths, and so forth. Some states are now specifying airport noise standards. California, as noted earlier, has such a state law, which establishes a Community Noise Exposure Level, or CNEL, for each airport. Finally a large number of states have a requirement to "pass through" all federal AIP money destined for local airports. This pass through requirement allows the regulating states to examine and influence how this money is to be spent.

States	Local Governments	Voluntary
(Each function does *not* apply to all states)	A. Operating budget	A. Airport Operators Council International—Operations manuals
A. Airport certification/ licensing	B. Operating rules	
	C. Zoning/building regulations—Codes	
B. Safety regulations	D. Environmental regulations	B. American Association of Airport Executives—Airport manager accreditation
C. Environmental regulations		
D. Pass-through laws for federal airport funds		

Local governments also have a large influence over airports. In fact, a large majority of the publicly owned airports in the United States are owned and operated by various types of local governments. As the owners and operators of so many airports, local governments therefore have a large voice in directing how the airport facilities are to be used. For example, it is through local airport regulations that airport-related use fees are established. Fees relate closely to expenditures, which are budgeted for locally controlled airports through the airport governing bodies. Also, the local government owner/operators establish airport safety regulations which complement those in place through state and federal regulations.

On the negative side, local governments may restrict the use of their own airports because of noise problems. Many airports—such as Lindbergh Field in San Diego—have airport curfews which restrict aircraft movements during certain night hours (usually 10:00 or 11:00 P.M. to 6:00 or 7:00 A.M.). Several airports are attempting to control noise through more direct means by establishing airport-specific rules such as engine run-up policies, noise abatement (take-off, landing) procedures, and preferential runway use plans. In cooperation with other local governments, the local airport authority may also establish compatible land use plans and zoning. A few airports have even worked to revise local building codes to require soundproofing of any new structures.

Voluntary organizations also have a regulatory impact on airports. The American Association of Airport Executives (AAAE) has fought the proposed expansion of the FAR Part 139 airport certification requirements to include the certification of airport managers. The AAAE has, instead, established a professional airport manager accreditation program. This program—which requires a combination of formal education (B.S. degree minimum), practical experience in airport management, successful completion of a written and an oral exam and the completion of a thesis—is very stringent. It results in the award of the Accredited Airport Executive (AAE) status.

Many airports are also members of the Airport Operators' Council International (AOCI). This organization has assembled a series of advisory standards which can be used by airports in the development of operation rules for their own facilities.

Case Study: State Regulation of Airport Safety. The Illinois Example

As explained in Chapter 4, the chief aviation regulatory functions of the states focus on the areas of safety, economics, environmental protection, airport promotion, and airport development/operations. The wide range of the airport regulatory functions of the states makes this form of regulation crucial to airport operators in many states. This range of airport-related regulatory functions at the state level includes: 1) safety-related powers, 2) environmental/ noise control powers, 3) zoning/height obstruction control powers, 4) miscellaneous airport operations powers (for those states which operate airports), 5) aviation education/airport promotion activities, and 6) airport finance/funding powers. Chief among this list of regulatory powers is the safety-related power entrusted to 39 states. In response to a survey distributed by the National Association of State Aviation Officials, 30 of the 50 states indicated that they license airports. (See Table 30.)

Obviously the state safety regulatory role varies widely from state to state. Some states have laws but do not enforce them. Other have laws applicable only to certain classes of airports, such as public-use airports only. Of those that have a wide range of power, Illinois is an example of a state which takes an active role in airport site approval and inspections. The Illinois approval process for new airport sites of all classes, including restricted landing areas (restricted to use of owners and their guests), involves a public hearing.[16] This is contrasted by the lack of an approval process of any kind in many states.

The airport safety regulations overseen by the Illinois Department of Transportation, Division of Aeronautics, affect both commercial airports (those open for public use, selling commercial products and services) and restricted landing areas (those open for private use only). The regulations specify minimum standards such as runway length for both classes of airports. Commercial airports in Illinois must have a minimum runway length of 2,400 feet, while restricted landing areas in Illinois must have a minimum runway length of 1,800 feet. In addition to dimensional standards, airport markings, obstructions, and minimum required facilities are covered in the Illinois regulations. For example, the minimum facilities required at all commercial airports in Illinois include: 1) hangar or office, 2) wind direction indicator, 3) fuel and oil facilities, 4) sanitary drinking water, 5) first aid kit, 6) sanitary toilets, 7) adequate fire protection equipment, 8) auto parking area (adequately fenced to separate it from the runway and aircraft parking areas), 9) reasonably accessible telephone, 10) adequate airport fencing, 11) adequate tie-down facilities, and 12) circle marker (segmented), where a nonstandard air traffic pattern is used.[17]

In addition to commercial airports for conventional aircraft, Illinois also has regulations which affect commercial heliports and balloon ports. Again, minimum standards, such as approach/departure slopes and facilities are

TABLE 30
STATES WITH SOME FORM OF AIRPORT LICENSING

Alabama	Michigan
Alaska	Minnesota
Arkansas	Montana
California	Nebraska
Delaware	New Hampshire
Florida	New Jersey
Hawaii	Oregon
Idaho	Pennsylvania
Illinois	Rhode Island
Indiana	South Carolina
Iowa	Tennessee
Kentucky	Utah
Louisiana	Virginia
Maine	Wisconsin
Maryland	Wyoming

Source: National Association of State Aviation Officials, 1978.

specified.[18] It is specified in the regulations that the operation of such facilities is unlawful without a certificate of approval.[19] Illinois is more restrictive in its approach to airport certification than at least 20 states without certification requirements, and many states that have such requirements. This is due to the fact that Illinois regulates the establishment of *both* publicly used *and* privately used airports.

In summary, then, airports can be heavily regulated at the state level depending upon the state in which they are located. If an airport is located in a state with strongly enforced airport safety powers, it would be crucial for the airport management to obtain information about the regulatory process in that state.

Fixed Base Operators

Overview

Table 31 illustrates the levels, numbers, and kinds of regulations affecting general aviation fixed base operators (FBOs). Aside from the airmen themselves, FBOs are considered to be the "grass roots" of aviation—they are the business through which the public learns to fly, purchases aircraft, maintains aircraft, charters aircraft, and obtains aerial spraying services. For this reason, the regulations focus on these functions. However, the focus has two perspectives—the purely aviation perspective and the purely business perspective.[20] For example:

Aviation Rules	Business Rules
1. Pilot certification	1. Excise Tax Laws (fuels, transportation, aircraft)
2. Flight school certification	2. Income tax laws
3. Repair station certification	3. Sales tax laws
4. Airworthiness certification	4. Stand-by fuel allocations
5. Charter operation certification, and so forth	5. Radio operators licensing, and so forth

To further complicate the situation, there are a number of regulatory bodies involved in the administration of both categories of rules. As with the other segments of the aviation industry already covered, the list of regulatory agencies is a long one. It is headed by the Federal Aviation Administration, which is responsible for the aviation safety regulations affecting FBOs. As noted in Table 31, there are four basic categories of aviation safety regulations faced by the FBO: flight instruction regulations, maintenance regulations, charter/air taxi regulations, and agricultural operators regulations. It should be noted at this point that there are individual businesses whose activity would encompass only one of these categories or two or three of these categories. As the FBO becomes more complex, so do its regulations.

In the flight instruction area, there are three crucial regulations. The first is FAR Part 61, "Certification of Pilots and Flight Instructors." This is the regulation under which all pilots learn to fly and are certificated as pilots or, later, as flight instructors. Recently, there has been increased emphasis on pilot proficiency and currency, thus emphasizing the importance of this regulation. Also important are FARs 141 ("Pilot Schools") and 143 ("Ground Instructors") which certificate the institutions within which flight instruction can be given and the people who give "ground school" instruction, respectively.

The aviation maintenance functions performed by FBOs are regulated chiefly by the FAR under which FAA-certified repair stations are established (FAR Part 145) and under the FARs which specify airworthiness standards for aircraft (Part 23, for utility aircraft), engines (Part 33), and propellers (Part 35), and which establish maintenance, preventive maintenance, rebuilding, and alteration standards (Part 43). Also crucial to keeping up with required maintenance steps is FAR Part 39, "Airworthiness Directives." Under this FAR, the FAA distributes information to aircraft operators, including FBOs, regarding corrective maintenance steps which must be undertaken on a particular aircraft type, engine type, or propeller type. Usually this information is based upon operator experience or FAA and/or NASA research which has indicated a need for corrective action.

Those FBOs which operate charter or air taxi operations are concerned with two regulations—FAR Part 91, "General Operating and Flight Rules," and FAR Part 135, "Air Taxi Operators and Commercial Operators of Small Aircraft." As was noted earlier in the Regional/Commuter Airline portion of this chapter, FAR Part 135 has undergone recent revisions which have made it more stringent, and more costly and time-consuming to comply with. The crucial requirement contained in the FAR is that each operator flying under FAR Part 135 must meet the requirements for and hold an Air Taxi/Commercial Operator (ATCO) Certificate from the FAA. The requirements within Part 135 for the ATCO Certificate include: record-keeping requirements, aircrew training, exlusive use of at least one aircraft that meets the operating requirements of the company, flight dispatch procedures, flight manuals, maintenance manuals, and ground operations manuals. In addition, general operating requirements under FAR Part 91 and under Part 135 must be followed. These requirements include everything from passenger briefings to IFR and night operations limitations. As was mentioned earlier, the tightening of crew competency and operations requirements under the revised FAR Part 135 have made the ATCO certificate tougher to acquire.

TABLE 31

OVERVIEW REGULATORY CHART FOR A FIXED BASE OPERATOR

Federal Aviation Administration	Other Federal	State	Local

A. Flight Instruction
  1. FAR Part 61—Certification: Pilots and Flight Instructors
  2. FAR Part 141—Pilot Schools
  3. FAR Part 143—Ground Instructors
B. Maintenance
  1. FAR Part 145—Repair Stations
  2. FAR Part 23—Airworthiness Standards: Normal, Utility, and Acrobatic Category Airplanes
	A. Treasury/Internal Revenue Service—Tax withholding (excise and income) laws for business
	B. Department of Energy (standby regulations for fuel allocation, price and delivery)
	C. Federal Communications Commission—(licensing for radio operators, radio transmission equipment, and avionics repair)
	D. Department of Agriculture (regulations regarding aerial spraying)
		A. Business license
		B. School licensing
		C. Aviation safety regulations (aircraft Registration, etc.)
		D. Sales taxes
		E. Workmen's compensation
			A. Lease from the local airport authority to operate
			B. Airport operating rules
			C. Zoning Requirements

E. Food and Drug Administration (regulations regarding aerial spraying)

F. Federal Trade Commission (administration of rules related to advertising and consumer protection)

G. Social Security Administration, U.S. Dept. of Health and Human Services (administration of Social Security, Medicare, and Unemployment tax laws)

H. U.S. Department of Labor (minimum wage rules)

I. Occupational Safety and Health Administration, U.S. Department of Labor (work safety rules)

3. FAR Part 33—Airworthiness Standards: Aircraft Engines

4. FAR Part 35—Airworthiness Standards: Propellers

5. FAR Part 39—Airworthiness Directives

6. FAR Part 43—Maintenance, Preventative Maintenance, Rebuilding and Alteration

C. Charter/Air Taxi
   1. FAR Part 135—Air Taxi Operators and Commercial Operators of Small Aircraft

   2. FAR Part 91—General Operating and Flight Rules

D. Agricultural Operators
   1. FAR Part 137—Agricultural Aircraft Operations

An atypical FBO is one which is involved in aerial spraying or applications. Such operators are important factors in the aviation community in several agricultural states. These operators are regulated under FAR Part 137, which specifies the definition of an agricultural operation, the acquisition of an agricultural aircraft certificate, operating rules, aircraft specifications, personnel requirements, and record-keeping requirements. It also should be pointed out that there are significant regulations on Part 137 operators from the United States Department of Agriculture, the United States Food and Drug Administration, and state agencies involved in aeronautics, public health, and agriculture.

Other federal regulations affecting FBOs in general are not usually as specific to aircraft operations as those affecting agricultural operators. In general the non-FAA regulations affecting FBOs fall into the business-related regulation category mentioned earlier. These regulations include withholding income tax and excise tax requirements of the Internal Revenue Service (IRS) of the Department of the Treasury. When an FBO complains of the cost of doing business, many times it is due to the fact that IRS requirements force some additional overhead costs to be added to a business. For example, the FBO must not only pay tax on the *income* generated by the business, it must also pay special *excise* taxes dictated several places in federal law. These taxes include civil aircraft use taxes, transportation taxes (for cargo as well as people), and fuel taxes. On top of taxes paid by the FBO itself, the FBO must collect the withholding tax paid by individuals earning income from the FBO and remit these taxes to IRS. In addition to the requirements of IRS taxes, the FBO must also meet the regulations of the Social Security Administration regarding unemployement, medicare, and FICA (Federal Insurance Contributions Act) contributions. Again the FBO as employer, must contribute the employer's share and submit the employee's share via withholding/deductions from earned income with the FBO.

Aside from the tax-related regulations, FBOs must meet the regulatory requirements of several other nonaviation federal agencies. The Federal Communications Commission licenses radio operators and radio equipment. This type of regulation is important to all FBOs operating aircraft with radio equipment aboard and is crucial to FBOs which specialize as avionics repair stations. The United States Department of Labor has important minimum hourly wage laws which the FBO must follow in its hiring practices. The Occupational Safety and Health Administration (OSHA), while recently limited in its actions due to budget cuts, is still a significant regulator of business in the area of workplace safety. The main effect of OSHA has been to increase the awareness of the FBO employer and employees of the need to monitor workplace safety. Finally, the Department of Energy has passed standby energy allocation and price rules for use in future energy emergencies. These rules will be crucial if there is an energy embargo or some similar problems restricting the flow of crude oil to the United States.

At the state level, there are numerous rules and regulations which affect the FBO. These include regulations affecting pilot and aircraft registration, licensing of airports (epecially those providing commercial services), agricultural operators, and parachutists. In some states, state education or training departments license flight schools much as they would any vocational training institution. Of course, a license to do business is crucial in most states for the FBOs. Once an FBO is licensed, it must comply with the state laws related to sales taxes (applicable to the sale of goods and services, with some exemptions) and workmen's compensation. Many states have considered relaxing tight state licensing requirements for business because of the benefits which new businesses could provide to the state economy.

At the local level, there is also some significant regulation of FBOs. The most important of these regulations is the lease under which the FBO operates at publicly owned airports. (At privately owned airports, the owner of the airport is usually also the FBO.) This lease is a form of regulation in that it specifies what the FBO can do (e.g., it is limited to certain aviation activities or it can be a full-service FBO). It also specifies the amount of rent or lease money that must be paid to the airport authority. The FBO must also follow airport operating rules passed by the airport authority. These would include fuel sales prices, curfew (if any), landing fees (if any), and so forth. Finally, many local governments have zoning and building code regulations which may affect the location of a new buildings or building additions at some airports. The local regulations may include automobile hauling requirements, advertising sign regulations, and construction-related requirements (wiring, drainage, sanitary sewer, and so forth).

Case Study: Regulations Affecting Fixed Base Operators' Leases and Operations

The key to a successful fixed base operation (FBO) on a publicly owned airport is the lease which the FBO negotiates with the airport. However, there are regulations which effect the terms of this lease. The regulations are both federal and local even though most publicly owned airports are locally owned. Some of these regulations are:

1. No exclusive rights. An FBO could not have exclusive rights to operate on a publicly owned airport receiving federal funds under the Airport Development Aid Program (ADAP).[21] The exclusive rights rule has been mentioned in federal law since 1938.[22] Its objective is to make sure federal money is not being spent on an airport which is allowing an anticompetitive

situation to exist. The impact on FBOs of this rule has been negative in its implementation. One aspect of its implementation is the "forced entry" concept. The concept of forced entry occurs when the FAA decides that additional competition is needed at an airport and requires an airport to bring in another FBO.[23] In some cases the additional competition forced upon an airport has created a situation where none of the FBO's can operate profitably. The result of the implementation of this regulation has meant the demise of some FBOs.[24] The Airport and Airway Improvement Act of 1982 gives an airport more flexibility in determining the number of FBOs it has. However, this will be subject to court tests.

2. Nondiscrimination. The FBOs operating in a federally funded airport must agree not to discriminate on the basis of race, creed, or national origin. This is a federal requirement.[25]

3. Minimum operating standards. Minimum operating standards are usually specified by the airport owners. These are requirements which must be met for an FBO to retain its lease. Many times these standards include a 24-hour-per-day operating requirement and other such service-related standards.

These and other regulations affect the daily operations of FBOs on publicly owned airports. The central vehicle for implementing these regulations is the lease between the FBO and the airport owner. The other vehicle for implementing these regulations is an inspection by the FAA.

CORPORATE FLIGHT DEPARTMENTS

Overview

As identified earlier, the corporate flight department is a special operating unit in the aviation industry. As such, one would expect it to have a regulation—or set of regulations—dedicated to it, as do airports, airlines, or aircraft manufacturers. Actually, only a *part* of a FAR is the "Bible" of this segment of aviation. As shown in Table 32, this regulation is FAR Part 91, Subpart D. It is this regulation which governs aircraft operations conducted by corporations for their own company purposes. FAR Part 125 also affects corporate activity if the corporation is operating large transport aircraft. Flight operations conducted "for hire" or on a scheduled basis for persons outside the owning company (or companies) are regulated through FAR Part 135 or FAR part 121. This regulation specifies everything from progressive maintenance planning for the aircraft operated to the flight attendants' ratio to the passenger capacity of the aircraft. Also included are operations manual requirements, minimum crew qualifications, and joint ownersip requirements (e.g., if more than one company own the aircraft, responsibilities for maintenance, flight crews, and so forth, must be specified).

Another very important rule affecting corporate flight department operations in general is FAR Part 36. As noted earlier, this regulation was developed to regulate aircraft noise at the source. The impact on corporate flight departments has been heaviest on those operating jet aircraft. All of the new model corporate jet aircraft now being produced by the manufacturers meet FAR Part 36 regulations. However, older model corporate jet aircraft— as well as older surplus airline aircraft (707s, 727-100s and DC-8s) that many corporations are looking at for corporate use—do not meet the regulation. Therefore, those corporations operating these older aircraft have an important reequipment versus retrofit decision to make by 1985 (the deadline for meeting FAR Part 36).

As with other segments of the aviation industry involved with aircraft operations, the airmen hired to operate the aircraft must be duly certificated under FAR Part 61. For example, a qualified copilot is required on large aircraft (12,500 pounds or over) or on multiengine jet aircraft certificated for more than one pilot. This second-in-command pilot must have a minimum of a private pilot's rating and an instrument rating. This regulation then, specifies operating standards for the certification of pilots and flight instructors. In addition to these standards are the medical certification standards for pilots contained in FAR Part 67.

Also important to the corporate flight department are the various airworthiness rules which must be followed by those performing aircraft maintenance for corporate operations. Obviously, FAR Part 23 must be used for "utility" aircraft (less than 12,500 pounds gross weight) and FAR Part 25 must be used for "transport" category aircraft (above 12,500 pounds gross weight). Also, FAR part 33 must be followed during engine maintenance and FAR Part 35 must be followed during propeller maintenance. FAR Part 43 establishes standards for maintenance, preventive maintenance, rebuilding, and alteration. Finally, airworthiness directives issued under FAR Part 39 require modifications to affected aircraft.

Other federal regulators which are important to corporate flight departments are the United States Department of the Treasury, Internal Revenue Service (IRS), and the Environmental Protection Agency (EPA). The IRS is important because of its ruling affecting the use of corporate aircraft as a business expense and because of rules related to the depreciation of aircraft equipment for tax purposes. The IRS also specifies rules for the payment of and collection of income taxes. The Environmental Protection Agency deserves mention due to its role in regulating aircraft noise emissions. In its role as environmental regulator, the EPA *proposes* the rules related to aircraft noise emissions. (In this case, the FAA is relegated to the role of making comments

TABLE 32

OVERVIEW REGULATORY CHART FOR A CORPORATE FLIGHT DEPARTMENT

Federal Aviation Administration*	Other Federal	State/Local	Other
A. Aircraft Operating Rules 1. FAR Part 91, Subpart D—General Operating and Flight Rules (for the operation of aircraft for noncommercial purposes within a corporate structure) 2. FAR Part 36, Noise Standards: Aircraft Type and Airworthiness Certification—Specifies maximum noise limits by type 3. FAR Part 125—Privately Owned Large Transport Aircraft	A. Internal Revenue Service—Excise and income tax laws, including limits on the business use of aircraft B. Environmental Protection Agency—Proposed environmental protection rules, including additional aircraft noise rules	A. Noise laws/curfews on turbo jet/fan aircraft B. Storage/hangaring (appropriate facilities)	A. Company relationship of flight department for the overall corporate structure—regulation of aircraft use, scheduling, crewing B. National Business Aircraft Association—Cites industry standards for corporate aircraft operations C. Insurance companies (specifications of premium and standards for premiums on corporate flight department operations)

154

B. Airman Certificate Rules

1. FAR Part 61—Certification: Pilots and Flight Instructors (appropriate type ratings for corporate crews, etc.)

2. FAR Part 67—Medical Standards and Certification (for medical certification standards for crews).

C. Aircraft Airworthiness Rules for Maintenance

1. Appropriate FAR for the aircraft type (FAR Part 23 is for "utility" aircraft and FAR Part 25 is for "transport" aircraft—those larger than 12,500 pounds gross weight)

2. FAR Part 33—Engine Airworthiness

*See Appendix 4 for the complete titles of the FARs cited here.

155

on EPA proposals but does not have to adopt proposals without a review of the safety implications of the given proposals). While most of the EPA's importance in the regulation of noise has already been felt by the operators of large aircraft, there may be future proposals regarding smaller general aviation aircraft operated by some corporations.

State regulations affecting corporate flight departments are restricted to aircraft and airmen registration requirements and laws which might affect the overall corporation itself. At the local level, however, are crucial regulatory matters which affect corporate flight departments. The first is the proliferation of noise-related actions by local governments which own major hub and reliever airports. This action can take several forms, including *curfews* on aircraft operations during late night and early morning hours, *bans* on jet aircraft preferential runway use, recommended power reductions on take-off and nonstandard noise abatement approach or departure paths to and from airports. The second area of local government impact on corporate flight departments has to do with the negotiation of long-term hangar use agreements. One of the major operational limitations faced by corporate flight departments is adequate airport facilities, including sufficient runway lengths as well as properly sized hangar facilities. This is particularly a problem in metropolitan areas where airports are congested. Many different arrangements regarding hangar use can be made, at the discretion of each individual airport operator. In a corporate flight department operating multiple aircraft from multiple locations, this means separate negotiations at each airport served conforming to the special requirements and conditions of each locale. For example, liability insurance for operations at each airport will be required. Also, one operation may be from an independently operated hangar while another may be from a large "community" hangar. All of these conditions merit separate attention in separate agreements.

Some of the "other" regulatory *factors* faced by corporate flight departments include the company itself, the insurance companies, and the National Business Aircraft Association. The company within which the corporate flight department operates provides the overall operating parameters for the flight department. That is, it specifies rules for aircraft use, aircraft scheduling, operations manuals, and even how the aircraft use will be "billed" within the company. The insurance companies have a role to play in corporate operations because they are in the position of assessing the overall health of the corporate flight department for insurance risk purposes. Therefore, the insurance companies assess crew qualifications, hours flown, aircraft types, and so forth, in making their decisions about the level of premiums charged. This, in turn, affects management decisions such as in the personnel and aircraft equipment areas. It also affects overall corporate flight department costs. Finally, the National Business Aircraft Association produces a *Recommended Standards Manual* for the operation of corporate aircraft. This manual sets the industry standard for the corporate flight department management, containing recommendations in the administration, flight operations, and maintenance areas.

Case Study: Regulations Affecting the Expansion of the Reliever Airport System

Because corporate flight departments depend so heavily on the availability of good reliever airports, this case study will examine the regulations affecting the expansion of the reliever airport system. The definition of a reliever airport has recently been broadened to the following: "an airport designated by the Secretary [of Transportation] as having the function of relieving congestion at a commercial service airport and providing more general aviation access to the overall community."[26] Most reliever airports, however, relieve general aviation traffic from major primary airports in large metropolitan areas. Relievers are important to corporate users because they provide an alternate destination for corporate aircraft bound for major, capacity-constrained airports. Frequently, the use of reliever airports reduces airspace usage delays as well as taxiing of aircraft. Also, reliever airports are, in most cases, more geared to handling corporate aircraft than the large air carrier airports.

Nearly all relievers are also owned by local government or by private entities. Local government and private owners find it difficult to expand reliever airports because:

1. Most existing reliever airports are located in suburban areas and also serve corporate jet aircraft. They therefore produce noise in the community. Some communities have passed restrictions on jet aircraft operations at local government owned relievers to reduce noise. Most reliever airports face community opposition to expansion because of this situation.

2. Reliever airports are normally located on expensive suburban land. This makes it very difficult to expand using neighboring property, which is also usually expensive.

3. Some crucial relievers are privately owned and were barred from receiving federal aid for development until 1982. Now that these relievers are eligible for federal funds, competition for such monies is fierce because of the expansion of the reliever definition.

4. Federal funding especially earmarked for relievers has only been available since 1976. Prior to that year, relievers "fought it out" with other categories of airports for federal funds.

Therefore, even though there has been a strong airport development aid program since 1970, many relievers have not received any direct federal aid because of these problems. Local noise regulations, high land costs, community opposition, restrictions on privately owned airports, limited federal funding, and fierce competition for federal funds are the primary problems facing those wanting to improve reliever airports. It is obvious that there is a broad range of legislative and regulatory problems to be overcome before reliever airports can be expected to be fully funded and supported nation-wide.

Corporate users are negatively affected by this situation. The National Business Aircraft Association, the industry association representing corporate aircraft users, made the following statement about relievers in their 1981 annual report. "The significance of reliever airports in the national airways system is often lost on local officials who must initiate requests for available funds from the federal government for their development. There is no question that the aviation community, especially those in business aviation know the value of reliever airports. These valuable airports take the traffic strain off major air carrier airports in larger cities."[27] The NBAA, together with two other related aviation industry user groups, are attempting to generate more local interest in relievers through the "Reliever Airport Project." However, the regulatory impact of the federal and local and state governments goes beyond the problem of generating more local interest in relievers. Specific action will have to be taken to resolve the reliever airport problem.

AIRMEN

Overview

There are a number of different types of airmen—pilots, airframe and powerplant mechanics, flight engineers, flight attendants, air traffic control tower and radio operators, and so forth. The regulation of all of these individuals is largely a responsibility of the Federal Aviation Administration through the FARs.

Two examples selected for further review are pilots and mechanics. As can be seen in Table 33, pilots are subjected to somewhat more non-FAA scrutiny than are mechanics. While pilots and mechanics are subject to various FAA certificate regulations (as noted in Table 33), pilots face additional restrictions from other federal agencies. For example, the IRS has specific rules to follow in reporting the business use of aircraft. Also, most states require the registration of pilots but not mechanics. In the area of "other" regulations, there are rules which a pilot must follow to rent an aircraft at a local airport. These rules are provided by the FBO or, in some cases, by the local airport authority. Finally, airlines, air taxi operators, and corporate flight departments all have company rules specifying minimum flight experience for pilots to be hired.

The mechanic and the pilot do have one thing in common: a long list of safety-related FARs which must be followed in their respective tasks. For the pilot there are the airspace and air traffic rules in the general subject areas of the FARs numbered in the 70s and the 90s. For the mechanic, all of the aircraft airworthiness FARs in the 20s and 30s general subject areas are important (see Tables 24, 26, and 32).

TABLE 33
OVERVIEW REGULATORY CHART FOR AIRMEN

I. PILOTS	II. AIRFRAMES AND POWERPLANT MECHANICS
Federal Aviation Administration★	Federal Aviation Administration★
A. Certification—FAR Part 61	A. Certification/Training
B. Training—FAR Parts 141 and 143	1. FAR Part 65—Airmen Other Than Flight Crewmembers
C. Medical—FAR Part 67	2. FAR Part 147—Aviation Maintenance Technician Schools
D. Previously cited airspace and air traffic rules	B. Airworthiness Certification
Other Federal	1. FAR Part 21—Certification Procedures for Products and Parts
A. Treasury/IRS—Tax laws re: business use of flying or aircraft if owner	2. FAR Part 23—Airworthiness Standards: Normal, Utility, and Acrobatic Category Airplanes
States (not all)	3. FAR Part 25—Airworthiness Standards: Transport Category Airplanes
A. Pilot registration	4. FAR Part 33—Airworthiness Standards: Aircraft Engines
B. Aircraft registration (if also an aircraft owner)	5. FAR Part 39—Airworthiness Directives
Other	6. FAR Part 43—Maintenance, Preventive Maintenance, Rebuilding and Alteration
A. FBO rules, enforcing FAA rules, re: aircraft rental (may require check rides, verification of credentials, credit checks, etc.)	7. FAR Part 45—Identification and Registration Marking
	8. FAR Part 47—Aircraft Registration
B. Airline rules specifying minimum experience requirements for pilots	C. Repair Facilities Certification
	1. FAR Part 145—Repair Stations
	2. FAR Part 147—Maintenance Technical School Certificates

★See Appendix 4 for the complete titles of the FARs cited here.

Case Study: Credentialing for Student and Private Pilots

There are four basic pilot certificates: student, private, commercial, and air transport. The pilot's basic introductory certificates, the student and private pilot ratings, are the lifeblood of general aviation. However, over the years, there have been abuses of the limits of these certificates which have led to many tragic accidents.[28] In 1982, the National Association of Flight Instructors proposed several basic changes in how airmen would be licensed at

TABLE 34

PROPOSED CHANGES IN STUDENT AND PRIVATE PILOT CREDENTIALING:
SAMPLE CHARACTERISTICS

Current System	Proposed System
1. Student—Minimum age 16; third class medical certificate.	1. Student—Minimum age 15.
2. Private—Minimum age 17; Biennial flight review; no checkout requirement for sophisticated single engine aircraft; third class medical certificate.	2. Private—Minimum age 16; checkout required before assuming pilot-in-command status in 200-plus horsepower or retractable gear and/or controllable-prop aircraft; annual flight review for pilots with fewer than 400 hours.
3. (No current rating of this type.)	3. Student recreational pilot rating—Age limit 14; cannot use tower-controlled airports; limited to aircraft of 200 horsepower or less and only one or two seats; may not operate above 10,000 feet above sea level or 2,000 feet above ground level, whichever is higher; three-mile minimum visibility; no night flying. No medical certificate requirements.
4. (No current rating of this type.)	4. Recreational pilot rating—Age limit 16; all other requirements as under no. 3 above.

Source: Richard Collins, "A Concensus on Licensing," *Flying Magazine*, July 1982, 76–78.

the basic levels.[29] Some of the characteristics of these proposed changes are summarized in Table 34. The key aspect of these proposed licensing changes is the proposal to create two basic licenses. These are the student recreational and recreational pilot certificates. These new licenses would supplement rather than replace the current student and private certificates. The key feature of the recreational categories is the limit placed on sophistication of aircraft that can be operated by a certificate holder. These aircraft may not be powered by an engine larger than 200 horsepower, may not have more than two seats, and may not be operated above 10,000 feet sea level or 2,000 feet above the ground, whichever is higher. In addition to these limits, there are prohibitions for recreational pilots on night flying and on operating from tower-controlled airports. These new recreational pilots would have the opportunity to begin training sooner, at age 14 (rather than 16 for the current student pilot certificate). Also, there are no minimum medical certificate requirements for recreational pilots.

The changes recommended for regular student and private pilot certificates start with lowering the age requirements—to 15 for student pilots and 16 for private pilots. In the private pilot cateogry, the proficiency requirements are even more far-reaching. For example, a pilot may not assume pilot-in-command status on a sophisticated aircraft (200-plus horsepower, retractable gear, controllable prop), without first being checked out on that aircraft by a flight instructor. Also, private pilots wishing to fly as pilot-in-command (PIC) and having less than 400 hours total time, and no PIC experience in the past 180 days, must be checked out by a flight instructor. In addition, an annual flight review is required for all private pilots with less than 400 hours. The regular biennial review would apply to those pilots with more than 400 hours. Finally, there are proposed visibility limits for day visual flight rules (three miles) and night visual flight rules (five miles) for flights by pilots with less than 400 hours.[30]

In summary, there are proposals being made which would significantly tighten the current student and private pilot rating requirements. These proposals would help the regulations affecting pilots keep pace with the sophistication of the aircraft being flown by student and private pilots. It is hoped that these new limits will have a positive impact on general aviation accident rates in the long term. However, sub-400-hour pilots will be faced with increased regulations. In addition to tightening the requirements for current ratings, these proposals also suggest two new certificates—the student recreational and recreational pilot certificates. These proposed certificates are an attempt to recognize a transition in the kind of flying being undertaken in America today.

8

Future Directions

THE FUTURE OF AVIATION INDUSTRY regulation can be examined in the context of legislation, regulators, regulatory instruments, and the regulated parts of the aviation industry described in previous chapters. The interrelationships among these aspects of aviation industry regulation will be summarized at the conclusion of this chapter.

LEGISLATION

The major focus of recent legislation in the aviation field has been in the economic area. The Airline Deregulation Act of 1978 has had an unexpected impact, which has prompted some legislators to call for "reregulation." Among the problems that have emerged are:

1. Airline survival. In a deregulated environment airlines are more vulnerable to adverse economic conditions. One major carrier has already failed and others face uncertain futures. Some contend that airline failures are a necessary by-product of a healthy marketplace. Others favor "bailing out" airlines that are in trouble.

2. Small community air service. While there is specific legislation guaranteeing essential air service to small communities, inadequate service levels and subsidies have prompted affected communities to press for legislative change.

3. Airport access. Airport capacity problems have interfered with the ability to obtain adequate gate space at selected facilities. Airport officials have developed policies or used the pricing mechanism to ration demand for airport services.

4. Carrier data reports. Deregulation has obviated certain carrier data reporting requirements. While this has liberated the carriers from burdensome paper-work requirements, it has also deprived industry planners and analysts of a valuable source of data. As a result, there has been congressional support for continuing some data reporting requirements.

Other unresolved issues with respect to deregulation relate to employee protection, antitrust immunity, consumer protection, and impartial decision-making for continued regulation.

In order to resolve these problems and issues, new legislation or amendments to existing legislation have been proposed. Some have suggested the acceleration of deregulation, including the dismantling of the CAB prior to 1985 and the immediate withdrawal of all federal authority over economic regulation. Others believe that the Deregulation Act should be "fine tuned" to clarify the transfer of regulatory authority to other agencies. Finally some legislators, dissatisfied with reductions in air service in some communities and concerned over the financial viability of the airlines, have proposed reregulating the industry and resurrecting some type of regulatory body to replace the CAB.

In the environmental area, the federal government has recently established a legislative precedent for maintaining its distance from local airport environmental issues. The 1979 Aviation Safety and Noise Abatement Act delegated much of the responsibility for resolving airport noise issues to state and local officials. Thus while federal legislative policy promotes airport/land use compatibility, it grants local officials considerable latitude in meeting environmental goals. This legislative framework is expected to continue in the future. The area of aviation safety is expected to experience considerable change at the federal level. The deregulation philosophy of the Reagan administration reflects a different approach to carrying out the safety mandate of the Federal Aviation Act of 1958. For example, the "regulation by objective" approach substitutes more generalized goal-oriented regulations for the "how-to" procedures in previous regulations and gives the regulated parties greater flexibility in complying with them.[1]

Legislative changes may be necessary to clarify and/or redefine the roles of the Federal Aviation Administration and the aviation division of the National Transportation Safety Board (NTSB). Historically these two agencies have engaged in extensive debates over proper safety procedures.

Another potential area for legislative change pertains to the FAA's role in promoting aviation. While the Federal Aviation Act of 1958 directs the

FAA to promote civil aviation, critics of the agency contend that it cannot regulate and promote aviation simultaneously without bias. Future legislation may therefore call for a reduction in promotional activities, which would have a significant impact on the FAA's airports and research and development programs.

REGULATORS

The Airline Deregulation Act of 1978 calls for the demise of the Civil Aeronautics Board in 1985. Aside from the reregulation debate, a more immediate issue is the transfer of some of the CAB's functions to other federal agencies. According to current plans, the United States Department of Transportation will assume responsibility for the essential air service program and general rulemaking functions; the Justice Department will handle antitrust issues as they relate to mergers and intercarrier agreements; the Post Office will negotiate mail contracts with air carriers; and the State Department, along with the Department of Transportation, will become more heavily involved in foreign and international air service matters. The precise manner in which these agencies will implement their new regulatory responsibilities may require further legislative clarification.

The Federal Aviation Administration, while in no way facing demise, does face significant change. The air traffic controllers' strike of 1981 has necessitated an internal review of air traffic management practices and has resulted in a 20-year plan for the improvement of the nation's airspace management system: The National Airspace System Plan. If implemented, this plan will entirely revamp the FAA's air traffic control system.

The overall goal of the National Airspace System Plan is to accommodate future air traffic demand in a safe and efficient manner. To achieve this goal, it proposes to: 1) consolidate air traffic control facilities and increase automation, 2) reduce the labor-intensive nature of the system, 3) use compatible and interlinked computers, 4) upgrade weather and flight services, 5) install improved navigation aids, 6) reduce system maintenance costs, and 7) implement a collision-avoidance system. The principal benefit of the plan is that it would increase the safety and capacity of the air traffic control system while improving its efficiency.[2]

The FAA has also considered pulling back from its commitment to the airport development program. Although federal airport funding legislation was passed in 1982, the agency, as a result of staffing reductions, has delegated a great deal of the responsibility for compliance with program requirements to local sponsors and their consultants.

The FAA's organizational structure is another item that has been subjected to close scrutiny. In 1981, a proposal to consolidate regional offices was withdrawn because of significant congressional, state, and local opposition. This issue may resurface at a later date, along with the potential restructuring of FAA district offices throughout the country. Related to changes in the structure of offices is the "lead region" concept for the certification of aircraft.

The FAA may also be called upon to tighten its enforcement of federal safety regulations. This demand has resulted from a discussion of the proper roles of the FAA and National Transportation Safety Board during major accident investigations. The NTSB and FAA maintain a continous dialogue, wherein the NTSB generally recommends more stringent enforcement or tighter safety rules and the FAA responds to these recommendations. Some have proposed that qualifications for NTSB members include aviation experience such as in engineering, safety, or some other field related to the aircraft accident investigation mission of the NTSB.

At the state level, there exists the possibility of increased involvement in airport finance and environmental controls. Many states have had strong, successful aviation programs in areas such as airport certification, aircraft registration, and safety promotion. As the FAA restructures its regulatory role, the states can be expected to respond accordingly to fill any voids.

At the local level, the primary areas of increased regulatory responsibility will most likely fall in the environmental and airport expansion areas. With respect to environmental regulations, there has been and will continue to be a greater interest in the development of noise regulations and ordinances. In the airport expansion area, some of the larger airport sponsors may assume more responsibility for financing development. This will hinge upon future efforts to "defederalize" major air carrier airports.

REGULATORY INSTRUMENTS

During the 1980s there has been an increasing emphasis on the use of various emergency regulatory instruments (Special Federal Aviation Regulations or SFARs) to handle special problems such as those resulting from the air traffic controllers' strike. The volatility of the aviation industry had contributed to the the methods employed to regulate it and brought about the need for more SFARs.

More recently there has been an effort within the FAA under President Reagan's first Administrator, J. Lynn Helms, to rewrite some of the FARs. This rewriting effort is guided by a new regulatory attitude which emphasizes objectives rather than specific standards. An example of the impact of this new philosophy is the condensation of the flight duty/crew scheduling portions of FAR Part 121 from several pages to eight lines.[3]

The proposed FAR Part 120, now rescinded, was another example of the "regulation by objective" concept. It would have replaced FAR Parts 121 and 135, which prescribe operational requirements for large and small commercial air carriers, and substitute safety objectives for many of the existing "how to" regulations. Each carrier would have been given greater flexibility to determine the means by which it met the required safety objectives, rather than being forced to adhere to specific procedures identified in FAR Parts 121 and 135.

Although this proposed FAR was touted as "revolutionary" it did not represent a dramatic departure from current safety practices. The so called "how to" regulations in FAR Parts 121 and 135 would have been transferred to FAA advisory circulars. Carriers would then have been given the option of using the specific procedures contained in these ACs, or, with the approval of the FAA, substituting their own procedures. Any new procedures would have had to meet the safety objectives prescribed in Part 120.[4]

Another change relates to the status of those regulations promulgated and enforced by the Civil Aeronautics Board. With the CAB "sunset," those federal agencies which assume some of its regulatory responsibilities will need to decide whether to maintain, revise, replace, or delete any applicable procedural or economic regulations. For example, in the essential air service area, the CAB has established economic regulation Part 325 which defines how essential air service determinations are to be made. This regulation is now subject to review by the United States Department of Transportation since the CAB has been eliminated.

The increasing volume of regulations and the strengthening of enforcement procedures can be expected to contribute to the proliferation of other regulatory instruments including orders, airworthiness directives, and advisory circulars. However, it is likely that there will be a reduction in the number of advisory circulars which are prepared and dispensed for strictly information purposes.

An alternative to the growth of government regulatory instruments is "self-regulation" by the aviation industry. Examples of such regulation include industrywide formats developed for technical manuals (flight, maintenance, parts, and so forth) by the Air Transport Association of America and the General Aviation Manufacturers Association, certification programs for airport managers formulated by the American Association of Airport Executives, and airport construction procedures defined by the Association of General Contractors. Self-regulation offers the advantage of peer pressure and direction rather than outside pressure from a government agency.

The future of self-regulation is crucial to the continued health and growth of the aviation industry. As budget constraints force the government to reduce it regulatory efforts, the industry must be prepared to exercise self-discipline and develop and enforce its own standards. Such standards could potentially relate to the collection of essential data and interline agreements among the airlines, monitoring airport construction by consulting engineers, developing a quality control program under the guidance of the aircraft manufacturers, and establishing pilot proficiency guidelines and testing procedures by professional pilot groups. Any attempt, however, by the industry to regulate and constrain certain competitive practices would face stiff opposition from the Justice Department. The airline industry, for example, would find it difficult to regulate rate-making standards and route capacity.

THE AVIATION INDUSTRY

The future of aviation-related legislation, the regulators, and instruments of regulation will be affected by the future structure and performance of the industry itself. And the industry's structure and performance are tied directly to the general economy.

> Prior to the mid-1970's, aviation growth appeared immune to the vicissitudes of general economic activity. Growth in general aviation and air carrier operations seemed almost immune to short-term fluctuations in general economic activity. The first sign that this long-term independence might be disintegrating occurred in the fall of 1973 when the Arab Oil Embargo and rapidly rising fuel prices led to a general economic recession and a no-growth year for the scheduled air carrier industry.[5]

After peaking in 1978–79, the economy and air transportation began a steady decline and bottomed out in 1982. The following general prediction is made by the FAA concerning the future. "Aviation activity is expected to reverse three straight years of losses in 1983, reflecting a return of the Air Traffic Control System to normalcy and an upturn in economic activity. Overall, the long-term outlook for aviation is for relatively strong growth throughout the forecast period [1983–94], consistent with forecasted long-term economic growth."[6] But, how does this translate into a comment about the future of each industry segment? The following paragraphs will further illustrate the future of each industry segment.

Aviation Manufacturing

The civilian aviation manufacturing industry was hit particularly hard in 1982 with some earlier-than-forecast production run shutdowns (L-1011) as well as by temporary and permanent plant closings (Piper, Beech, and Cessna small aircraft lines). Certainly, on the civilian side, 1982 was a year or retrenchment for the aircraft manufacturers. Luckily for many of the manufacturers, strong military aircraft orders have helped balance an otherwise gloomy picture. Some of current problems which this industry segment faces—and which will shape the future of the industry—are:

1. The general state of the economy and its impact on the purchasing power of aircraft buyers in the aviation community.

2. The health of other segments of the aviation industry. The success of airline and general aviation businesses which use new aircraft are critical to the success of the aircraft manufacturers.

3. Foreign competition in both the air transport and general aviation aircraft fields is growing. A key example of this is the dominancy of foreign manufacturers in the commuter airline aircraft market. Of course, this foreign dominance is due to both the aggressiveness of the foreign producers as well as the historical restraints on the size of aircraft operated by United States commuter airlines. Air transport and general aviation aircraft exports play an important positive part in the United States balance of payments picture. As the United States market share is reduced, so is this benefit.

4. Government policies. Any revisions in the "safe harbor" leasing provisions of 1981 tax legislation or changes in United States support for the Export-Import Bank will have a negative impact on the major airframe manufacturers as well as on the major airlines. Safe harbor leasing provisions allow the airlines significant tax advantages from aircraft lease arrangements. There has been talk of reversing this tax advantage.

The Export-Import Bank is a federally supported method of financing major foreign purchases of United States goods at competitive interest rates. This concept is also under congressional and administration scrutiny.

It is difficult to make an exact statement about the future of aviation manufacturers because of all the variables that must be considered. However, consider the following combination of statements, beginning with the FAA's prediction concerning the domestic air carrier fleet. "Based upon projections of air carrier traffic, seat capacity and load factor, the U.S. commercial airline fleet is forecast to increase from 2,483 large jet aircraft in 1982 to 3,120 aircraft in 1994. The growth in the air carrier averages 1.9 percent or 53 aircraft annually."[7]

The Aerospace Industries Association states it a little differently.

On the basis of backlog figures, AIA estimates civil aircraft sales in 1983 at $11.4 billion up only $200 million—meaning a decline in inflation-adjusted terms. Transport aircraft constitute by far the largest element of the industry's civil aircraft sales and manufacturers estimate the transport market at $100–120 billion over the next decade; the question is when the financial health of the world's airlines will permit them to resume aircraft orders. The answer hinges largely on a turnaround in the world economy.[8]

The future of the general aviation manufacturing area is viewed a little more cautiously.

The industry will experience a continuation of slow growth in the general aviation fleet in the 1983–1985 time period. There will be variations in the number of aircraft added to the fleet each year due in part to changes in economic conditions. However, the net addition to the fleet will average approximately 8,500 aircraft per year between 1982 and 1994. Active single-engine and multi-engine piston aircraft are forecast to grow approximately 3.2 percent per year. The number of turbine powered aircraft is projected to more than double from 7,900 in 1982 to 16,600 in 1994. The rotorcraft fleet is also expected to show significant growth, increasing at the rate of 5 percent per year.[9]

Overall, civil aircraft manufacturing will slowly begin to come out of a long period of decline by the mid-1980s. Manufacturers of two-engine narrow-body and wide-body transport aircraft and turbine-powered general aviation aircraft will do best in the next decade. It should be pointed out that, even though civil aviation manufacturing has been in decline and will be slowly recovering in the 1980s, defense and space related aviation manufacturing will continue their already well-established growth trends. In 1983 defense sales were up 11 percent over 1982 and space sales were up 12 percent over 1982.[10]

Major/National Airlines

The large airlines are facing one of their most turbulent times ever. In 1981, the major/national airlines suffered their worst losses in history. In May 1982, Braniff Airlines went under Chapter 11 bankruptcy. What does the future hold? The Federal Aviation Administration notes:

Air carrier domestic enplanements increased by 3.1 percent in 1982 to 272.6 million, reversing a two year decline in enplanements. This reversal is expected to continue throughout the forecast period, with enplanements projected to increase 4.3 percent in 1983, 7.1 percent in 1984 and 6.0 percent in 1985. For the entire forecast period, growth in domestic enplanements is expected to increase at an average annual rate of 4.7 percent to 471.1 million passengers in 1994.[11]

However, the number of major/national airlines, their operating styles, and their size will vary considerably from the historical airline industry structure that everyone is familiar with. For example, the number of major and national airlines has already begun to drop—as noted in chapter 1. This trend is expected to continue for three reasons: mergers, bankruptcies (and other financial reasons), and competition from new carriers.

The operating styles are expected to change to conform to the new "free-wheeling" route structure allowed under deregulation—as tempered by the Braniff experience. Carriers will continue to experiment with route structures with most major and national carriers moving to some sort of "hub and spoke" concept to maximize the "feed" to flights on its own system. There will be decreasing emphasis on flights on domestic routes under 500 and over 1,500 miles in length.[12]

The size of individual major/national carriers can be expected to grow through mergers, response to bankruptcies, and general expansion. An example of this kind is American Airlines, which has grown in recent years due to general expansion and through response to the Braniff bankruptcy. However, substantial growth in the overall industry can be expected only if the nation's economy continues its recovery from the doldrums of 1981–82. Also, the amount of growth from carrier to carrier will depend greatly on the impact of "new entrant" airlines. These airlines, over twenty of which are now in operation (among them Midway, Air One, New York Air, People Express, Muse Air, Jet America, and Florida Express) are providing low fare, high frequency competition to major/national carriers with jet aircraft. There are many more "new entrants" waiting for improvement in the nation's economy before initiating operations. Even if only a few of these carriers succeed, there will be an impact on existing major/national carriers in certain markets.

Regional/Commuter Airlines

While the regional/commuter airline sector of the aviation industry has been historically the most volatile, its future looks optimistic. According to the FAA:

> After a brief slowdown in the demand for commuter service in 1982, the forecast shows that the strong growth in commuter activity relative to other segments of the aviation industry will resume in 1983. The forecast anticipates a higher growth rate in the early years of the forecast period and a gradual decline in the magnitude of that growth as 1994 is approached. . . . the expected average growth rate between 1982 and 1994 is 8.4 percent for enplanements and 10.2 percent for passenger miles. This forecast implies that enplanements will more than double their 1982 level during the forecast period to 41.5 million enplanements in 1994. Revenue passenger miles will more than triple their 1982 level to 6.9 billion in 1994.[13]

As already noted, the exit of larger carriers from small community markets will help commuters. Even more significant, however, is the recognition by the world's aircraft manufacturers that the smaller airlines are viable. There is also a greater selection of commuter airline aircraft from which to choose. This, in turn, will improve the marketability of the commuters to the public. The financing arrangements which manufacturers must use to attract commuter customers will have to be very creative, especially for smaller, undercapitalized carriers.

Another area of importance to the future of commuters is the competition from the automobile. Auto fuel costs, airport auto parking costs/availability, highway improvements, highway maintenance, and auto speed limits (and their enforcement) are factors in the choice of personal automobiles over commuter airlines. Fare levels, through-baggage checking, aircraft size/comfort, safety record, and service frequencies are factors which play a role in the choice of commuter airlines over the automobile.

Finally, fuel costs and availability and the airport access issue will also affect the future of commuter/regional airlines. Fuel costs will be an issue for commuters because commuters have less of a revenue base across which to spread any additional costs. Availability is an issue because the commuters are relatively small fuel users as compared to the major and national airlines at most airports. The airport access issue is important from two aspects: first, whether or not a commuter/regional carrier can gain gate space at major hub airports; second, whether or not gate space can be obtained in a reasonable location on the airport. These factors will need to be decided on an individual carrier basis with the decisions affecting the overall success of this segment of the industry.

Airports

The future of the nation's airport system depends largely upon the ability of various units of local government to continue to operate and maintain their airports. It also depends upon the continuation of national airport and airways legislation which helps local airports.

Although the total number of airports available in America has increased steadily in recent years, the *quality* of airports has declined. The number of publicly owned and public-use airports both have decreased steadily in recent years. The FAA even publishes a list of airports in danger of closing, most of which are reliever airports on or near metropolitan areas. Thus, most of the growth has been in privately owned, private-use airports in rural areas.

The future of the nation's airport system is discussed in the National Plan of Integrated Airport Systems. The most recent revision of this document, issued under the old title of National Airport System Plan, forecast the need for $12.67 billion in airport investment (in 1979 dollars) in 3,621 airports through 1989.[14] It is unclear how the new NPIAS to be issued under the new definitions and guidelines of the Airport and Airway Improvement Act of 1982 will change the airport development picture. However, the funding levels for airports contained in this legislation indicate that a high level of airport support will remain available through the 1980s. The future of airports, then, depends largely upon the ability of the airport system to serve changing aviation needs. It also depends upon the willingness of local, state, and federal governments to continue to support investments of public money in the airport system.

Fixed Base Operators

The FBOs also face a future in which the changing composition of aviation activity will be a major factor. Table 35 illustrates the FAA forecast of active general aviation aircraft by aircraft type. Single engine piston aircraft, the primary type of instructional/training aircraft used by FBOs, are the single largest group of aircraft throughout the forecast period, but are declining as a percentage of total aircraft. This forecast portends a shift in the types of aircraft used and sold toward multiengine equipment.

Another important indicator of the future of FBOs is the forecast of fuel sales to general aviation. FAA data reveal that jet fuel accounts for a larger share of the market than aviation gasoline in terms of total sales volume.[15] This trend will continue with jet fuel accounting for about 70 percent of the total general aviation fuel market by 1994.[16]

The table also shows that the percentage increase in the general aviation jet fuel market will be larger than the percentage increase in the general aviation gasoline market. These figures demonstrate significant trends in aircraft usage which have an impact on FBOs. First is the decline of "pleasure" flying due to the rising cost of fuel, which affects general aviation gas sales; second is the increasing sophistication of aircraft, a trend already pointed out in the aviation manufacturing section; third is the increasing business use of general aviation aircraft.

Table 36, which lists the number of active pilots by certificate type, indicates some interesting trends of importance to the FBOs. First is the continued increase in the number of student pilots, which is forecast to increase at a rate of 44.5 percent for the 1982–94 period. Student pilots are important to FBOs because they are an indicator of people who are entering the aviation field and may have a need for their services. Second, private pilots are expected to increase at a rate of 33.2 percent for the 1982–94 period. The largest pilot group, private pilots, is expected to increase at a lower rate than nearly all other categories because the higher costs of flying will hold down pleasure flying. Third is the continued increase in instrument–rated pilots at a rate of 50.8 percent for the 1982–94 period. This increase illustrates a greater sophistication and a need for greater all-weather flying for business purposes. Also many of these instrument ratings will be earned in the FBOs. Fourth is the even higher rate of increase (62.3 percent for the 1982–94 period) for airline transport pilot certificates. Again more business use, and increases in commuter airline and corporate aviation, will encourage this growth. The FBOs will benefit from this because they will provide the training for the upgraded pilots.

With the increasing emphasis on the business user, the various services offered by FBOs to this class of user will have to improve. Also, with jet fuel dominating sales to the general aviation market, FBOs must adapt their marketing, their service personnel, and their facilities to this potentially growing market. On the other hand, FBOs must continue to offer fueling and other services to the piston aircraft owner since the number of aircraft being served in this category will still dominate the general aviation portion of the industry.

Corporate Aviation

As previously illustrated in the aviation manufacturing and fixed base operation sections, turbine aircraft (both props and jets) will increase dramatically through the early 1990s (as noted in Table 35). The total number of turbine aircraft (including both turboprop and turbojet) in the national fleet will increase from 7,900 aircraft in 1982 to 16,600 in 1994. The larger share of this total will belong to the turboprop portion of the fleet. A total of 10,400 turboprops are forecast to be in the fleet by 1994 as compared with 6200 turbojets/fans. Also, the percentage increase in turboprops will be larger than in turbojets, indicating a much larger annual rate of increase in the turboprop category throughout the 1982–94 period.

The FAA comments on its data illustrate some of the factors which are spurring this growth: "Over the past several years general aviation has become increasingly important as a means of transportation for business use. Events which have contributed to this are changes in tax legislation, rapid escalation of fuel prices, business dispersion and centralized management, changing air carrier route structures and the cost advantage of general aviation relative to other competing modes of transportation."[17]

The future of corporate aviation, in terms of aircraft flown, looks very promising. With more than a doubling of turboprop and turbojet (and fan) aircraft, the corporate fleet will also become very sophisticated. Also of note, however, in the data in Table 35 are the increases noted for the turbine rotorcraft, piston rotorcraft, and multiple-engine piston categories. While not all corporate airplanes, the aircraft in these categories are a significant part of corporate aviation. Together with the turboprop and turbojet categories,

TABLE 35

ESTIMATED ACTIVE GENERAL AVIATION AIRCRAFT BY TYPE OF AIRCRAFT (THOUSANDS)

As of January 1	FIXED WING					ROTORCRAFT		Balloons Dirigibles Gliders
	Total	Piston		Turbo-prop	Turbo-jet	Piston	Tur-bine	
		Single Engine	Multi-engine					
Historical								
1978	184.3	149.3	21.5	2.9	2.3	2.7	2.1	3.6
1979	198.8	160.7	23.2	3.1	2.5	2.8	2.5	4.0
1980	210.3	168.4	25.1	3.5	2.7	3.1	2.7	4.8
1981	211.0	168.4	24.6	4.1	3.0	2.8	3.2	4.9
1982	213.2	167.9	25.2	4.7	3.2	3.3	3.7	5.0
Forecast								
1983	215.0	168.1	26.1	5.0	3.3	3.4	3.9	5.2
1984	217.1	168.5	26.9	5.4	3.4	3.5	4.1	5.3
1985	221.9	171.7	28.0	5.9	3.5	3.6	4.3	5.5

1986	229.1	175.6	29.2	6.4	3.8	3.7	4.7	5.7
1987	237.3	181.3	30.4	6.9	4.0	3.8	5.0	5.9
1988	246.5	187.5	31.8	7.5	4.2	3.9	5.3	6.3
1989	257.1	194.9	33.2	8.0	4.5	4.1	5.6	6.8
1990	268.7	203.4	34.7	8.5	4.8	4.3	5.8	7.2
1991	280.2	211.4	36.3	9.0	5.1	4.6	6.1	7.7
1992	291.7	219.9	37.5	9.4	5.4	4.8	6.5	8.2
1993	303.5	228.4	38.8	9.9	5.8	5.0	6.9	8.7
1994	315.2	236.8	40.1	10.4	6.2	5.2	7.3	9.2

Sources: Department of Transportation, Federal Aviation Administration, *Aviation Forecasts, Fiscal Years 1983–1994* (Washington, D.C., Feb. 1983), 50; and FAA *Statistical Handbook of Aviation, Fiscal Year 1981* (Washington, D.C., 1982).

Note: Detail may not add to total because of rounding.

An active aircraft must have a current registration and must have been flown at least one hour during the previous calendar year.

all of the aircraft used for corporate purposes will increase significantly by 1994.

Airmen

As already noted in Table 36 active pilots are expected to increase at an overall rate of 35.0 percent for the 1982–94 period. Also, student, airline transport, glider, helicopter, and instrument rated pilots are increasing at a higher rate than the overall rated while private and commercial rated pilots are increasing at lower rates than overall. In all, the pilots flying in America in 1994 are expected to be a more sophisticated group with stronger instrument skills.

The airframes and powerplant mechanics group—a much smaller group at 115,000 or so—is *not* expected to grow rapidly because of traditional constraints on pay scales for mechanics. Also, limits related to the ability of certified mechanics' training schools to expand their capacity for students will probably hold down growth in this field. This is true even though the aviation field—aircraft, avionics, and so forth—will grow in size and sophistication.

CONCLUSIONS

This book has provided an overview of federal regulation of the aviation industry, and in the process covered an extensive amount of material. While differences of opinion exist with respect to the advantages and disadvantages of regulations, and the impact of the regulatory agencies, the following observations are considered to be as objective as possible:

1. Deregulation

Although some economic regulations have been eliminated, government continues to be involved in the functioning of the airline industry and interferes with market forces. The FAA uses slot allocations or develops special regulations to ration capacity at saturated airports, rather than using the pricing mechanism. Local airport operators, sensitive to user demands and political pressures, rely on policy to determine who will use overcrowded facilities rather than raising user fees to determine who really needs to use the facility and therefore is willing to pay for the right. In addition, airlines are not completely free to serve whatever market they wish because of the application of individual local airport policies, rather than price, to determine access. Noise sensitive communities also have a detrimental effect on airport access. Finally, mandated "essential air service to small communities" is a constant reminder of the type of economic regulatory authority once exercised on a broader scale.

Although deregulation has not occurred in a total sense, it is certainly possible to draw a general conclusion on the impact of the Airline Deregulation Act. If the measure of the act's success is whether it has brought about better air service to more people at a lower price, then it appears to have had a positive effect. However, this has resulted in a concentration of air service and low fares in the top 40 or so markets (these account for some 70 percent of all airline passengers), while small and medium sized communities admittedly have not reaped the benefits that deregulation once promised. This has resulted in widespread dissatisfaction and opposition.

Airline financial woes, blamed by some on deregulation, can also be blamed on adverse economic conditions, the actions of the airlines themselves, and the fact that the industry is no longer protected from the swings of the business cycle. Nevertheless some airlines manage to prosper, and based on past experience, it is not clear that "reregulation" would markedly enhance the carriers' economic status.

2. The Federal Aviation Administration and Its Regulatory Role

Because of the vastness of the aviation industry and the impossibility of overseeing every activity that has a bearing on safety, FAA employees have become in effect regulatory managers rather than regulators. More and more regulatory functions have been delegated to industry, with the FAA performing a supervisory and watchdog role to assure that safety measures are adhered to. Nevertheless the FAA continues to play a predominant role in establishing the standards for achieving a safe and efficient aviation system.

Budget limitations have also reduced some of the FAA's promotion activities. Whether or not New Federalism initiatives are implemented, giving state and local governments more responsibility for airport development, the FAA's airport functions have diminished. Staffing constraints have made it difficult or impossible for the FAA Airports Division to review preliminary engineering, monitor construction, and undertake extensive planning activities. Many of these functions have been delegated to consultants and local sponsors. It appears that a major FAA initiative is to revamp the air traffic control system to make it more cost effective and more responsive to the needs of the flying public.

3. Regulations and the Regulatory Process

Despite problems with regulations and the burdensome nature of the regulatory process described in Chapter 3, there will continue to be the

TABLE 36

ACTIVE PILOTS BY TYPE OF CERTIFICATE (THOUSANDS)

As of January 1	Total	Students	Private	Com-mercial	Airline Transport	Heli-copter	Glider	Other	Instrument Rated*
Historical									
1978	783.9	203.5	327.5	188.8	50.1	4.8	6.2	3.1	266.3
1979	798.8	204.9	337.6	185.8	55.9	4.9	6.5	3.2	236.3
1980	814.7	210.2	343.3	182.1	63.7	5.2	6.8	3.4	247.1
1981	827.0	199.8	357.5	183.4	69.6	6.0	7.0	3.7	260.5
1982	764.2	179.9	328.6	168.6	70.3	6.5	7.4	3.0	252.5
Forecast									
1983	776.4	182.0	332.4	169.6	74.3	7.0	7.9	3.2	261.1
1984	792.4	187.2	337.4	170.0	78.9	7.4	8.3	3.3	269.9
1985	810.4	193.2	344.4	170.1	82.9	7.7	8.7	3.4	280.8

Year								
1986	832.7	202.9	351.9	170.2	86.9	8.1	9.2	3.5	292.0
1987	856.9	211.5	361.9	170.3	91.5	8.4	9.6	3.7	303.7
1988	877.3	216.7	371.5	171.0	95.5	8.7	10.0	3.9	315.8
1989	900.7	224.3	382.3	172.1	98.5	9.0	10.4	4.1	325.3
1990	924.5	230.9	393.3	174.2	101.7	9.3	10.8	4.3	335.0
1991	949.6	237.5	404.4	177.5	104.9	9.6	11.2	4.5	345.1
1992	976.5	244.6	415.8	181.7	108.1	9.9	11.7	4.7	355.4
1993	1,003.9	252.2	426.8	186.7	111.1	10.2	12.0	4.9	369.7
1994	1,031.6	260.0	437.6	192.0	114.1	10.5	12.3	5.1	380.7
Percentage increase for 1983–94 period:	35.0	44.5	33.2	13.9	62.3	61.5	66.2	70.0	50.8

Sources: Department of Transportation, Federal Aviation Administration, *Aviation Forecasts, Fiscal Years 1983–1994* (Washington, D.C., Feb. 1983), 64; and FAA *Statistical Handbook of Aviation, Fiscal Year 1981* (Washington, D.C., 1982).

Note: Detail may not add to total because of rounding.

*Should not be added to other categories in deriving total.

initiation of new regulations, and the updating of existing ones. Nevertheless efforts will be made to minimize regulatory proliferation, and most efforts will be concentrated in the area of aviation safety. Also, promotional efforts of federal regulatory agencies can be expected to decline because of budget limitations.

4. State and Local Regulatory Role

The regulatory role of the states and of local governments remains on the periphery of aviation regulation. However, in recent years, it has grown in a couple of keys areas such as the environmental area and in airport licensing. Local governments have a role in aviation regulation which is limited primarily to proprietary issues on airports owned and operated by local governments. Taken together, however, state and local government regulation of aviation is significant. Also, as federal regulation becomes less pervasive in the future, state and local regulations can be expected to supplement federal regulations in additional areas.

5. Self-Regulation

Due to the delegation of many federal regulatory functions, the aviation industry regulates itself in a number of ways. Examples include certified flight examiners, certified airframe and powerplant examiners and designated engineering representatives (at the manufacturers). In addition, the industry regulates itself through such efforts as the accredited airport executive program of the American Association of Airport Executives. It appears that industry self-regulation will become increasingly important as the federal government cuts its regulatory effort because of budget difficulties.

In summary, the regulation of the aviation industry has evolved from a tool to promote a fledgling industry to a body of rules governing many of the operations of a maturing industry. It is clear from this review of aviation industry regulations that the process of evolution of both the aviation industry and it's regulations is not complete. Also, the regulatory process is not yet as strong and adaptable as it needs to be. However, the evolution of the industry, government's ability and desire to intervene in the industry, and the process of merging industry and government interests will result in a strong future system of aviation industry regulation. With the potential civilian applications of aerospace vehicles such as the space shuttle, there must be flexibility in both the industry and it regulations to adapt to the future.

Appendixes
Notes
Selected Bibliography
Index

Appendix 1

Petition for Rulemaking—
Published in the *Federal*
Register (45 FR 10802),
February 19, 1980

DEPARTMENT OF TRANSPORTATION
Federal Aviation Administration
14 CFR Ch. 1
[Docket No. 19749; Petition Notice No. PR 80-3]
Petition for Rule Making of William Becker

AGENCY: Federal Aviation Administration (FAA), DOT.

ACTION: Publication of petition for rulemaking; request for comments.

SUMMARY: By letter dated September 13, 1979, Captain William Becker petitioned the Federal Aviation Administration (FAA) to amend § 121.587 of the Federal Aviation Regulations (FAR) to allow the closing and locking of the flightcrew compartment to be at the discretion of the captain.

DATES: Comments must be received on or before April 21, 1980.

ADDRESS: Send comments on the petition in duplicate to: Federal Aviation Administration, Office of the Chief Counsel, Attn: Rules Docket (AGC-24), Docket No. 19749, 800 Independence Avenue S.W., Washington, D.C. 20591.

FOR FURTHER INFORMATION CONTACT: Mr. Raymond E. Ramakis, Chief, Regulatory Projects Branch (AVS-24), Federal Aviation Administration, 800 Independence Avenue S.W., Washington, D.C. 20591; Telephone (202) 755-8716.

SUPPLEMENTARY INFORMATION:

Comments Invited

Interested persons are invited to submit such written data, views, or arguments on the petition for rule making as they desire. Communications should identify the regulatory docket number or petition notice number and be submitted in duplicate to: Federal Aviation Administration, Office of the Chief Counsel, Attention: Rules Docket, AGC-24, 800 Independence Avenue S.W., Washington, D.C. 20591. All communications received on or before will be considered by the Administrator before taking action on the petition for rule making. All comments submitted will be available, both before and after the closing date for comments, in the Rules Docket for examination by interested persons. A report summarizing each substantive public contact with FAA personnel concerned with this rule making will be filed in the docket.

Background Information

On September 13, 1979, Captain William Becker submitted a petition for rule making, in accordance with Part 11 of the FAR, to amend § 121.587. This petition is published in its entirety as part of this notice.

Section 121.587 states, in pertinent part, that the pilot in command of a large airplane carrying passengers shall ensure that the door separating the flightcrew compartment from the passenger compartment is closed and locked during flight.

The petitioner contends that closing and locking the flightcrew compartment door during flight has not been a deterrent to hijacking and could cause delays in case of an emergency evacuation. Additionally, petitioner states the flightcrew compartment can become excessively warm, which can have a detrimental effect on a pilot's performance.

Although this notice sets forth the contents of the petition as received by the FAA without changes, it should be understood that its publication to receive public comment is in accordance with FAA procedures governing the processing of petitions for rule making. It does not propose a regulatory rule for adoption, represent an FAA position, or otherwise commit the agency on the merits of the petition. The FAA intends to proceed to consider the petition under the applicable procedures of Part 11 and to reach a conclusion on the merits of Captain Becker's proposal after it has had an opportunity to carefully evaluate it in light of the comments received and other relevant matters presented. If the FAA concludes that it should initiate public rulemaking procedures on the petition, appropriate rulemaking action, including an evaluation of the proposal, will be published.

The Petition

Accordingly, the Federal Aviation Administration publishes verbatim for public comment the following petition for rule making of Captain William Becker dated September 13, 1979.

Issued in Washington, D.C., on February 11, 1980

Edward P. Faberman,

Acting Assistant Chief Counsel, Regulations and Enforcement Division.

Olmito, Texas, September 13, 1979.

Mr. Langhorne Bond, Administrator, Federal Aviation Agency, 800 Independence Ave., S.W., Washington, D.C.

Dear Mr. Bond: As a commercial airline captain with 27 years of flying experience, I am writing to ask for a change in FAR 121.587, which requires that the cockpit door of a large airplane carrying passengers be kept closed and locked during flight. My reasons for requesting this change are:

1. Having the door closed and locked has never been a deterrent to a hijacking. In fact, after carefully researching every hijacking occuring during the last several years, I found that every one took place while the door was closed and locked. All that person need do is to threaten any crew member or passenger, and his demand to enter the cockpit must be met. The door may be left open while passengers are boarded at the gate, or while taxiing, so why is a hijacking only considered to be a threat during flight?

2. In the event of an accident on take-off or landing, this door could and has become a hazard to safe evacuation by the pilots by becoming distorted and jammed. I have four documented cases of accidents which occured during landing where the door did prevent the pilots from escaping aft through the cabin exits, which according to the aircraft flight manual are the primary emergency escape routes. The manual also states that the pilots shall proceed to the cabin to assist the passengers in evacuating. However, they were forced to use the cockpit windows, thus preventing them from carrying out this important duty. Suppose the cockpit windows had become jammed or shattered? Why should a pilot be forced into a potentially blocking off one avenue of escape? Three of these accidents occurred on the DC-9, which I am flying.

3. On the DC-9, especially during the summer months, the cockpit becomes extremely warm. I have recorded temperatures of up to 110° with the door closed. When the door was opened for comparative purposes, the temperature dropped to 94°. Obviously temperatures in the 100° range can have a detrimental effect on a pilot's performance, especially on a day with several approaches and landings such as we frequently operate under.

It is for these reasons that I request a change in this FAR. If a Captain can be assumed to be responsible enough to operate a multi-million dollar aircraft with a hundred or more human lives entrusted to his care, he should be responsible enough to use his own judgment as to when, and if, his cockpit door should be closed and locked.

I request that a copy of your reply be sent to each of the persons named below.

Sincerely,
William Becker,
Capt., EAL.

Appendix 2
Notice of Proposed Rulemaking— Published in the *Federal Register* (47 FR 3068), January 21, 1982

DEPARTMENT OF TRANSPORTATION
Federal Aviation Administration
14 CFR Part 121
[Docket No. 20843; Notice No. 82-1]
Number of Flight Attendants Required
During Intermediate Stops

AGENCY: Federal Aviation Administration (FAA), DOT.

ACTION: Notice of proposed rulemaking (NPRM).

SUMMARY: This notice proposes to change the regulations by reducing by one-half the number of flight attendants required to remain on board the aircraft during intermediate stops when passengers remain on board. Current regulations are interpreted as providing that the required number of flight attendants must remain on board during these stops. This proposal arose as a result of a petition for rulemaking submitted by the Air Transport Association of America (ATA) on October 9, 1980, and is consistent with Executive Order 12291.

DATE: Comments must be received on or before March 22, 1982.

ADDRESS: Send comments on this proposal in duplicate to: Federal Aviation Administration, Office of the Chief Counsel, Attn: Rules Docket (AGC-204), Docket No. 20843, 800 Independence Avenue, SW., Washington, D.C. 20591; or deliver comments in duplicate to: Room 916, 800 Independence Ave., SW., Washington, D.C. Comments may be examined in the Rules Docket weekdays, except Federal holidays, between 8:30 a.m. and 5 p.m.

FOR FURTHER INFORMATION CONTACT: Joseph A. Sirkis, Regulatory Projects Branch (AVS-24), Safety Regulations Staff, Associate Administrator for Aviation Standards, Federal Aviation Administration, 800 Independence Avenue SW., Washington, D.C. 20591; telephone (202) 755-8716.

SUPPLEMENTARY INFORMATION:

Comments Invited

Interested persons are invited to participate in the making of the proposed rule by submitting such written data, views, or arguments as they may desire. Communications should identify the regulatory docket or notice number and be submitted in duplicate to: Federal Aviation Administration, Office of the Chief Counsel, Attention: Rules Docket (AGC-204), 800 Independence Avenue SW., Washington, D.C. 20591. All communications received on or before the closing date for comments will be considered by the Administrator before taking action on the proposed rule. The proposal contained in this notice may be changed in the light of comments received. All comments submitted will be available, both before and after the closing date for comments, in the Rules Docket for examination by interested persons. A report summarizing each substantive public contact with FAA personnel concerned with this rulemaking will be filed in the docket.

Commenters wishing the FAA to acknowledge receipt of their comments submitted in response to this notice must submit with those comments a self-addressed, stamped postcard on which the following statement is made: "Comments to Docket No. 20843." The postcard will be date/time stamped and returned to the commenter.

Availability of NPRM

Any person may obtain a copy of this notice of proposed rulemaking (NPRM) by submitting a request to the Federal Aviation Administration, Office of Public Affairs, Attention: Public Information Center, APA-430,

800 Independence Avenue SW., Washington, D.C. 20591, or by calling (202) 426-8058. Communications must identify the notice number of this NPRM. Persons interested in being placed on a mailing list for future NPRM's should also request a copy of Advisory Circular No. 11-2, "Notice of Proposed Rulemaking Distribution System," which describes the application procedure.

Background Information

On October 9, 1980, ATA submitted a petition for rulemaking in accordance with the provisions of § 11.25 of the Federal Aviation Regulations (FAR). A summary of this petition was published in the *Federal Register* on February 19, 1981 (46 FR 12981). No comments were received. This petition requested clarification of § 121.391(a) in regard to the number of flight attendants required to be on board airline passenger-carrying aircraft other than during flight time.

The current regulation states that each certificate holder shall provide at least the following flight attendants on each passenger-carrying airplane used:

1. For airplanes having a seating capacity of more than 9 but fewer than 51 passengers—1 flight attendant.

2. For airplanes having a seating capacity of more than 50 but fewer than 101 passengers—2 flight attendants.

3. For airlines having a seating capacity of more than 100 passengers—2 flight attendants plus 1 additional flight attendant for each unit (or part of a unit) of 50 passenger seats above a seating capacity of 100 passengers.

ATA states in its petition that by memorandum of June 2, 1980, from the FAA's Acting Chief, Air Transportation Division, FAA regions were advised of a new interpretation from the Office of the Chief Counsel in regard to § 121.391. This interpretation states that the minimum complement of flight attendants required by § 121.391 must be on the aircraft whenever passengers are on the aircraft. This includes the periods of time during the boarding process and during intermediate stops. The interpretation also states that if an individual (e.g., a gate agent) replaced a flight attendant and that flight attendant was part of the minimum crew complement, then the individual replacing the flight attendant would have to receive crewmember emergency training on that aircraft in accordance with § 121.417.

ATA further states in its petition that its member airlines strongly disagree with this interpretation and "difficulties associated with the application of the June 2 FAA interpretation would adversely affect the airlines operationally, economically, and could well create unnecessary hardship to the traveling public."

After review and analysis of the ATA petition, the FAA concurs with the ATA that the current regulations contain unnecessary requirements. As already noted, the current regulation provides that all required flight attendants not only must be on the aircraft during flight time but must also remain on board during intermediate stops. Analysis of the safety issues involved reveals that this is not necessary and precludes such personnel from performing other related duties. Such duties include aiding elderly or handicapped passengers, accompanying minors, and coordinating with ground personnel.

Sections 25.803 and 121.291 and Appendix D to Part 121 of the FAR require that during a demonstration of emergency evacuation procedures, not more than 50 percent of the emergency exits in the sides of the fuselage of an airplane may be used for the demonstration. Similarly, in exemptions granted from § 121.291 of the FAR, the FAA requires the flight attendants to open 50 percent of the required emergency floor-level exits and 50 percent of the required emergency nonfloor-level exits and to deploy 50 percent of the emergency exit slides within 15 seconds. The 50 percent figure reflects the probability that one-half of the emergency exits may be rendered inoperative in a crash situation due to fuselage damage or fire. At an intermediate stop, however, at least one floor-level exit will remain open and time will not be lost in preparing that exit for evacuation during an emergency situation. In addition, most other exits should normally be operable.

Therefore, the FAA proposes to reduce the number of required flight attendants who must remain on board during intermediate stops. Intermediate stops are stops where passengers remain on board and proceed on that aircraft to another destination. They are usually of short duration. During such stops, the aircraft is in a static mode, in a level attitude with the engines stopped. This is in contrast with a crash situation in which the aircraft often comes to rest in an unusual attitude with cabin contents dislodged and with exits blocked or inoperable because of impact damage. The FAA proposes that during such stops each certificate holder shall provide and maintain on board the aircraft at least one-half (rounded to the next higher figure) the required number of flight attendants.

Additionally, the FAA proposes that the certificate holder must ensure that at least one floor-level exit on that aircraft remains open during that stop and that such exit provides for the rapid deplaning of passengers. One or more additional exits may be open for servicing the galleys and lavatories. As part of their emergency evacuation duties, the required flight attendants on board are required by the certificate holder, to open, if necessary, additional emergency exits to provide for the rapid deplaning of passengers. Also, at most intermediate stops, flight crewmembers, mechanics, baggage handlers, security personnel, and other ground personnel are nearby to assist in the event of an emergency. Furthermore, the aircraft's engines are shut down while the aircraft is at the gate. This factor should mitigate the chances of an emergency that may arise from engine torching or overheating.

Additionally, this proposal would allow the substitution for required flight attendants of other personnel qualified in the emergency evacuation procedures for that aircraft required in § 121.417 of the FAR as long as they are identified to the passengers. Personnel such as passenger agents, customer service representatives, and ticket agents who have been trained in accordance with § 121.417 of the FAR would be allowed to perform safety-related flight attendant duties in the absence of the required flight attendants at intermediate stops. These normally required flight attendants may be performing other related duties such as aiding unaccompanied children or ill passengers.

Finally, it has been determined that during many intermediate stops only a small number of passengers remain on board the aircraft. In most cases, passengers have the opportunity to proceed to a lounge or to other appropriate places instead of remaining on board the aircraft during any prolonged intermediate stop. Therefore, if the airplane is stationary, the engines are not operating, and one or more exits are open, then allowing one-half of those flight attendants required by § 121.391 to remain on board the airplane at an intermediate stop would provide a necessary level of safety for all passengers and crewmembers.

Cost Impact

This rulemaking responds to an industry petition for relief from the current regulation. No formal cost/benefit analysis was completed with respect to this proposal for regulatory relief. A regulatory evaluation was conducted for this action to preliminarily assess the cost and economic impact. While the ATA petition did not summarize current staffing practices for periods when occupied aircraft are at intermediate stops, the FAA concludes that there are no apparent direct or indirect (nonindustry) costs associated with granting the requested relief. The ATA petition indicates that the cost of literal compliance with present § 121.391(a) could involve millions of dollars yearly in added cost per carrier. The FAA agrees with the general estimates provided by ATA. It is therefore expected that the benefits of granting the relief far outweigh any direct costs associated with changing the present regulation. We invite further comment on this matter.

The Proposed Amendment

PART 121—CERTIFICATION AND OPERATIONS: DOMESTIC, FLAG, AND SUPPLEMENTAL AIR CARRIERS AND COMMERCIAL OPERATORS OF LARGE AIRCRAFT

Accordingly, the FAA proposes to amend § 121.391 of the Federal Aviation Regulations (14 CFR 121.391) by adding a new paragraph (e) to read as follows:

§ 121.391 Flight attendants.
. . . .

(e) At stops where passengers remain on board and proceed on that aircraft to another destination, each certificate holder shall provide and maintain on board the aircraft during that stop at least one-half (rounded to the next higher figure) of the flight attendants as provided in paragraph (a) of this section or the same number of other personnel qualified in the emergency evacuation procedures for that aircraft as required in § 121.417 and provided those personnel are identified to the passengers. Additionally, the certificate holder must ensure that the aircraft engines are shut down and at least one floor-level exit on that aircraft remains open during that stop and that such exit provides for the deplaning of passengers.

(Secs. 313, 314, and 601 through 610, Federal Aviation Act of 1958, as amended (49 U.S.C. 1354, 1355, 1421 through 1430); sec. 6(c), Department of Transportation Act (49 U.S.C. 1655(c)); and 14 CFR 11.45)

Note.—The FAA has determined that this proposal relaxes requirements and allows more flexibility to affected Part 121 operators as it will reduce by one-half the number of flight attendants required to remain on board the aircraft during intermediate stops when passengers remain on board. There are no apparent direct or indirect (nonindustry) costs associated with granting the requested relief, and the benefits far outweigh any direct costs associated with changing the present regulation. Therefore, it has been determined that this is not a major regulation under Executive Order 12291. I certify that, under the criteria of the Regulatory Flexibility Act, the proposed rule, if promulgated, will not have a significant economic impact on a substantial number of small entities. This proposal applies to certificated air carriers, few of which are considered to be small entities. It would allow all carriers to reduce the number of employees which must be on aircraft during certain parts of the operations, thus reducing overall costs. In addition, the FAA has determined that this proposed revision is not significant under the Department of Transportation Regulatory Policies and Procedures (44 FR 11034; February 26, 1979). The draft evaluation prepared for this action is

contained in the regulatory docket. A copy of it may be obtained by contact-
ing the person identified under the caption "FOR FURTHER INFORMA-
TION CONTACT."

Issued in Washington, D.C. on December 18, 1981.

Kenneth S. Hunt,
Director of Flight Operations.

Appendix 3
FAA Orders by Identification Number and Category

ID Number	Category
0000	Checklists and Indexes
1000	Administration, Management, Policies—General
1100	Organization, Authorities, and Functions
1200	External Relations
1300	Management Programs
1400	Affirmative Action
1500	Travel and Transportation
1600	Security
1700	Administrative Services
1800	Program Management and Appraisal
1900	Defense Readiness and Civil Defense
2000–2300	Legal
2400	Financial Management—General
2500	Budget
2600	Accounting
2900	Auditing
3000–3100	Training
3200–3800	Personnel Management

ID Number	Category
3900	Employee Health and Safety
4000–4300	Agency Aircraft Management
5000–5200	Airports—General
5300	Airport Design, Construction, and Maintenance
5400	Federally Owned or Operated Airports
5900	Planning Grant Program
6000	Airway Facilities
6100	Data Systems
6200	Test Equipment
6300	Radar
6450	Central Operations Facilities
6500	Communications and Flight Assistance Facilities
6600	Communications and Equipment
6700–6800	Navigational Aids
6900	Plant and Structures
7000	Air Traffic Management—General
7100	Air Traffic Procedures
7200	Air Traffic Operations and Standards
7300	Communication Operations
7400	Airspace Allocation and Use
7700	Air Traffic Regulations
7900	Flight Information
8000	Flight Safety, Standards, and Procedures—General
8100	Airworthiness Certification
8200	Flight Inspection and Procedures
8300	Maintenance Certification and Surveillance
8400	Operations, Certification, and Surveillance
8500	Aeromedical Certification
9000	Aviation Medicine—General
9500	Research and Development

Appendix 4
FAA Advisory Circular—
AC 00-2TT, March 15, 1981,
Department of Transportation,
Federal Aviation Administration

1. PURPOSE. This circular transmits the revised checklist of current FAA advisory circulars (AC's) as of March 15, 1981.

2. CANCELLATION. AC 00-SS, Advisory Circular Checklist, dated July 15, 1980 is cancelled.

3. EXPLANATION OF AC SYSTEM. The FAA issues advisory circulars to inform the aviation public in a systematic way of nonregulatory material of interest. Unless incorporated into a regulation by reference, the contents of an advisory circular are not binding on the public. Advisory circulars are issued in a numbered-subject system corresponding to the subject areas of the Federal Aviation Regulations (FAR's) (Title 14, Code of Federal Regulations, Chapter I, Federal Aviation Administration). An AC is issued to provide guidance and information in its designated subject area or to show a method acceptable to the Administrator for complying with a related Federal Aviation Regulation. This checklist is issued as necessary to list all current advisory circulars.

4. The Circular Numbering System.

a. General. The advisory circular numbers relate to the FAR subchapter titles and correspond to the Parts, and when appropriate, to the specific sections of the Federal Aviation Regulations.

b. General and specific subject numbers. The subject numbers and related subject areas are as follows:

General Subject Number[1]	Specific Subject Number[2]	Subject
00		GENERAL
	1	Definitions and Abbreviations
10		PROCEDURAL RULES
	11	General Rule-Making Procedures
	13	Enforcement Procedures
20		AIRCRAFT
	21	Certification Procedures for Products and Parts
	23	Airworthiness Standards: Normal, Utility, and Acrobatic Category Airplanes
	25	Airworthiness Standards: Transport Category Airplanes
	27	Airworthiness Standards: Normal Category Rotorcraft
	29	Airworthiness Standards: Transport Category Rotorcraft
	31	Airworthiness Standards: Manned Free Balloons
	33	Airworthiness Standards: Aircraft Engines
	35	Airworthiness Standards: Propellers
	36	Noise Stantandards: Transport Category Rotorcraft
	31	Airworthiness Standards: Manned Free Balloons
	33	Airworthiness Standards: Aircraft Engines
	35	Airworthinnance, Rebuilding and Alteration

General Subject Number[1]	Specific Subject Number[2]	Subject
	159/20	Dulles International Airport
	169	Expenditures of Federal Funds for Nonmilitary Airports or Air Navigational Facilities Thereon
170		NAVIGATIONAL FACILITIES
	171	Non-Federal Navigation Facilities
180		ADMINISTRATIVE REGULATIONS
	183	Representatives of the Administrator
	185	Testimony by Employees and Production of Records in Legal Proceedings
	187	Fees
190		WITHHOLDING SECURITY INFORMATION; WAR RISK INSURANCE; AIRCRAFT LOAN GUARANTEE PROGRAM
	191	Withholding Security Information from Disclosure Under the Air Transportation Security Act of 1974
210		FLIGHT INFORMATION
	211	Aeronautical Charts and Flight Information Publications
	212	Publication Specifications—Charts and Publications

[1]Based on FAR Subchapter Titles.
[2]Based on FAR Part Titles.

Within the General Subject Number Areas, specific selectivity in advisory circular mail lists is available corresponding to the applicable FAR Parts. For example: under the 60 general subject area, separate mail lists for advisory circulars issued in the 61, 63, 65, or 67 series are available. An AC numbered "60" goes to all numbers in the 60 series—61, 63, 65, 67.

c. Breakdown of subject numbers. When the volume of circulars in a series warrants a subsubject breakdown, the general number is followed by a slash and a subsubject number. Material in the 150 series, Airports, is issued under the following subsubjects:

Number and Subject

Appendix 5

Advisory Circulars Referenced in FAR Part 152

APPENDIX B—LIST OF ADVISORY CIRCULARS INCORPORATED BY § 152.11

(A) CIRCULARS AVAILABLE FREE OF CHARGE.

Number and Subject

150/5100-12—Electronic Navigationsl Aids Approved for Funding Under the Airport Development Aid Program (ADAP).

150/5190-3A—Model Airport Hazard Zoning Ordinance.

150/5210-7A—Aircraft Fire and Rescue Communications.

150/5210-10—Airport Fire and Rescue Equipment Building Guide.

150/5300-2C—Airport Design Standards—Site Requirements for Terminal Navigational Facilities.

150/5300-4B—Utility Airports—Air Access to National Transportation.

150/5300-6—Airport Design Standards—General Aviation Airports—Basic and General Transport.

150/5300-8—Planning and Design Criteria for Metropolitan STOL Ports.

150/5320-6B—Airport Pavement Design and Evaluation.

150/5320-10—Environmental Enhancement at Airports—Industrial Waste Treatment.

150/5320-12—Methods for the Design, Construction, and Maintenance of Skid Resistant Airport Pavement Surfaces.

150/5325-2C—Airport Design Standards—Airports Served by Air Carriers—Surface Gradient and Line-of-Sight.

150/5325-4—Runway Length Requirements for Airport Design.

150/5325-6A—Airport Design Standards—Effect and Treatment of Jet Blast.

150/5325-8—Compass Calibration Pad.

150/5335-1A—Airport Design Standards—Airports Served by Air Carriers—Taxiways.

150/5335-2—Airport Aprons.

150/5335-3—Airport Design Standards—Airports Served by Air Carriers—Bridges and Tunnels on Airports.

150/5335-4—Airport Design Standards—Airports Served by Air Carriers—Runway Geometrics.

150/5340-1D—Marking of Paved Areas on Airports.

150/5340-4C—Installation Details for Runway Centerline and Touchdown Zone Lighting Systems.

150/5340-5A—Segmented Circle Airport Marker System.

150/5340-8—Airport 51-foot Tubular Beacon Tower.

150/5340-14B—Economy Approach Lighting Aids.

150/5340-17A—Standby Power for Non-FAA Airport Lighting System.

150/5340-18—Taxiway Guidance Sign System.

150/5340-19—Taxiway Centerline Lighting System.

150/5340-20—Installation Details and Maintenance Standards for Reflective Markers for Airport Runway and Taxiway Centerlines.

150/5340-21—Airport Miscellaneous Lighting Visual Aids.

AC/5340-22—Maintenance Guide for Determining Degradation and Cleaning of Centerline and Touchdown Zone Lights.

150/5340-23A—Supplemental Wind Cones.

150/5340-24—Runway and Taxiway Edge Lighting System.

150/5340-25—Visual Approach Slope Indicator (VASI) Systems.

150/5345-1E—Approved Airport Lighting Equipment.

150/5345-2—Specification for L-810 Obstruction Light.

150/5345-3C—Specification for L-821 Panels for Remote Control of Airport Lighting.

150/5345-4—Specification for L-829 Internally Lighted Airport Taxi Guidance Sign.

150/5345-5—Specification for L-847 Circuit Selector Switch. 5,000 Volt 20 Ampere.

150/5354-7C—Specification for L-824 Underground Electrical Cable for Airport Lighting Circuits.

150/5345-10C—Specification for L-828 Constant Current Regulators.

150/5345-11—Specification for L-812 Static Indoor Type Constant Current Regulator. Assembly; 4 KW and 7½ KW. With Brightness Control for Remote Operation.

150/5345-12A—Specification for L-801 Beacon.

150/5345-13—Specification for L-841 Auxiliary Relay Cabinet Assembly for Pilot Control of Airport Lighting Circuits.

150/5345-18—Specification for L-811 Static Indoor Type Constant Current Regulator Assembly; 4 KW; With Brightness Control and Runway Selection for Direct Operation.

150/5345-21—Specification for L-813 Static Indoor Type Constant Current Regulator Assembly; 4 KW and 7½ KW; for Remote Operation of Taxiway Lights.

150/5345-26A—Specification for L-823 Plug and Receptacle. Cable Connectors.

150/5345-27A—Specification for L-807 Eight-foot and Twelve-foot Unlighted or Externally Lighted Wind Cone Assemblies.

150/5345-28C—Specification for L-851 Visual Approach Slope Indicators and Accessories.

150/5345-36—Specification for L-808 Lighted Wind Tee.

150/5345-39A—FAA Specification for L-853, Runway and Taxiway Retroreflective Markers.

150/5345-42A—FAA Specification L-857, Airport Light Bases, Transformer Housings, and Junction Boxes.

150/5345-43B—FAA/DOD Specification L-856, HIgh Intensity Obstruction Lighting Systems.

150/5345-44A—Specification for L-858 Retroreflective Taxiway Guidance Sign.

150/5345-45—Lightweight Approach Light Structure.

150/5345-46—Specification for Semiflush Airport Lights.

150/5345-47—Isolation Transformers for Airport Lighting Systems.

150/5345-48—Specification for Runway and Taxiway Edge Lights.

150/5360-6—Airport Terminal Building Development with Federal Participation.

150/5360-7—Planning and Design Considerations for Airport Terminal Building Development.

150/5370-7—Airport Construction Controls to Prevent Air and Water Pollution.

150/5370-9—Slip-Form Paving—Portland Cement Concrete.

150/5370-11—Use of Nondestructive Testing Devices in the Evaluation of Airport Pavements.

(B) CIRCULARS FOR SALE.

Number and Subject

150/5320-5B—Airport Drainage; $1.30.
150/5370-10—Standards for Specifying Construction of Airports; $7.25.
150/5390-1A—Heliport Design Guide; $1.50.
[Docket No. 19430, 45 FR 34795, May 22, 1980]

Appendix 6
Regulations Contained in the
Code of Federal Regulations,
Title 14, Chapter II, Pages 3–7
(Covers changes as of January 1982.)

CHAPTER II—CIVIL AERONAUTICS BOARD
(PARTS 200 TO 1199)

NOTE: For nomenclature changes made to Chapter II, see 37 FR 18909, Sept. 16, 1972; ER-1023, 42 FR 47825, Sept. 22, 1977; ER-1085, 43 FR 59829, Dec. 22, 1978.

SUBCHAPTER A—ECONOMIC REGULATIONS

SUBCHAPTER B—PROCEDURAL REGULATIONS

Subchapter C—[Reserved]

Subchapter D—Special Regulations

Subchapter E—Organization

Subchapter F—Policy Statements

Notes

CHAPTER 1. THE AVIATION INDUSTRY AND ITS REGULATION

1. Aerospace Industries Association of America, *1983 Aerospace Year-End Review and Forecast—An Analysis* (Washington, D.C., Dec. 16, 1983), Table I.

2. "Masters of the Air: Boeing Captures the Cruise Missile Contract and Dominates World Aviation," *Time*, Apr. 7, 1980, 52.

3. Aerospace Industries Association, 12.

4. Aerospace Industries Association, 12.

5. Commuter Airline Association of America, *Commuter Airline Industry 1980 Annual Report* (Washington, D.C., Nov. 1980), 6–8.

6. "Airline Yearbook 1982," *Airline Executive*, May 1982.

7. Gellman Research Associates for the National Air Transportation Association, *Analysis of Competition in, and Profile of, the FBO Industry* (Washington, D.C., Dec. 1979), 27.

8. General Aviation Manufacturers Association, *The General Aviation Story* (Washington, D.C., 1979).

9. *Webster's New World Dictionary*, 2nd college ed. (New York: William Collins and World Publishing, 1978), 1197.

CHAPTER 2. THE EVOLUTION OF AVIATION INDUSTRY REGULATION

1. Charles Kelly Jr., *The Sky's the Limit*, (New York: Coward-McCann, 1963), 16.

2. Carl Solberg, *Conquest of the Skies: A History of Commercial Aviation in America*, (Boston: Little, Brown, 1979), 6.

3. C. Kelly, 17.

4. Fred Kelly, *The Wright Brothers*, (New York: Harcourt, Brace, 1943), 77–78.

5. C. Kelly, 16.

6. Solberg, 7–8.

7. Robert M. Kane and Allan D. Vose, *Air Transportation*, 7th ed. (Dubuque, Iowa: Kendall/Hunt Publishing, 1979), pp. 3-23 to 3-24.

8. Douglas Rolfe and Alexis Dawydoff, *Airplanes of the World*, (New York: Simon and Schuster, 1954), 49–51.

9. Arch Whitehouse, *The Sky's the Limit* (New York: Macmillan, 1971), 24–44.

10. R. E. G. Davies, *A History of the World's Airlines* (London: Oxford Univ. Press, 1964), 40.

11. Davies, 41.

12. Davies, 41.

13. Caroll V. Glines, *The Saga of the Air Mail*, (Princeton, N.J.: D. Van Nostrand, 1968), 74–75.

14. Davies, 41–42.

15. Whitehouse, 13–14.

16. Whitehouse, 14.

17. Davies, 43.

18. Davies, 43.

19. Davies, 44.

20. Solberg, 32.

21. Solberg, 37.

22. Davies, 44.

23. Donald R. Whitnah, *Safer Skyways: Federal Control of Aviation, 1925–1966* (Ames: Iowa State Univ. Press, 1966), 20–21.

24. Whitnah, 17.

25. Whitnah, 26.

26. Whitnah, 27.

27. Whitnah, 8–9.

28. C. Kelly, 39.

29. 43 Stat. 805.

30. Nick A. Komons, *Bonfires to Beacons*, (Washington, D.C.: GPO, 1978), 192–93.

31. 44 Stat. 568.

32. 44 Stat. 574, 575.

33. 44 Stat. 571.

34. Robert Burkhardt, *The Federal Aviation Administration*, (New York: Frederick A. Praeger, 1967), 37.

35. *Congressional Record*, 69th Congress, First Session, (Apr. 12) 1926, Vol. 67, Pt. 7: 7312–23.

36. Whitnah, 39.

37. Komons, 197–99.

38. 46 Stat. 259.

39. Kane and Vose, p. 5-8.

40. Whitehouse, 167.

41. Davies, 133.

42. Davies, 133–36.

43. Norman E. Borden, Jr., *Air Mail Emergency 1934*, (Freeport: Bond Wheelwright, 1968), 135–36.

44. Komons, 263–65.

45. Whitehouse, 201–2.

46. Kane and Vose, p. 5-14.

47. Solberg, 146–47.

48. Davies, 137.

49. Davies, 137.

50. 52 Stat. 973.

51. 54 Stat. 1231.

52. 54 Stat. 1231.

53. 52 Stat. 988.

54. 52 Stat. 998.

55. 52 Stat. 1000–1004.

56. Whitnah, 152–53.

57. Whitnah, 189–90.

58. 60 Stat. 170.

59. 60 Stat. 170.

60. Office of the Federal Register, National Archives and Records Service, General Services Administration, CFR, Title 14, Aeronautics and Space, Pt. 151, 1965.

61. Kane and Vose, p. 6-2.

62. 72 Stat. 731.

63. 72 Stat. 731.

64. Whitnah, 281–83.

65. 80 Stat. 931.

66. 80 Stat. 938.

67. 88 Stat. 2156.

68. 84 Stat. 219.

69. 87 Stat. 88.

70. 90 Stat. 871.

71. 91 Stat. 1278.

72. 92 Stat. 1705.

73. 94 Stat. 35.

74. 94 Stat. 50.

75. 94 Stat. 50 (Title 1).

76. National Association of State Aviation Officials, "Analysis of Airport Improvement Act of 1982," Washington, D.C., Oct. 1982.

77. J. J. Corbett, "Reflections on the New Airport/Airway Trust Fund Law," *Airport Services Management*, Sept. 1982, 26–30.

CHAPTER 3. THE FEDERAL REGULATORS

1. 80 Stat. 931.

2. Department of Transportation, Federal Aviation Administration, Order 1100.2A, *Organization—FAA Headquarters*, June 1980.

3. Federal Aviation Administration, Order 1105A, *FAA Organization—Field*, 1977.

4. Federal Aviation Administration, "Flight Standards Field Offices," Washington, D.C., November 1980, 5.

5. Telephone interviews by Harry P. Wolfe with Federal Aviation Administration personnel in the Phoenix, Arizona, Air Carrier District Office and the Scottsdale, Arizona, General Aviation District Office, July 1982.

6. 72 Stat. 731.

7. Department of Transportation, "Federal Aviation Administration Activities in the Agency's 50th Year," Washington, D.C., 1977, 20–25.

8. 49 USC 1423.

9. Department of Transportation, "Federal Aviation Administration Activities in the Agency's 50th Year," 25–29.

10. Federal Aviation Administration, Airworthiness Directive 75-15-05.

11. 49 USC 1423(b).

12. 49 USC 1423(c).

13. 49 USC 1425.

14. Interview by Harry P. Wolfe with Federal Aviation Administration personnel in the Phoenix Air Carrier District Office, January 13, 1981.

15. Interview by Harry P. Wolfe with Federal Aviation Administration personnel in the Scottsdale General Aviation District Office, July 6, 1982.

16. 49 USC 1426.

17. Office of the Federal Register, National Archives and Records Service, General Services Administration, CFR, Title 14, Aeronautics and Space, Revised as of Jan. 1, 1982, Pt. 171.

18. 14 CFR Pts. 141, 143, 145.

19. 14 CFR Pt. 147.

20. 85 Stat. 492.

21. 14 CFR Pt. 139.

22. 14 CFR Pt. 139.

23. 14 CFR Pt. 139.

24. Department of Transportation, "Federal Aviation Administration Activities in the Agency's 50th Year," 42–56, 91–100, 103–9.

25. 49 USC 1348 (a) (b).

26. Department of Transportation, "Federal Aviation Administration Activities in the Agency's 50th Year," 118–43.

27. 90 Stat. 871.

28. 90 Stat. 871 (Title 2).

29. This discussion of the construction process is based upon Harry P. Wolfe's experience in airport development procedures.

30. Department of Transportation, "Federal Aviation Administration Activities in the Agency's 50th Year," 250–95.

31. 80 Stat. 931.

32. 88 Stat. 2156.

33. National Transportation Safety Board, "Safety Board: What It Is and What It Does," Washington, D.C., 1980.

34. 49 CFR Pt. 830.

35. National Transportation Safety Board, 5–6.

36. Robert M. Kane and Allan D. Vose, *Air Transportation*, 7th ed. (Dubuque: Kendall/Hunt Publishing, 1979), p. 8-11.

37. 49 USC 1443.

38. Interview by Harry P. Wolfe with Terry Armentrout, National Transportation Safety Board, Los Angeles Regional Office, Dec. 2, 1980.

39. 49 USC 1442.

40. National Transportation Safety Board, 7–8.

41. Based on Harry P. Wolfe's experience and general knowledge of arguments pertaining to the deregulation issue.

42. Charles S. Rhyne, *Civil Aeronautics Act Annotated*, (Washington, D.C.: National Law Book, 1939), 119.

43. 52 Stat. 973, as amended by 54 Stat. 1231.

44. Paul W. McAvoy and John W. Snow, eds., *Regulation of Passenger Fares and Competition Among Airlines*, (Washington, D.C.: American Enterprise Institute for Public Policy Research, 1977), 4.

45. Rhyne, 119.

46. Nawal K. Taneja, *The Commercial Airline Industry*, (Lexington, Mass.: D. C. Heath, Lexington Books, 1976), 192.

47. Taneja, 197.

48. Taneja, 197–216.

49. McAvoy and Snow, 4.

50. Kane and Vose, p. 10-18.

51. Kane and Vose, pp. 14-11 to 14-18.

52. Taneja, 246–50.

53. Rhyne, 119.

54. Based on Harry P. Wolfe's recollection as a participant in the deregulation debate, while working for the Illinois Department of Transportation from 1975 to 1978.

55. Based on Harry P. Wolfe's personal observations and experience.

56. United States Senate, Committee on the Judiciary, Subcommittee on Administrative Practice and Procedures, *Civil Aeronautics Board, Practices and Procedures*, Report 175, 94th Congressional Session, 1977.

57. Based on Harry P. Wolfe's personal observations and experience.

58. 92 Stat. 1705.

59. 92 Stat. 1732, and 49 USC 1389.

60. Civil Aeronautics Board, Order 79-10-203, *Essential Air Service Determination for the State of Arizona*, Oct. 1979.

61. Based on Harry P. Wolfe's personal observations and experience.

CHAPTER 4. STATE AND LOCAL REGULATORS

1. Robert C. Lieb, *Transportation: The Domestic System*, (Reston, Va.: Prentice-Hall, 1978), 207.

2. Lieb, 207.

3. Lieb, 210.

4. Lieb, 210. The Wabash Ruling (1886) held that the states could not regulate interstate railroads regardless of federal inactivity on the subject.

5. Letter to David A. NewMyer dated January 27, 1982, from the National Association of State Aviation Officials (NASAO).

6. 49 USC 1301.

7. National Association of Regulatory Utility Commissioners, "Analysis of State Regulatory Functions," Washington, D.C., 1977.

8. 49 USC 1305(a)(1).

9. Letter of January 27, 1982, from NASAO.

10. National Association of State Aviation Officials, "Survey of Airport Regulatory/Safety Powers," Washington, D.C., 1978, 3.

11. National Association of State Aviation Officials, "Survey of Powers," 3.

12. National Association of State Aviation Officials, *NASAO Databank*, Washington, D.C., Mar. 1982, 4.

13. *California Statutes*, Title 4, Department of Aeronautics, Subchapter 6, "Noise Standards," Register 70, No. 48, Nov. 28, 1970.

14. *California Statutes*, Title 4, Department of Aeronautics, Subchapter 6, "Noise Standards."

15. Department of Transportation, Office of the Secretary, and the Federal Aviation Administration, *Aviation Noise Abatement Policy* (Washington, D.C., Nov. 1976), 51.

16. Los Angeles, California, Ordinance Nos. 152, 455, May 31, 1979.

CHAPTER 5. THE REGULATORY FRAMEWORK

1. Department of Transportation, Federal Aviation Administration, Order 2100.13, *Rulemaking Policies*, June 1, 1976.

2. Office of the Federal Register, National Archives and Records Service, General Services Administration, CFR, Title 14, Aeronautics and Space, Revised as of Jan. 1, 1982, Pt. 11.

3. 14 CFR Pt. 11, Subpts. B and C.

4. 14 CFR Pt. 11, Sec. 11.23.

5. 14 CFR Pt. 11, Sec. 11.25.

6. 14 CFR Pt. 11, Secs. 112.7 (b) and (c).

7. Office of the Federal Register, National Archives and Records Service, General Services Administration, FR, Vol. 45, No. 34, Tues., Feb. 19, 1980, 10802–3.

8. 14 CFR Pt. 11, Sec. 11.27 (f).

9. 14 CFR Pt. 11, Sec. 11.27.

10. Federal Aviation Administration, Order 2100.13, *Rulemaking Policies*, June 1, 1976, 6–8.

11. 14 CFR Pt. 11, Sec. 11.29.

12. 47 FR 3068–69.

13. 14 CFR Pt. 11, Secs. 11.31, 11.33, 11.37.

14. 14 CFR Pt. 11, Secs. 11.47, 11.49, 11.51.

15. 49 USC 1301.

16. Peter Jan Honigsberg, *Gilbert Law Summaries: Legal Research*, 1st ed. (New York: Harcourt Brace Jovanich Legal and Professional Publications, 1980), 64.

17. 72 Stat. 731.

18. 84 Stat. 219.

19. 92 Stat. 1705.

20. 94 Stat. 50.

21. 94 Stat. 35.

22. 83 Stat. 852.

23. 14 CFR Pt. 36.

24. 72 Stat. 731.

25. 14 CFR.

26. 49 CFR.

27. 40 CFR.

28. 24 CFR.

29. 49 USC 1422.

30. 49 USC 1423.

31. 49 USC 1424.

32. 49 USC 1427.

33. 49 USC 1432.

34. 49 USC 1426.

35. Department of Transportation, Federal Aviation Administration, "Western Region Headquarters Directives Checklist," WE 0000, Los Angeles, Apr. 30, 1981.

36. Federal Aviation Administration, "Directives Checklist."

37. 14 CFR Pt. 11.

38. Federal Aviation Administration, Order 2100.13, *FAA Rulemaking Policies*, June 1, 1976.

39. 14 CFR Pt. 152.

40. Federal Aviation Administration, Order 1050.1c, *Policies and Procedures for Considering Environmental Impacts*, Jan. 1980.

41. 14 CFR Pt. 36.

42. Federal Aviation Administration, Order 1100.128, *Implementation of Noise Type Certification Standards*, Feb. 1971, first time issued.

43. Department of Transportation, Order 5610.1C, *Environmental Impact Assessment Procedures*, 1979.

44. Office of the Federal Register, National Archives and Records Service, General Services Administration, *A Codification of Presidential Proclamations and Executive Orders*, Jan. 20, 1961, to Jan. 20, 1981, Chapter XIV, Aeronautics and Space, Nov. 30, 1981, 239–46.

45. Office of the Federal Register, *A Codification of Presidential Proclamations and Executive Orders*, 239–40.

46. Office of the Federal Register, *A Codification of Presidential Proclamations and Executive Orders*, 241–42.

47. Office of the Federal Register, *A Codification of Presidential Proclamations and Executive Orders*, 242–44.

48. Office of the Federal Register, *A Codification of Presidential Proclamations and Executive Orders*, 246.

49. 3 CFR Pts. 100 and 101 (Executive Order 12291).

50. 14 CFR Pt. 39.

51. Department of Transportation, Federal Aviation Administration, "Advisory Circular Checklist," AC 00-2TT, Washington, D.C., Mar. 15, 1981, 1–2.

52. 14 CFR Pt. 152, Appendix B.

53. Federal Aviation Administration, "Advisory Circular Checklist," 1–2.

CHAPTER 6. THE REGULATIONS

1. *U.S. Air Service Newsletter*, Jan. 2, 1920, borrowed from Feb. 1982 *CAP News*.

2. Office of the Federal Register, National Archives and Records Service, General Services Administration, CFR, Title 14, Revised as of Jan. 1, 1982.

3. 14 CFR Chapter II.

4. 14 CFR Pts. 300, 302.

5. 14 CFR Pts. 312, 313.

6. 14 CFR Pt. 325.

7. 14 CFR Pt. 372.

8. 14 CFR Pts. 384, 385, 387, 389.

9. 14 CFR Pt. 399.

10. 14 CFR Pt. 1.

11. 14 CFR Pt. 11.

12. 14 CFR Pt. 13.

13. 14 CFR Pt. 21.

14. 14 CFR Pt. 23.

15. 14 CFR Pt. 25.

16. 14 CFR Pt. 36.

17. 14 CFR Pt. 43.

18. 14 CFR Pt. 45.

19. 14 CFR Pt. 47.

20. 14 CFR Pt. 49.

21. 14 CFR Pt. 61.

22. 14 CFR Pt. 63.

23. 14 CFR Pt. 65.

24. 14 CFR Pt. 67.

25. 14 CFR Pt. 71.

26. 14 CFR Pt. 73.

27. 14 CFR Pt. 75.

28. 14 CFR Pt. 77.

29. 14 CFR Pt. 77.

30. 14 CFR Pt. 91.

31. 14 CFR Pt. 93.

32. 14 CFR Pt. 95.

33. 14 CFR Pts. 97, 99.

34. 14 CFR Pt. 101.
35. AOPA Air Safety Foundation, "Federal Aviation Regulation Part 103, Released," Bethesda, Md., Oct. 1982.
36. 14 CFR Pt. 105.
37. 14 CFR Pt. 107.
38. 14 CFR Pt. 108,
39. 14 CFR Pt. 121, Subpt. B.
40. 14 CFR Pt. 121, Subpt. E.
41. 14 CFR Pt. 121, Subpt. G.
42. 14 CFR Pt. 121, Subpt. H.
43. 14 CFR Pt. 121, Subpt. I.
44. 14 CFR Pt. 121, Subpt. J.
45. 14 CFR Pt. 121, Subpt. K.
46. 14 CFR Pt. 121, Subpt. T.
47. 14 CFR Pt. 121, Subpt. M.
48. 14 CFR Pt. 121, Subpt. N.
49. 14 CFR Pt. 121, Subpt. Q.
50. 14 CFR Pt. 135, Subpt. B.
51. 14 CFR Pt. 135, Subpt. C.
52. 14 CFR Pt. 135, Subpt. D.
53. 14 CFR Pt. 135, Subpt. I.
54. 14 CFR Pt. 135, Subpt. J.
55. 14 CFR Pt. 137.
56. 14 CFR Pt. 139, Subpt. C.
57. 14 CFR Pt. 139, Subpt. D.
58. 14 CFR Pt. 139, Subpt. E.
59. 14 CFR Pt. 141.
60. 14 CFR Pt. 143.
61. 14 CFR Pt. 145.
62. 14 CFR Pt. 147.
63. 14 CFR Pt. 150.
64. 14 CFR Pt. 152, Subpt. B.
65. 14 CFR Pt. 152, Subpt. C.
66. 14 CFR Pt. 152, Subpt. G.
67. 14 CFR Pt. 154.
68. 14 CFR Pt. 155.
69. 14 CFR Pt. 157.
70. 14 CFR Pt. 159.
71. 14 CFR Pt. 171.
72. 14 CFR Pt. 183.
73. 14 CFR Pt. 185.
74. 14 CFR Pt. 187.
75. 14 CFR Pt. 189.
76. 14 CFR Pt. 191.
77. 14 CFR Pt. 198.
78. 14 CFR Pt. 199.

79. 42 USC 4321.

80. 42 USC 1857.

81. 40 CFR Pt. 1500, Sec. 1500.1.

82. Department of Transportation, Federal Aviation Administration, Order 1050.1C, Paragraph 301, as contained in FR, Vol. 45, No. 7, Jan. 10, 1980, 2251–52.

83. 14 CFR Pt. 36.

84. 14 CFR Pt. 36, Appendix A.

85. 46 USC 1431.

86. Department of Transportation, Office of the Secretary, and the Federal Aviation Administration, *Aviation Noise Abatement Policy* (Washington, D.C., Nov. 1976).

87. Office of the Federal Register, National Archives and Records Service, General Services Administration, FR, Vol. 46, No. 16.

88. 46 FR 8328–31.

89. 46 FR 8321–22.

90. 46 FR 8320.

91. 46 FR 8322.

92. 46 FR 8326.

93. Office of the Federal Register, National Archives and Records Service, General Services Administration, CFR, Title 49, Transportation, Revised as of Oct. 1, 1981, Part 21.

94. 49 CFR Pt. 23.

95. 49 CFR Pt. 25.

96. 49 CFR Pt. 27.

97. 49 CFR Pt. 81.

98. 49 CFR Pt. 91.

99. 49 CFR Pt. 93.

100. 49 CFR Pt. 175.

101. 49 CFR Pt. 821.

102. 49 CFR Pt. 830.

103. 49 CFR Pt. 831.

CHAPTER 7. THE REGULATED: HOW THE MAJOR SEGMENTS OF THE AVIATION INDUSTRY ARE REGULATED

1. Boeing Commercial Airplane Company, Public Relations Department, "The Boeing 767 Twinjet," Background Information No. S-2745, June 1982.

2. Boeing Commercial Airplane Company, 4–5.

3. Federal Aviation Administration, Northwest Mountain Region, *Directorate Approach to the Airworthiness and Operation of Transport Airplanes*, Seattle, Mar. 1982, 2.

4. Letter to David A. NewMyer dated June 9, 1982, from John H. Newland, Public Relations Director, New Airplane Programs, Boeing Commercial Airplane Company, concerning the Boeing 767 Flight Test Program.

5. Letter of June 9, 1982, from John H. Newland, Boeing Commercial Airplane Company.

6. Pierre Condom, "Boeing's New Transports in a Flight Test Marathon," *Interavia*, July 1982, 695–97.

7. Condom, 695–97.

8. "Europeans Object to U.S. FAA Lead Region Certification Plan," *Aviation Week and Space Technology*, Vol. 114, No. 13, Mar. 30, 1981, 34.

9. "Midway Airlines President Says Controllers' Strike May Affect Expansion Plans," *Aviation Daily*, Feb. 4, 1982, 177.

10. "Midway Airlines President Says Controllers' Strike May Affect Expansion Plans," 177.

11. Michael Feazel, "New Entrants Attack FAA Rules," *Aviation Week and Space Technology*, Vol. 116, No. 1, Jan. 25, 1982, 28.

12. "Carriers Warned to Provide for New Entrants at Airports, DOT Says," *Aviation Daily*, Feb. 5, 1982, 185.

13. Joan M. Feldman, "Pacific Express: Borrowing Bits from Other Airlines' Successful Formulas," *Air Transport World*, Sept. 1981, 30.

14. Commuter Airline Association of America, *Commuter Airline Industry 1980 Annual Report* (Washington, D.C., 1981), 9–11.

15. This section is based largely on a review of two sources: Commuter Airline Association of America, *Annual Report 1980*, and the North Carolina Department of Transportation, *North Carolina Small Community Airline Service Route and Marketing Study* (Raleigh, N.C., 1980).

16. Illinois Department of Transportation, Division of Aeronautics, *Aviation Safety Rules and Regulations* (Springfield, Ill., 1978), 39–43.

17. Illinois Department of Transportation, 24.

18. Illinois Department of Transportation, 24–25.

19. Illinois Department of Transportation, 29.

20. J. D. Richardson, in *Essentials of Aviation Management*, 2nd ed. (Dubuque, Iowa: Kendall/Hunt Publishing, 1981), reviews this aviation and business "split" in detail on pages 79–129.

21. National Air Transportation Association, *Negotiating Aviation Agreements* (Washington, D.C., 1981), 38–40.

22. National Air Transportation Association, *Negotiating Aviation Agreements*, 39.

23. National Air Transportation Association, *FBO's Today. . . . Whats Ahead Tomorrow* (Washington, D.C., 1981), 4.

24. National Air Transportation Association, *FBO's Today*, 4.

25. National Air Transportation Association, *Negotiating Aviation Agreements*, 56.

26. 49 USC 2202 (b) 18.

27. National Business Aircraft Association, *Annual Report, 1981* (Washington, D.C., 1982), 7.

28. Richard Collins, "A Consensus on Licensing," *Flying Magazine*, July 1982, 76–78.

29. Collins, 76–78.

30. Collins, 76–78.

CHAPTER 8. FUTURE DIRECTIONS

1. "Proposed New Safety Rules Will Permit Individual Flexibility," *Aviation Daily*, Sept. 17, 1982, 92.

2. Federal Aviation Administration, *National Airspace System Plan, Summary* (Washington, D.C., 1982).

3. FR, Vol. 47, No. 182, Mon., Sept. 20, 1982, Notice No. 82-13, Air Transportation Regulation, 41486–507.

4. 47 FR 41486–507.

5. Department of Transportation, Federal Aviation Administration, *Aviation Forecasts, Fiscal Years 1983–1994* (Washington, D.C., Feb. 1983), 3.

6. Federal Aviation Administration, *Aviation Forecasts, Fiscal Years 1983–1994*, 3.

7. Federal Aviation Administration, *Aviation Forecasts, Fiscal Years 1983–1994*, 28.

8. Aerospace Industries Association of America, "Aerospace Review and Forecasts 1982/1983," *Aerospace*, Vol. 21, No. 2 (Washington, D.C., Feb. 1983), 13.

9. Federal Aviation Administration, *Forecasts Fiscal Years 1983–1994*, 16.

10. Aerospace Industries Association of America, 13.

11. Federal Aviation Administration, *Aviation Forecasts, Fiscal Years 1983–1994*, 27.

12. McDonnell Douglas Corporation, "The Changing Aviation Industry: A Manufacturer's Perspective," paper presented at the FAA Aviation Forecasting and Planning Review Conference, Oct. 18, 1981, Long Beach, Calif.

13. Federal Aviation Administration, *Aviation Forecasts, Fiscal Years 1983–1994*, 31.

14. Federal Aviation Administration, *National Airport System Plan, Revised Statistics, 1980–1989* (Washington, D.C., 1980).

15. Federal Aviation Administration, *Aviation Forecasts, Fiscal Years 1983–1994*, 53.

16. Federal Aviation Administration, *Aviation Forecasts, Fiscal Years 1983–1994*, 53.

17. Federal Aviation Administration, *Aviation Forecasts, Fiscal Years 1982–1993* (Washington, D.C., 1982).

Selected Bibliography

BOOKS/PUBLICATIONS

Aerospace Industries Association of America. *Aerospace Review and Annual Report Forecast, 1981–1982.* Washington, D.C., Winter 1982.
———. *1983 Aerospace Year-End Review and Forecast—An Analysis.* Tables I. VII, and IX. Washington, D.C., Dec. 16, 1983.
Air Transport Association of America. *Air Transport 1983.* Washington, D.C., June 1983.
AOPA Air Safety Foundation. "Federal Aviation Regulation Part 103, Released," Bethesda, Md., Oct. 1982.
Berman, Benjamin A. "Regulatory Lag and CAB Fare Policy," in *Airline Deregulation: The Early Experience.* Boston: Auburn House, 1981.
Boeing Commercial Airplane Company, Public Relations Department. "The Boeing 767 Twinjet." Background Information No. S-2745, June 1982.
Borden, Norman E., Jr. *Air Mail Emergency 1934.* Freeport: Bond Wheelwright, 1968.
Burkhardt, Robert. *The Federal Aviation Administration.* New York: Frederick A. Praeger, 1967.
Commuter Airline Association of America. *Commuter Airline Industry 1980 Annual Report.* Washington, D.C., Nov. 1980.
Davies, R. E. G. *A History of the World's Airlines.* London: Oxford Univ. Press, 1964.
Gellman Research Associates for the National Air Transportation Association. *Analysis of Competition in, and Profile of, the FBO Industry.* Washington, D.C., Dec. 1979.

General Aviation Manufacturers Association. *The General Aviation Story*. Washington, D.C., 1979.

Glines, Carol V. *The Saga of the Air Mail*. Princeton, N.J.: D. Van Nostrand, 1968.

Honigsberg, Peter Jan. *Gilbert Law Summaries: Legal Research*. 1st ed. New York: Harcourt Brace Jovanovich Legal and Professional Publications, 1980.

Kane, Robert M., and Allan D. Vose. *Air Transportation*. 7th ed. Dubuque, Iowa: Kendall/Hunt Publishing, 1979.

————. *Air Transportation*. 8th ed. Dubuque, Iowa: Kendall/Hunt Publishing, 1982.

Kelly, Charles, Jr. *The Sky's the Limit*. New York: Coward-McCann, 1963.

Kelly, Fred. *The Wright Brothers*. New York: Harcourt, Brace, 1943.

Komons, Nick A. *Bonfires to Beacons*. Washington, D.C.: GPO, 1978.

Lieb, Robert C. *Transportation: The Domestic System*. Reston, Va.: Prentice-Hall, 1978.

McAvoy, Paul W., and John W. Snow, eds. *Regulation of Passenger Fares and Competition Among Airlines*. Washington, D.C.: American Enterprise Institute for Public Policy Research, 1977.

McDonnell Douglas Corporation. "The Changing Aviation Industry: A Manufacturer's Perspective." Paper presented at the FAA Aviation Forecasting and Planning Review Conference, Oct. 13, 1981, Washington, D.C.

National Air Transportation Association. *FBO's Today. . . . What's Ahead Tomorrow*. Washington, D.C., 1981.

————. *Negotiating Aviation Agreements*. Washington, D.C., 1981.

National Association of Regulatory Utility Commissioners. "Analysis of State Regulatory Functions." Washington, D.C., 1977.

National Association of State Aviation Officials. "Analysis of Airport Improvement Act of 1982." Washington, D.C., Oct. 1982.

————. *NASAO Databank*. Washington, D.C., Mar. 1982.

————. "Survey of Airport Regulatory/Safety Powers." Washington, D.C., 1978.

National Business Aircraft Association. *Annual Report, 1981*. Washington, D.C., 1982.

————. *NBAA Aircraft Fleet as of 3/30/84*. Washington, D.C., 1984. Pp. 1–4.

Rhyne, Charles S. *The Civil Aeronautics Act Annotated*. Washington, D.C.: National Law Book, 1939.

Richardson, J. D. *Essentials of Aviation Management*. 2nd ed. Dubuque, Iowa: Kendall/Hunt Publishing, 1981.

Richmond, Samuel B. *Regulation and Competition in Air Transportation*. New York: Columbia Univ. Press, 1961.

Rolfe, Douglas, and Alexis Dawydoff. *Airlines of the World*. New York: Simon and Schuster, 1954.

Solberg, Carl. *Conquest of the Skies: A History of Commercial Aviation in America*. Boston: Little, Brown, 1979.

Taneja, Nawal K. *The Commercial Airline Industry*. Lexington, Mass.: D. C. Heath, Lexington Books, 1976.

Webster's New World Dictionary. 2nd college ed. New York: Williams Collins and World Publishing, 1978.

Whitnah, Donald R. *Safer Skyways: Federal Control of Aviation, 1925–1966.* Ames: Iowa State Univ. Press, 1966.
Whitehouse, Arch. *The Sky's the Limit.* New York: Macmillan, 1971.

GOVERNMENT DOCUMENTS/PUBLICATIONS

California Statutes. Title 4, Department of Aeronautics, Subchapter 6, "Noise Standards." Register 70, No. 48, Nov. 28, 1970.
City of Los Angeles. Ordinance Nos. 152, 455, May 31, 1979.
City of Phoenix. Ordinance G-969, "Airport Field Rules and Regulations." City of Phoenix, Ariz., Aviation Department, Mar. 1970.
Civil Aeronautice Board. Order 79-10-203, *Essential Air Service Determination for the State of Arizona.* Washington, D.C., Oct. 30, 1979.
Congressional Quarterly, Inc. *Federal Regulatory Directory, 1981–1982.* Washington, D.C., 1982.
Congressional Record. 69th Congress, First Session, (Apr. 12) 1926, Vol. 67, Pt. 7: 7312–23.
Department of Transportation. "Civil Aircraft Landing Facilities Increased in 1983." *News.* Washington, D.C.: DOT, Mar. 22, 1984.
———. Order 5610.10, *Environmental Impact Assessment Procedures.* Washington, D.C., 1979.
Department of Transportation, Federal Aviation Administration. "Advisory Circular Checklist." AC 00-2TT. Washington, D.C., Mar. 15, 1981.
———. *Aviation Forecasts, Fiscal Years 1982–1993.* Washington, D.C., 1982.
———. *Aviation Forecasts, Fiscal Years 1983–1994.* Washington, D.C., Feb. 1983.
———. *Aviation Forecasts, Fiscal Years 1984–1995.* Washington, D.C., Feb. 1984.
———. "Federal Aviation Administration Activities in the Agency's 50th Year." Washington, D.C., 1977.
———. "Flight Standards Field Offices." FAA-P-8740-31, Washington, D.C., Nov. 1980.
———. *National Airport System Plan, Revised Statistics, 1980–1989.* Washington, D.C., 1980.
———. *National Airspace System Plan, Summary.* Washington, D.C., 1982.
———. Order 1050.1C, *Policies and Procedures for Considering Environmental Impacts.* Washington, D.C., Jan. 1980.
———. Order 1100.2A, *Organization—FAA Headquarters.* Washington, D.C., June 1980.
———. Order 1100.5A, *FAA Organization—Field.* Washington, D.C., 1977.
———. Order 1100.128, *Implementation of Noise Type Certification Standards.* Washington, D.C., Feb. 1971.
———. Order 2100.13, *FAA Rulemaking Policies.* Washington, D.C., June 1, 1976.
———. *Statistical Handbook of Aviation, Fiscal Year 1981,* Washington, D.C., 1982.
———. *Statistical Handbook of Aviation, Fiscal Year 1982.* Washington, D.C., 1983.
———. *Statistical Handbook of Aviation, Fiscal Year 1983.* Washington, D.C., 1984.

————. *Summary of Airworthiness Directives.* Bk. 2, Vol. II. Oklahoma City: FAA Aeronautical Center, Jan. 1982.

————. "Western Region Headquarters Directives Checklist." WE 0000. Los Angeles, Apr. 30, 1981.

Department of Transportation, Federal Aviation Administration, Northwest Mountain Region. *Directorate Approach to the Airworthiness and Operation of Transport Airplanes.* Seattle, Mar. 1982.

Department of Transportation, Office of the Secretary, and the Federal Aviation Administration. *Aviation Noise Abatement Policy.* Washington, D.C., Nov. 18, 1976.

General Accounting Office. *Lower Airline Costs Per Passenger Are Possible in the United States and Could Result in Lower Airfares.* Report to the Congress of the United States by the Comptroller General of the United States, Washington, D.C., 1977.

Illinois Department of Transportation, Division of Aeronautics. *Aviation Safety Rules and Regulations.* Springfield, Ill., 1978.

National Transportation Safety Board. "The Safety Board: What It Is and What It Does." Washington, D.C., 1980.

North Carolina Department of Transportation. *North Carolina Small Community Airline Service Route and Marketing Study.* Raleigh, N.C., 1980.

Office of the Federal Register, National Archives and Records Service, General Services Administration. *Code of Federal Regulations* (CFR). Title 3, Executive Orders and Proclamations, Revised as of Jan. 1, 1982.

————. CFR. Title 14, Aeronautics and Space, Pt. 151, 1965.

————. CFR. Title 14, Aeronautics and Space, Revised as of Jan. 1, 1982, Pts. 1 to 59.

————. CFR. Title 14, Aeronautics and Space, Revised as of Jan. 1, 1982, Pts. 60–139.

————. CFR. Title 14, Aeronautics and Space, Revised as of Jan. 1, 1982, Pts. 140–99.

————. CFR. Title 14, Aeronautics and Space, Revised as of Jan. 1, 1982, Pts. 200–1199.

————. CFR. Title 24, Housing and Urban Development, Revised as of Apr. 1, 1983, Pts. 0–199.

————. CFR. Title 40, Environment, Revised as of July 1, 1982, Pts. 0–51.

————. CFR. Title 49, Transportation, Revised as of Oct. 1, 1981, Pts. 1–99.

————. CFR. Title 49, Transportation, Revised as of Oct. 1, 1981, Pts. 100–399.

————. CFR. Title 49, Transportation, Revised as of Oct. 1, 1981, Pts. 400–999.

————. *A Codification of Presidential Proclamations and Executive Orders.* Jan. 20, 1961, to Jan. 20, 1981, Chapter XIV, Aeronautics and Space, Nov. 30, 1981.

————. *Federal Register* (FR). Vol. 45, No. 34, Tues., Feb. 19, 1980, Petition Notice No. PR 80-3, Petition for Rulemaking of William Becker, 10802–3.

————. FR. Vol. 46, No. 16, Mon., Jan. 26, 1981, Dockets 16279, 18691, Establishment of New Part 150 to Govern the Development and Submission of Airport Operators' Noise Compatibility Planning Programs and the FAA's Administrative Process for Evaluating and Determining the Effects of Those Programs, 8316–57.

———. FR. Vol. 47, No. 14, Thurs., Jan. 21, 1982, Notice No. 82-1, Number of Flight Attendants Required During Intermediate Stops, 3068–69.

———. FR. Vol. 47, No. 182, Mon., Sept. 20, 1982, Notice No. 82-13, Air Transportation Regulation, 41486–507.

———. *United States Government Manual. 1981–1982*, "Federal Aviation Administration," Washington, D.C., 1981, 415–16.

43 *Statutes at Large* (Stat.) 805. Air Mail Act of 1925. Public Law (Pub. L.) 63-359, Feb. 2, 1925.

44 Stat. 568. Air Commerce Act of 1926. Pub. L. 69-254, May 20, 1926.

46 Stat. 259. Air Mail Act of 1930. Pub. L. 71-178, Apr. 29, 1930.

48 Stat. 933. Air Mail Act of 1934. Pub. L. 73-308, June 12, 1934.

52 Stat. 973. Civil Aeronautics Act of 1938. Pub. L. 75-706, June 23, 1938.

54 Stat. 1231. Civil Aeronautics Authority Reorganization Plan (Plan 3). Apr. 2, 1940.

60 Stat. 170. Federal Airport Act of 1946. Pub. L. 79-377, May 13, 1946.

72 Stat. 731. Federal Aviation Act of 1958. Pub. L. 85-726, Aug. 23, 1958.

80 Stat. 931. Department of Transportation Act of 1966. Pub. L. 89-670, Oct. 15, 1966.

83 Stat. 852. National Environmental Policy Act of 1969. Pub. L. 91-190, Jan. 1, 1970.

84 Stat. 219. Airport and Airway Development Act of 1970. Pub. L. 91-258, May 21, 1970.

85 Stat. 492. Amendment to the Airport and Airway Development Act of 1970. Pub. L. 92-174, Nov. 27, 1971.

87 Stat. 88. Airport Development Acceleration Act of 1973. Pub. L. 93-44, June 18, 1973.

88 Stat. 2156. Independent Safety Board Act of 1974. Pub. L. 93-633, Jan. 3, 1975.

90 Stat. 871. Airport and Airway Development Act Amendments of 1976. Pub. L. 94-353, July 12, 1973.

91 Stat. 1278. Federal Aviation Act of 1958, Insurance Risks. Pub. L. 95-163 (one section of this act deregulates the air cargo industry), Nov. 9, 1977.

92 Stat. 1705. Airline Deregulation Act of 1978. Pub. L. 95-504, Oct. 24, 1978.

94 Stat. 35. International Air Transportation Competition Act of 1979. Pub. L. 96-192, Feb. 15, 1980.

94 Stat. 50. Aviation Safety and Noise Abatement Act of 1979. Pub. L. 96-193, Feb. 18, 1980.

96 Stat. 671. Airport and Airway Improvement Act of 1982. Pub. L. 97-248, Aug. 1982.

U.S. Air Service Newsletter. January 2, 1920. (Borrowed from Feb. 1982 *CAP News.*)

United States Code (USC), 1976 ed. Vol. 11, Titles 43–50. Washington, D.C.: GPO, 1977.

USC, 1976 ed. Supplement IV, Vol. 5, Titles 43–50. Washington, D.C.: GPO, 1981.

USC, 1976 ed. Supplement V, Vol. 6, Titles 43–50. Washington, D.C.: GPO, 1982.

United States House of Representatives, Committee on Government Operations.

"Executive Orders and Proclamations: A Study of a Use of Presidential Powers," Washington, D.C., Dec. 1957.

United States Senate, Civil Aeronautics Board Sunset Act of 1982 (Proposed). S. 1426, 97th Congress, First Session, 1981.

United States Senate, Committee on the Judiciary, Subcommittee on Administrative Practice and Procedures. *Civil Aeronautics Board, Practices and Procedures.* Report 175, 94th Congressional Session, 1977.

PERIODICALS

Aerospace Industries Association of America. "Aerospace Review and Forecasts 1982/83." *Aerospace*, Vol. 21, No. 2, Washington, D.C., Feb. 1983, 13.

Airline Pilots Association. *Airline Pilot*, Washington, D.C., Dec. 1982, 14–15.

"Airline Yearbook 1982." *Airline Executive.* May 1982.

Aviation Daily, Mar. 15, 1984, 81–82.

———. Apr. 13, 1984, back of p. 250.

"Carriers Newly Certificated or with Pending Applications." *Aviation Daily*, Jan. 29, 1982.

"Carriers Warned to Provide for New Entrants at Airports, DOT Says." *Aviation Daily*, Feb. 5, 1982, 185.

Collins, Richard. "A Consensus on Licensing." *Flying Magazine*, July 1982, 76–78.

Condom, Pierre. "Boeing's New Transports in a Flight Test Marathon." *Interavia*, July 1982, 695–97.

Corbett, J. J. "Reflections on the New Airport/Airway Trust Fund Law." *Airport Services Management*, Sept. 1982, 26–30.

"Europeans Object to U.S. FAA Lead Region Certification Plan." *Aviation Week and Space Technology*, Vol. 114, No. 13, Mar. 30, 1981, 34.

Feazel, Michael. "New Entrants Attack FAA Rules." *Aviation Week and Space Technology*, Vol. 116, No. 1, Jan. 25, 1982, 28.

Feldman, Joan M. "Pacific Express: Borrowing Bits from Other Airlines' Successful Formulas." *Air Transport World*, Sept. 1981, 30.

"Masters of the Air: Boeing Captures the Cruise Missile Contract and Dominates World Aviation." *Time* Apr. 7, 1980, 52.

"Midway Airlines President Says Controllers' Strike May Affect Expansion Plans." *Aviation Daily*, Feb. 4, 1982, 177.

"1983 Financial Results." *Aviation Daily*, Feb. 28, 1984, 313–14.

"Present Federal Regulatory Role." *Congressional Digest.* Vol. 57, No. 6–7. Washington, D.C., June–July 1978.

"Proposed New Safety Rules Will Permit Individual Flexibility." *Aviation Daily*, Sept. 17, 1982, 92.

Standard & Poor's. *Industry Surveys: Aerospace Basic Analysis.* New York, Oct. 7, 1982, A-24 to A-29.

Standard & Poor's. *Industry Surveys: Aerospace Current Analysis.* New York, Apr. 15, 1982.

Standard & Poor's. *Industry Surveys: Air Transport Basic Analysis.* New York, Dec. 10, 1981.

Letters to David A. NewMyer

Letter dated Jan. 27, 1982, from the National Association of State Aviation Officials.
Letter dated June 9, 1982, from John H. Newland, Public Relations Director, New Airplane Programs, Boeing Commercial Airplane Company, concerning the Boeing 767 Flight Test Program.

Interviews by Harry P. Wolfe

Dec. 2, 1980. Interview with Terry Armentrout, National Transportation Safety Board, Los Angeles Regional Office.
Jan. 13, 1981. Interview with Federal Aviation Administration personnel in the Phoenix, Arizona, Air Carrier District Office.
July 6, 1982. Interview with Federal Aviation Administration personnel in the Scottsdale, Arizona, General Aviation District Office.
July 1982. Telephone interviews with Federal Aviation Administration personnel in the Phoenix Air Carrier District Office and the Scottsdale General Aviation District Office.

Index

Harry P. Wolfe holds B.A. and M.A. degrees from Tulane University and the University of Texas at Austin respectively. Beginning in 1975 he spent three and one-half years as an Aviation Planning and Programming Specialist for the Illinois Department of Transportation. In 1978 he became Airport Planning Program Manager for the Arizona Department of Transportation. Since 1980 Wolfe has operated an aviation consulting business in Phoenix, Arizona. He complements his consulting activities by teaching aviation regulation and planning courses for Southern Illinois University, and he has also served as a Faculty Associate at Arizona State University.

David A. NewMyer holds a B.A. degree from the University of Redlands, an M.A. degree from Drew University, and an M.S. degree from Northwestern University. He is presently Coordinator, Aviation Management, and a member of the faculty in the Division of Advanced Technical Studies, School of Technical Careers, Southern Illinois University at Carbondale, where he has worked since 1977. He was the Director of Planning and Manager, Airport System Planning, for the Chicago Area Transportation Study from 1972 through 1977. NewMyer is also an aviation and airport consultant with research interests in aviation education, aviation industry regulation, and airport planning.